# THE COMPLETE
# INSTANT POT
## COOKBOOK FOR BEGINNERS

**550** Quick and Delicious Instant Pot Recipes
for Smart People on a Budget

Michelle Jones

# Contents

## PASTA, BEANS & GRAINS..........................................................41

## SOUPS AND SIDE DISHES ........................................................58

## POULTRY ...........................................................................80

## BEEF, PORK AND LAMB ..........................................................................108

## FISH AND SEAFOOD ........................................................................................158

## APPETIZERS .................................................................................173

## BROTHS & SAUCES .....................................................................183

## DESSERTS ...................................................................................189

# Introduction

Hello...and welcome to my book with 550 Quick and Delicious Instant Pot Recipes for Smart People on a Budget. Let me share all my favorite and amazing recipes with you, so you can make delicious and scrumptious meals for your family and friends. I'll also share what the Instant Pot is all about, so you can see how easy is to use it.

Let me start by saying that I absolutely love my Instant Pot! This is the kitchen tool I can't live without. I've perfected the art of using the Instant Pot pressure cooker and I hope that by sharing with you my experience, you will have one more reason to shine at every meal and occasion with your friends and family.

So let's find out what the Instant Pot is all about.

# What is the Instant Pot?

The buzz about the Instant Pot is true. It uses cutting-edge technology to let you cook foods fast as well as get all the benefits of a pressure cooker...all in one! You're probably wondering how that can be possible - to have several very different kitchen appliances in one. It's easy. The Instant Pot can be everything for everyone.

It won't take you long to learn how to use the Instant Pot. Because the Instant Pot is more than just a kitchen appliance! It can roast, broil, make soups and stews...and it can pressure cook as well.

Having this one amazing appliance means you can get rid of your dehydrator, roasting pan, slow cooker, even your oven. Just think of all the kitchen space you'll have when you just have one appliance, the Instant Pot, doing all the cooking for you.

Let's look a closer look at all the benefits of using the Instant Pot.

## BENEFITS OF USING THE INSTANT POT

### Prepare meals ahead of time

We all live busy lives. The Instant Pot lets you prepare food ahead of time – when you have the time and not when you're under pressure to get dinner on the table. Prep in the morning or the night before. Just follow one of the recipes in this book and get all the ingredients ready to go. If you're using the pressure cooker or slow cooker function, just put the ingredients into the Instant Pot, set to the right time, and dinner cooks on its own. Or have all the ingredients in the fridge, ready to go for when you arrive home at the end of the day.

### Prepare budget-friendly and healthy meals

The Instant Pot also lets you cook cheaper cuts of meat to perfection. When you pressure cook a beef shank, it comes out tender and juicy, cooked with sealed in moisture taste that you don't get when you cook it any other way.

### Cooks faster than the slow cooker

With the slow cooker, beans take from 4 to 5 hours cook. With the Instant Pot, you can get that time down to under 30 with the pressure cooking functions. And that includes the time it takes for the Instant Pot to get the pressure up to the right level! What does this mean for you? Simple – you can come home and have a bean soup or stew on the table in no time at all.

## USING THE INSTANT POT

When you first get your Instant Pot, it can be a little intimidating with all those functions and buttons to press. I certainly felt that way. But trust me...it won't take you long to get the hang of using the Instant Pot. Let's take a quick look at the basics of using the Instant Pot.

### Easy to read display

The display on the Instant Pot is easy to read. All of the functions are there for you just to press and set. You are also able to select the temperature, pressure levels, and time controls, as well as the Start/Stop button. As I said, don't let all these buttons make you think you'll never learn how to use the Instant Pot. The learning curve is fast – after making just one of my recipes you'll know what you're doing.

**Pressure cooking:** When you use the lid for the pressure cooker, you'll be able to cook all kinds of foods at low or high pressure. Just set the timer for one-minute increments all the way up to one hour. After an hour, you'll be able to up the time in five-minute increments and cook all the way to four hours for some foods, such as certain cuts of meat.

**Slow cooker:** You're never going to use your slow cooker again after you use this function on the Instant Pot. After putting all the ingredients in the pot, seal the pressure lid in the venting position. Then just use the Instant Pot the same as you would a slow cooker that cooks food for up to 10 hours. I like this function when I want to have the Instant Pot cook dinner for me overnight. It's perfect for chili or beef stew.

**Steaming:** Steaming fish and veggies is a breeze with the Instant Pot. And the great thing is that there will be no more over-steaming, causing foods to be limp and tasteless. The Instant Pot will cook the food so that it's tender but still crisp and flavorful.

**Sauté and Brown:** I use the sauté or brown function for many of my favorite recipes. This setting lets you brown and sear foods before or after cooking them. After browning foods, you can add a bit of liquid, and make some great tasting gravies. Sautéing foods in the Instant Pot is just like sautéing them on your stovetop.

**Easy cleanup:** Cleanup takes no time! Once the food is cooked, and the Instant Pot has cooled down, it's just a matter of cleaning the inner steel pot, in warm soapy water.

## TIPS AND TRICKS FOR YOUR INSTANT POT!

### Anyone can use the Instant Pot!

The technology of the Instant Pot makes this the perfect appliance for anyone to use…no matter how much you or your family think you can't cook! There are just three little things you need to do:

- Choose one of my foolproof recipes.
- Gather the ingredients and get them all prepped.
- Put the ingredients into the Instant Pot– choose one of the multiple settings, seal the lid…and walk away until you hear the timer.

### Forget to take the meat out of the freezer…no problem!

Did you forget to take dinner out of the freezer, so it can thaw in time for tonight's dinner? No problem at all. The Instant Pot takes frozen meats, such as chicken, and quickly pressure cooks it to defrost and cook at the same time.

### Rice is nice

You may think that sticking to your old way of cooking rice on the stovetop is faster and easier than using the Instant Pot. You'll want to rethink that old cooking method! Not only is using the Instant Pot is faster and easier on the cleanup, but you'll also never mess up the rice again when you don't get the proportions of rice to water just right. The pressure cooker cooks rice perfectly each time.

### Read the digital screen

When you are pressure cooking using the Instant Pot, you have to guess what the pressure level is inside the pot. With the Instant Pot, you can use the digital screen, so there's no more guessing! Make sure you take advantage of this handy little feature.

**Use the steaming rack to make baked desserts**

The Instant Pot is your perfect dessert-maker. Whip up the batter for a cheesecake or brownies…and layer the batter in the same pan you'd pop in the oven. But instead of using the oven, place that pan on the steaming rack or trivet that comes with the Instant Pot, which will hold the pan securely. Set the function to cake, and your favorite dessert will be done in no time.

# INSTANT POT RECIPES

The recipes in this book are my absolute favorite…and they're a great introduction to the Instant Pot, highlighting just what this amazing kitchen tool can do for you. Before you start cooking, here's some valuable information for using my recipes in the Instant Pot.

Brown and sear some food before putting into the Instant Pot

In some of my recipes, I'll have you brown or sear some of the ingredients, particularly meats before you start the cooking process. This is so that the juices are sealed into the food, making it cook up that much more tender.

Check some foods to avoid over-cooking

Some foods are easy to over-cook, such as baked foods. In my recipes, I'll remind you if you need to check to avoid over-cooking.

Adding Ingredients at the end of cooking time

When layering food in the Instant Pot, lay them flat and close together so that you make the most of the space in the pot. I'll guide you in my recipes when there are any foods that shouldn't be stacked or overlapped.

Use hot water when pressure cooking

If you add a tbsp or two of hot water when you're using the pressure cooker, the pressure will build up faster.

Adjusting cooking time

If you're using fewer ingredients, then my recipe calls for, remember to adjust the cooking time to a little less. The same goes if you're using more ingredients than my recipe calls for…adjust, so the Instant Pot cooks a little longer. Just be sure to check near the end of cooking time to see if needs to cook longer.

From a Slow Cooker to an Instant Pot

Foods cooked in a slow cooker for 4 hours on high, can be quickly cooked in the Instant Pot for only 25 to 30 minutes! In my recipes…I might have you add a bit more liquid than if you were cooking in a slow cooker. Please note that some different Instant Pot models may require more liquid than the recipe would suggest. Alsways double-check there's enough liquid to build up pressure inside your Instant Pot, to avoid burning the food and unnecessary waste of time.

Always press Cancel when changing the functions

It may be omitted on some recipes, but right before releasing the pressure or changing the function from Sauté to any pressure cooking mode, always press Cancel, and then the function you'd like to use.

As you can see, the Instant Pot is just what you need in your life. You'll be cooking exceptional meals in no time! I hope you enjoy my favorite recipes…these are the ones I make over and over again for my family and friends.

It's time to choose your first recipe…and get your Instant Pot cooking great food!

# *Morning Recipes*

## Chicken Sandwiches with Barbecue Sauce

Serving Size: 4 | Total Time: 45 minutes

### Ingredients

4 chicken thighs, boneless and skinless
Salt to taste
2 cups barbecue sauce
1 onion, minced
2 garlic cloves, minced

2 tbsp minced fresh parsley
1 tbsp lemon juice
1 tbsp mayonnaise
1 ½ cups iceberg lettuce, shredded
4 burger buns

### Directions

Season the chicken with salt, and transfer into the pot. Add in garlic, onion and barbecue sauce. Coat the chicken by turning in the sauce. Seal the lid and cook on High Pressure for 15 minutes.

Do a natural release for 10 minutes. Use two forks to shred the chicken and mix into the sauce. Press Keep Warm and let the mixture simmer for 15 minutes to thicken the sauce, until desired consistency.

In a bowl, mix lemon juice, mayonnaise, salt, and parsley; toss lettuce into the mixture to coat. Separate the chicken into equal parts to match the burger buns; top with lettuce and complete the sandwiches.

## Light & Fruity Yogurt

Serving Size: 12 | Total Time: 24hr

### Ingredients

1 pound hulled and halved raspberries
1 cup sugar
3 tbsp gelatin

1 tbsp fresh orange juice
8 cups milk
¼ cup Greek yogurt containing active cultures

### Directions

In a bowl, mash the raspberries with a potato masher. Add sugar and stir well to dissolve; let soak for 30 minutes at room temperature.

Add in orange juice and gelatin and mix well until dissolved.

Remove the mixture and place in a sealable container, close, and allow to sit for 12 hrs to 24 hrs at room temperature before placing in the fridge. Refrigerate for a maximum of 2 weeks.

Into the cooker, add milk and close the lid. The steam vent should be set to Venting then to Sealing.

Select Yogurt until "Boil" is displayed on the display. When complete there will be a display of "Yogurt" on the screen.

Open the lid and using a food thermometer ensure the milk temperature is at least 185°F.

Transfer the steel pot to a wire rack and allow to cool for 30 minutes until the milk has reached 110°F.

In a bowl, mix ½ cup warm milk and yogurt. Transfer the mixture into the remaining warm milk and stir without having to scrape the steel pot's bottom.

Take the steel pot back to the base of the Instant Pot and seal the lid. Select Yogurt mode and cook for 8 hrs.

Allow the yogurt to chill in a refrigerator for 1-2 hrs.

Transfer the chilled yogurt to a large bowl and stir in fresh raspberry jam.

# Yummiest Vegetable Soup with Coconut Milk

Serving Size: 5 | Total Time: 40 minutes

## Ingredients

2 tbsp olive oil
1 leek, chopped
2 cloves garlic, minced
2 carrots, diced
1 celery stalk, chopped
4 potatoes, quartered
½ cup coconut milk

1 red bell pepper, diced
¼ tsp red pepper flakes
Salt and black pepper to taste
1 ½ cups vegetable stock
2 tbsp parsley

## Directions

Heat olive oil on Sauté. Add garlic and leek and Sauté for 5 minutes. Add in red bell pepper, carrots, salt, potatoes, red pepper flakes, celery stalk, and pepper. Mix in vegetable stock.

Seal the lid and cook for 15 minutes on High Pressure. Release pressure naturally for 10 minutes. Add parsley and coconut milk to the soup. Use an immersion blender to blitz the soup until smooth.

# Vanilla Chai Latte Oatmeal

Serving Size: 4 | Total Time: 10 minutes

## Ingredients

3 ½ cups milk
½ cup raw peanuts
1 cup steel-cut oats
¼ cup agave syrup
1 tsp coffee
1 ½ tsp ground ginger
1 ¼ tsp ground cinnamon

½ tsp salt
¼ tsp ground allspice
¼ tsp ground cardamom
1 tsp vanilla extract
2 tbsp chopped fresh tea leaves
¼ tsp cloves

## Directions

With a blender, puree peanuts and milk to obtain a smooth consistency. Transfer into the cooker. To the peanuts mixture, add in agave syrup, oats, ginger, allspice, cinnamon, salt, cardamom, tea leaves, and cloves, and mix well.

Seal the lid and cook on High Pressure for 12 minutes. Let pressure to release naturally on completing the cooking cycle. Add vanilla extract to the oatmeal and stir well before serving.

# Pumpkin Steel Cut Oats with Cinnamon

Serving Size: 4 | Total Time: 25 minutes

## Ingredients

1 tbsp butter
2 cups steel cut oats
¼ tsp cinnamon
3 cups water

1 cup pumpkin puree
½ tsp salt
3 tbsp maple syrup
½ cup pumpkin seeds, toasted

## Directions

Melt butter on Sauté. Add in cinnamon, oats, salt, pumpkin puree and water.

Seal the lid, select Porridge and cook for 10 minutes on High Pressure to get a few bite oats or for 14 minutes to form oats that are soft. Do a quick release. Open the lid and stir in maple syrup. Top with pumpkin seeds to serve.

# Spinach & Feta Egg Pie with Cherry Tomatoes

Serving Size: 2 | Total Time: 30 minutes

## Ingredients

4 eggs
Salt and black pepper to taste
½ cup heavy cream
1 cup cherry tomatoes, halved

1 cup baby spinach, chopped
1 spring onion, chopped
¼ cup feta cheese, crumbled
1 tbsp parsley, chopped

## Directions

Grease a baking dish with cooking spray and add in the spinach and onion.

In a bowl, whisk the eggs, heavy cream, salt, and pepper. Pour over the spinach and arrange the cherry tomato halves on top. Sprinkle with the feta cheese.

Add a cup of water to the Instant Pot and insert a trivet. Place the dish on the trivet.

Seal the lid, press Manual and cook on High pressure for 15 minutes. Release pressure naturally for 10 minutes. Scatter parsley to serve.

# Greek Yogurt with Honey & Walnuts

Serving Size: 10 | Total Time: 15hr

## Ingredients

2 tbsp Greek yogurt
8 cups milk
¼ cup sugar honey

1 tsp vanilla extract
1 cup walnuts, chopped

## Directions

Add the milk, seal the lid and press Yogurt until display shows boil. When the cooking cycle is over, the display will show Yogurt. Open the lid and check that milk temperature is at least 175°F. Get rid of the skin lying on the milk's surface. Let cool in an ice bath until it becomes warm to touch.

In a bowl, mix one cup of milk and yogurt to make a smooth consistency. Mix the milk with yogurt mixture. Transfer to the pot and place on your Pressure cooker. Seal the lid, press Yogurt mode and adjust the timer to 9 hrs. Once cooking is complete, strain the yogurt into a bowl using a strainer with cheesecloth.

Chill for 4 hours. Add in vanilla and honey and gently stir well. Spoon the yogurt into glass jars. Serve sprinkled with walnuts and enjoy.

# Simple Homemade Chicken & Quinoa Soup

Serving Size: 6 | Total Time: 15 minutes

## Ingredients

1 tbsp canola oil
6 spring onions, chopped
2 garlic cloves, finely diced
1 carrot, chopped
2 celery stalks, chopped finely

2 chicken breasts, boneless, skinless, cut into chunks
6 cups chicken broth
1 cup quinoa
Salt and black pepper, to taste
2 tbsp chopped fresh parsley leaves

## Directions

Heat canola oil on Sauté. Add in celery, spring onions, garlic, and carrot. Cook for 5 minutes until tender. Add in chicken, quinoa, 1 tsp salt, chicken broth, and black pepper.

Seal the lid, select Soup/Broth and cook for 15 minutes on High. Do a quick release, and add in parsley.

# Savory Roast Beef Sandwiches

Serving Size: 8 | Total Time: 1 hour 20 minutes

## Ingredients

2 ½ pounds beef roast
2 tbsp olive oil
1 onion, chopped
4 garlic cloves, minced
½ cup dry red wine

2 cups beef broth stock
1 tsp dried oregano
16 slices Fontina cheese
8 split hoagie rolls
Salt and black pepper, to taste

## Directions

Season the beef with salt and pepper. Warm oil on Sauté and brown the beef for 2 to 3 minutes per side. Set aside on a plate. Add onion and cook for 3 minutes, until translucent. Stir in garlic and cook for one a minute until soft. Set aside.

Add red wine to deglaze. Scrape the cooking surface to remove any brown sections of the food using a wooden spoon flat edge. Mix in beef broth and take back the juices and beef to your cooker.

Over the meat, scatter some oregano. Seal the lid and cook on High Pressure for 50 minutes.

Release the pressure naturally for 10 minutes. Preheat a broiler. Transfer the beef to a cutting board and slice. Roll the beef and top with onion. Each sandwich should be topped with 2 slices Fontina cheese. Place the sandwiches under the broiler for 2-3 minutes until the cheese melts.

# Honey Butternut Squash Cake Oatmeal

Serving Size: 4 | Total Time: 35 minutes

## Ingredients

3 ½ cups coconut milk
1 cup steel-cut oats
1 cup shredded butternut squash
½ cup sultanas
1/3 cup honey
¾ tsp ground ginger
½ tsp sugar

½ tsp salt
½ tsp orange zest
¼ tsp ground nutmeg
¼ cup toasted walnuts, chopped
½ tsp vanilla extract

## Directions

In the cooker, mix sultanas, orange zest, ginger, milk, honey, butternut squash, salt, oats, and nutmeg. Seal the lid and cook on High Pressure for 12 minutes. Do a natural release for 10 minutes.

Into the oatmeal, stir in the vanilla extract and sugar. Top with walnuts and serve.

# Simple Apple Cider with Orange Juice

Serving Size: 6 | Total Time: 30 minutes

## Ingredients

6 green apples, cored and chopped
3 cups water

¼ cup orange juice
2 cinnamon sticks

## Directions

In a blender, add orange juice, apples, and water and blend until smooth; use a fine-mesh strainer to strain and press using a spoon. Get rid of the pulp.

In the pot, mix the strained apple puree, and cinnamon sticks. Seal the lid and cook for 10 minutes on High Pressure. Release the Pressure naturally for 15 minutes. Strain again and do away with the solids.

# Spiced & Warming Mulled Wine

Serving Size: 6 | Total Time: 30 minutes

## Ingredients

3 cups red wine
2 tangerines, sliced
¼ cup honey
6 whole cloves
6 whole black peppercorns

2 cardamom pods
8 cinnamon sticks
1 tsp fresh ginger, grated
1 tsp ground cinnamon
6 tangerine wedges

## Directions

Add red wine, honey, cardamom, 2 cinnamon sticks, cloves, tangerines sliced, ginger, and peppercorns. Seal the lid and cook for 5 minutes on High Pressure. Release Pressure naturally for 20 minutes. Using a fine mesh strainer, strain the wine. Discard spices. Divide the warm wine into glasses and add tangerine wedges, ground cinnamon, and a cinnamon stick for garnishing before serving.

# Broccoli, Potatoes & Cheese Cream Soup

Serving Size: 4 | Total Time: 30 minutes

## Ingredients

1/3 cup butter
1 head broccoli, cut into florets
2 cloves garlic, minced
1 onion, chopped
2 ½ pounds potatoes, peeled and chopped

4 cups vegetable broth
½ cup heavy cream
Salt and black pepper to taste
Cheddar cheese, grated for garnish
½ cup fresh chopped scallions, for garnish

## Directions

Melt butter on Sauté. Add onion and garlic and Sauté for 5 minutes. Add in broth, potatoes, and broccoli, and mix well. Press Cancel. Seal the lid and cook for 5 minutes on High Pressure. Release pressure naturally for 10 minutes. Transfer the potato mixture to a blender and blend until smooth.

Add in heavy cream and season with pepper and salt. Divide among bowls and top with cheese and scallions.

# Honey Homemade Almond Milk

Serving Size: 4 | Total Time: 15 minutes

## Ingredients

1 cup raw almonds, soaked overnight, peeled
1 cup cold water
2 dried apricots, chopped

2 tbsp honey
4 cups water
1 vanilla bean

## Directions

In the pot, mix a cup of cold water with almonds and apricots. Seal the lid and cook for 1 minute on High.

Release the pressure quickly. The almonds should be soft and plump, and the water should be brown and murky. Use a strainer to drain almonds; rinse with cold water for 1 minute.

To a high-speed blender, add the rinsed almonds, vanilla bean, honey, and 4 cups water. Blend for 2 minutes until well combined and frothy. Line a cheesecloth to the strainer.

Place the strainer over a bowl and strain the milk. Use a wooden spoon to press milk through the cheesecloth and get rid of solids.

Place almond milk in an airtight container and refrigerate.

# Lazy Steel Cut Oats with Coconut Milk

Serving Size: 2 | Total Time: 18 minutes

## Ingredients

1 tsp coconut oil
1 cup steel-cut oats
1 ½ cups water

¾ cup coconut milk
Salt, to taste

## Directions

Warm coconut oil on Sauté, until foaming. Add oats and cook as you stir until soft and toasted. Press Cancel. Add milk, salt and water and stir. Seal the lid, and Press Porridge. Cook for 12 minutes on High Pressure. Set steam vent to Venting to release the pressure quickly. Open the lid. Add oats as you stir to mix any extra liquid.

# Strawberry Jam

Serving Size: 6 | Total Time: 30 minutes

## Ingredients

1 pound strawberries, chopped
1 cup sugar

½ lemon, juiced and zested
1 tbsp mint, chopped (optional)

## Directions

Add the strawberries, sugar, lemon juice and zest to the Instant Pot. Seal the lid, select manual, and cook for 2 minutes on High. Release Pressure naturally for 10 minutes. Open the lid and stir in chopped mint. Select Sauté and continue cooking until the jam tickens, about 10 minutes. Let to cool before serving.

# Homemade Spanish-Style Horchata

Serving Size: 4 | Total Time: 15 minutes

## Ingredients

4 cups cold water
½ cup short-grain rice
¼ stick cinnamon

Zest from 1 lemon
2 tbsp sugar
1 tbsp cinnamon powder

## Directions

In the pot, combine cinnamon, rice and 2 cups of water. Seal the lid cook on High Pressure for 5 minutes. Release Pressure naturally for 10 minutes.

In a blender, puree the rice mixture with the lemon zest and sugar. Strain the blended mixture into the remaining water. Mix well and place in the refrigerator until ready for serving. Serve sprinkled with cinnamon.

# Speedy Soft-Boiled Eggs

Serving Size: 4 | Total Time: 10 minutes

## Ingredients

4 large eggs
1 cup water

Salt and black pepper, to taste

## Directions

To the pressure cooker, add water and place a wire rack. Place eggs on it. Seal the lid, press Steam and cook for 3 minutes on High Pressure. Do a quick release. Allow to cool in an ice bath. Peel the eggs and season with salt and pepper before serving.

# Mushroom, Onion & Goat Cheese Omelet

Serving Size: 2 | Total Time: 25 minutes

## Ingredients

4 eggs
½ cup fresh goat's cheese
¼ cup milk
1 cup button mushrooms
1 large onion, finely chopped

1 tsp dried oregano
¼ tsp salt
2 tsp olive oil
Fresh parsley, to garnish

## Directions

Grease the pot with olive oil. Stir-fry onion for a few minutes, until translucent. Stir in oregano, salt and button mushrooms. Cook for 5-6 minutes, stirring occasionally.

Crack the eggs into a bowl, and mix with goat cheese and milk. Remove the mushrooms and set aside. Pour the egg mixture in the pot and cook for 2 minutes, stirring constantly, on Sauté.

Serve with button mushrooms and topped with parsley.

# Goat Cheese & Beef Egg Scramble

Serving Size: 3 | Total Time: 25 minutes

## Ingredients

6 oz lean ground beef
1 onion, chopped
6 eggs
¼ cup skim milk
¼ cup goat cheese

¼ tsp garlic powder
¼ tsp rosemary powder
1 tbsp tomato paste
½ tsp salt
2 tbsp olive oil

## Directions

Grease the inner pot with olive oil. Stir-fry the onion, for 4 minutes, until translucent, on Sauté. Add beef and tomato paste. Cook for 5 minutes, stirring twice.

Meanwhile, Whisk the eggs, milk, goat cheese, rosemary, garlic, and salt. Pour the mixture into the pot and stir slowly with a wooden spatula. Cook until slightly underdone. Remove from the heat and serve.

# Frittata with Vegetables & Cheese

Serving Size: 4 | Total Time: 30 minutes

## Ingredients

4 eggs
8 oz spinach, finely chopped
½ cup cheddar cheese, shredded
½ cup ricotta cheese, crumbled
3 cherry tomatoes, halved
¼ cup red bell pepper, chopped

1 cup chopped broccoli, pre-cooked
4 tbsp olive oil
Salt and black pepper to taste
¼ tsp dried oregano
½ cup fresh celery leaves, finely chopped

## Directions

Heat olive oil on Sauté. Add spinach and cook for 5 minutes, stirring occasionally. Add tomatoes, peppers, and broccoli and stir-fry for 3-4 more minutes.

In a bowl, Whisk eggs, cheddar cheese, and ricotta cheese. Pour in the pot and cook for 5-7 minutes. Season with salt, black pepper, and oregano; press Cancel.

Serve with chopped celery leaves.

# Spanish Tortilla Omelet with Cottage Cheese

Serving Size: 4 | Total Time: 25 minutes

## Ingredients

1 lb tomatoes, peeled and diced
1 tbsp tomato paste
1 cup cottage cheese
4 eggs, beaten

3 tbsp olive oil
1 tbsp Italian seasoning mix
¼ cup fresh parsley, chopped
¼ tbsp salt

## Directions

Grease the inner pot with olive oil. Press Sauté and add tomatoes, Italian seasoning, parsley, tomato paste and salt. Cook for 10 minutes until the tomatoes soften. Stir occasionally. Mix eggs and cottage cheese. Pour the mixture into the pot stir well. Cook for 3 more minutes. Serve immediately.

# Kale & Parmesan Omelet

Serving Size: 6 | Total Time: 20 minutes

## Ingredients

6 large eggs
2 tbsp heavy cream
½ tsp freshly grated nutmeg

Salt and black pepper to taste
1 ½ cups kale, chopped
¼ cup grated Parmesan cheese

## Directions

In a bowl, beat eggs with the rest of the ingredients. Grease a cake pan. Place egg mixture into the prepared pan. Pour in 1 cup of water, set a steamer rack over the water. Lay the pan onto the rack. Seal the lid and cook for 10 minutes on High Pressure. Release the pressure quickly.

# Power Swiss Chard & Spinach Omelet

Serving Size: 2 | Total Time: 20 minutes

## Ingredients

1 cup spinach, chopped
1 cup Swiss chard, chopped
4 eggs

2 tbsp olive oil
½ tsp salt
¼ tsp red pepper flakes

## Directions

Grease the inner pot with olive oil. Stir-fry the Swiss chard and spinach for 5 minutes on Sauté. Set aside. Whisk the eggs, salt, and red pepper flakes. Pour the mixture in the pot. Spread the eggs with a wooden spatula and cook for 3-4 minutes on Sauté. With a spatula, ease around the edges and slide to a serving plate. Add Swiss chard and spinach and fold it over in half.

# Ham Omelet with Red Bell Pepper

Serving Size: 2 | Total Time: 20 minutes

## Ingredients

1 red bell pepper, chopped
4 eggs, beaten
2 tbsp olive oil

2 garlic cloves, crushed
½ cup ham, chopped
1 tsp Italian seasoning mix

## Directions

Grease the pot with olive oil. Stir-fry the pepper and garlic for 5 minutes. Mix the eggs with ham and season with Italian seasoning. Pour the mixture into the pot and cook for 2-3 minutes, or until set. Using a spatula, loosen the edges and gently slide onto a plate. Fold over to serve.

# *Vegan & Vegetarian*

## Cheesy Mashed Potato Balls with Tomato Sauce

Serving Size: 4 | Total Time: 40 minutes

### Ingredients

2 potatoes, peeled
1 onion, peeled, chopped
1 lb fresh spinach, torn
¼ cup mozzarella cheese, shredded
2 eggs, beaten
Salt and black pepper to taste

1 tsp dried oregano, crushed
1 cup whole milk
¼ cup flour
¼ cup corn flour
2 garlic cloves

*Tomato sauce:*

1 lb fresh tomatoes, peeled, roughly chopped
1 large onion, peeled, chopped
2 garlic cloves, peeled, crushed
3 tsp olive oil
¼ cup white wine

1 tsp sugar
1 tsp dried rosemary, crushed
½ tsp salt
1 tsp tomato paste

### Directions

Place the potatoes in your instant pot and add enough water to cover. Seal the lid and cook on High Pressure for 13 minutes. Do a quick release. Add 1 cup of milk and mash with a potato masher.

Whisk in eggs, one at the time and mix well. Add the remaining ingredients and mix with hands. Shape into balls and set aside. Press Sauté, warm olive oil and stir-fry onion, garlic, until translucent.

Stir in tomatoes and cook until tender, for about 10 minutes. Pour in wine, add sugar, rosemary, and salt. Stir in 1 tsp of tomato paste and mix well. Cook for five more minutes. Place the potato balls in the cooker and seal with the lid. Cook on High Pressure for 5 minutes. Do a natural release, for 5 minutes.

## Spicy Vegetable Pilau with Cilantro & Lemon

Serving Size: 4 | Total Time: 30 minutes

### Ingredients

3 tbsp olive oil
1 tbsp ginger, minced
1 cup onion, chopped
1 cup green peas
1 cup carrots, chopped
1 cup mushrooms, chopped
1 cup broccoli, chopped
1 tbsp chili powder

½ tbsp ground cumin
1 tbsp garam masala
½ tbsp turmeric powder
1 cup basmati rice, rinsed and drained
2 cups vegetable broth
1 tbsp lemon juice
2 tbsp chopped fresh cilantro
Salt and black pepper to taste

### Directions

Warm 1 tbsp olive oil on Sauté. Add in onion and ginger and cook for 3 minutes until soft. Stir in broccoli, green peas, mushrooms, and carrots; cook for 1 more minute. Add turmeric powder, chili powder, garam masala, salt, pepper, and cumin; cook for 1 minute until soft.

Add ¼ cup broth to deglaze; scrape the bottom to get rid of any browned bits. To the vegetables, add the remaining broth and rice. Seal the lid and cook for 1 minute on High Pressure. Release the pressure quickly. Use a fork to fluff rice, sprinkle with lemon juice. Divide into plates and garnish with cilantro.

# Quinoa Pesto Bowls with Brussels Sprouts & Broccoli

Serving Size: 2 | Total Time: 30 minutes

## Ingredients

1 cup quinoa, rinsed
2 cups water
Salt and black pepper to taste
1 small beet, peeled and cubed
1 cup broccoli florets
1 carrot, peeled and chopped

½ pound Brussels sprouts
2 eggs
1 avocado, chopped
¼ cup pesto sauce
Lemon wedges, for serving

## Directions

In the pot, mix water, salt, quinoa and pepper. Set trivet over quinoa and set steamer basket on top. To the steamer basket, add eggs, Brussels sprouts, broccoli, beet cubes, carrots, pepper and salt.

Seal the lid and cook for 1 minute on High Pressure. Release pressure naturally for 10 minutes, then release any remaining pressure quickly. Remove steamer basket and trivet from the pot and set the eggs to a bowl of ice water. Peel and halve the eggs. Use a fork to fluff quinoa.

Divide quinoa, broccoli, avocado, carrots, beet, Brussels sprouts, eggs between two bowls, and top with a dollop of pesto. Serve alongside a lemon wedge.

# Minestrone Soup with Green Vegetables

Serving Size: 4 | Total Time: 30 minutes

## Ingredients

2 tbsp olive oil
1 head broccoli, cut into florets
4 celery stalks, chopped thinly
1 leek, chopped thinly
1 zucchini, chopped

1 cup green beans
2 cups vegetable broth
3 whole black peppercorns
Salt to taste
2 cups chopped kale

## Directions

Add broccoli, leek, beans, salt, peppercorns, zucchini, and celery. Mix in vegetable broth, oil, and enough water to cover. Seal the lid and cook on High Pressure for 4 minutes. Release pressure naturally for 5 minutes, then release the remaining pressure quickly. Stir in kale; set on Sauté, and cook until tender.

# Homemade Gazpacho Soup

Serving Size: 4 | Total Time: 2 hours 20 minutes

## Ingredients

1 pound trimmed carrots
1 pound tomatoes, chopped
1 cucumber, peeled and chopped
¼ cup olive oil
2 tbsp lemon juice

1 red onion, chopped
2 cloves garlic
2 tbsp white wine vinegar
Salt and black pepper to taste

## Directions

Add carrots, salt and enough water to cover the carrots. Seal the lid and cook for 10 minutes on High Pressure. Do a quick release.

In a blender, add carrots, cucumber, red onion, pepper, garlic, oil, tomatoes, lemon juice, vinegar, 4 cups of water, and salt. Blend until very smooth.

Place gazpacho into a serving bowl, chill while covered for 2 hours.

# Steamed Artichokes with Lime Aioli

Serving Size: 4 | Total Time: 20 minutes

### Ingredients

2 large artichokes
2 cups water
2 garlic cloves, smashed

½ cup mayonnaise
Salt and black pepper to taste
Juice of 1 lime

### Directions

Using a serrated knife, trim about 1 inch from the top of artichokes. Into the pot, add water and set trivet over. Lay the artichokes on the trivet. Seal lid and cook for 14 minutes on High Pressure.

Release the pressure quickly. Mix the mayonnaise with garlic and lime juice. Season with salt and pepper. Serve artichokes in a platter with garlic mayo on the side.

# Weekend Burrito Bowls

Serving Size: 4 | Total Time: 30 minutes

### Ingredients

2 tbsp olive oil
1 onion
2 garlic cloves, minced
1 tbsp chili powder
2 tbsp ground cumin
2 tbsp paprika
Salt and black pepper to taste
¼ tbsp cayenne pepper
1 cup quinoa, rinsed

1 (14.5-ounce) can diced tomatoes
1 (14.5-ounce) can black beans
1 ½ cups vegetable stock
1 cup frozen corn kernels
2 tbsp chopped cilantro
1 tbsp roughly chopped fresh coriander
Cheddar cheese, grated for garnish
1 avocado, chopped

### Directions

Warm oil on Sauté. Add in onion and stir-fry for 3 to 5 minutes, until fragrant. Add garlic and Sauté for 2 more minutes until soft and golden brown. Add in chili powder, paprika, cayenne pepper, salt, cumin, and black pepper and cook for 1 minute until spices are soft.

Pour quinoa into onion and spice mixture and stir to coat quinoa completely in spices. Add diced tomatoes, black beans, vegetable stock, and corn; stir to combine.

Seal the lid and cook for 7 minutes on High Pressure. Release the pressure quickly. Open the lid and let sit for 6 minutes until flavors combine. Use a fork to fluff quinoa and season with pepper and salt. Into quinoa and beans mixture, stir in cilantro and divide into plates. Top with cheese, avocado slices and coriander.

# Buttery Mashed Cauliflower

Serving Size: 4 | Total Time: 15 minutes

### Ingredients

2 cups water
1 head cauliflower
1 tbsp butter

Celery salt and black pepper to taste
¼ cup heavy cream
1 tbsp fresh parsley, chopped

### Directions

Into the pot, add water and set trivet on top. Lay cauliflower head onto the trivet. Seal the lid and cook for 8 minutes on High Pressure. Release the pressure quickly. Remove trivet and drain the liquid from the pot.

Take back the cauliflower to the pot alongside the pepper, heavy cream, salt and butter. Use an immersion blender to blend until smooth. Top with parsley and serve.

# Parsley Lentil Soup with Vegetables

Serving Size: 4 | Total Time: 30 minutes

## Ingredients

1 tbsp olive oil
1 onion, chopped
1 cup celery, chopped
2 garlic cloves, chopped
3 cups vegetable stock

1 ½ cups dried lentils, rinsed
4 carrots, halved lengthwise
½ tsp salt
A handful of fresh parsley, chopped

## Directions

Warm olive oil on Sauté. Add in onion, garlic, and celery, and Sauté for 5 minutes until onion is soft. Mix in lentils, carrots, and vegetable stock. Seal the lid and cook on High Pressure for 10 minutes. Release the pressure quickly. Mix lentils with salt and serve topped with parsley.

# Garlic & Herbed Potatoes

Serving Size: 4 | Total Time: 30 minutes

## Ingredients

1 ½ pounds potatoes
3 tbsp butter
3 cloves garlic, chopped
2 tbsp fresh rosemary, chopped

½ tsp fresh thyme, chopped
½ tsp fresh parsley, chopped
Salt and black pepper to taste
½ cup vegetable broth

## Directions

Use a small knife to pierce each potato to ensure there are no blowouts when placed under pressure. Melt butter on Sauté. Add in potatoes, rosemary, parsley, pepper, thyme, and garlic, and cook for 10 minutes until potatoes are browned and the mixture is aromatic.

Stir in the vegetable broth. Seal the lid and cook for 5 minutes on High Pressure. Release the pressure quickly.

# Cauliflower & Potato Curry with Cilantro

Serving Size: 4 | Total Time: 40 minutes

## Ingredients

1 tbsp vegetable oil
1 head cauliflower, cored and cut into florets
1 potato, peeled and diced
1 tbsp ghee
2 tbsp cumin seeds
1 onion, minced
4 garlic cloves, minced
1 tomato, cored and chopped

1 jalapeño pepper, deseeded and minced
1 tbsp curry paste
1 tbsp ground turmeric
½ tsp chili pepper
1 cup water
Salt and black pepper to taste
A handful of cilantro leaves, chopped

## Directions

Warm oil on Sauté mode. Add in potato and cauliflower and cook for 8 to 10 minutes until lightly browned; season with salt. Set the vegetables to a bowl. Add ghee to the pot.

Mix in cumin seeds and cook for 10 seconds until they start to pop; add onion and cook for 3 minutes until softened. Mix in garlic; cook for 30 seconds.

Add in tomato, curry paste, chili pepper, jalapeño pepper, and turmeric; cook for 4 to 6 minutes. Return potato and cauliflower to the pot. Stir in water. Seal the lid and cook on High Pressure for 4 minutes. Quick release the pressure. Top with cilantro.

# Savory Spinach with Mashed Potatoes & Chives

Serving Size: 6 | Total Time: 30 minutes

## Ingredients

3 pounds potatoes, quartered
1 ½ cups water
½ tbsp salt
½ cup milk

1/3 cup butter
2 tbsp chopped fresh chives
Salt and black pepper to taste
2 cups spinach, chopped

## Directions

In the cooker, mix water, salt and potatoes. Seal the lid and cook on High Pressure for 8 minutes. Release the pressure quickly. Drain the potatoes, and reserve the liquid in a bowl. In a bowl, mash the potatoes.

Mix with butter and milk; season with pepper and salt. With reserved cooking liquid, thin the potatoes to attain the desired consistency. Put the spinach in the remaining potato liquid and stir until wilted; Season to taste. Drain and serve with potato mash. Garnish with cracked black pepper and chives.

# Plant-Based Indian Curry

Serving Size: 3 | Total Time: 25 minutes

## Ingredients

1 tsp vegan butter
1 onion, chopped
2 cloves garlic, minced
1 tsp ginger, grated
1 tsp ground cumin
1 tsp red chili powder
1 tsp salt

½ tsp ground turmeric
1 (15-ounce) can chickpeas, drained and rinsed
1 tomato, diced
1/3 cup water
5 cups collard greens, chopped
½ tsp garam masala
1 tsp lemon juice

## Directions

Melt butter on Sauté. Toss in the onion to coat. Seal the lid and cook for 2 minutes until soft. Mix in ginger, cumin, turmeric, red chili powder, garlic, and salt and cook for 30 seconds until crispy. Stir in tomato. Into the cooker, mix in water, tomato and chickpeas.

Seal the lid and cook on High Pressure for 4 minutes. Release the pressure quickly. Press Sauté.

Into the chickpea mixture, stir in lemon juice, collard greens and garam masala, until well coated. Cook for 2 to 3 minutes until collard greens wilt, on Sauté. Serve over rice or naan.

# Easy Tahini Sweet Potato Mash

Serving Size: 4 | Total Time: 25 minutes

## Ingredients

1 cup water
2 lb sweet potatoes, peeled and cubed
2 tbsp tahini
1 tbsp sugar

¼ tsp ground nutmeg
Chopped fresh chives, for garnish
Salt and black pepper to taste

## Directions

Into the cooker, add 1 cup cold water and insert a steamer basket. Add sweet potato cubes into the steamer basket. Seal the lid and cook for 8 minutes at High Pressure. Release the pressure quickly.

In a bowl, add cooked sweet potatoes and slightly mash. Using a hand mixer, whip in nutmeg, sugar, and tahini until the sweet potatoes attain desired consistency. Add salt and pepper to taste and top with chives to serve.

# Monday Night Rice with Red Beans

Serving Size: 4 | Total Time: 50 minutes

## Ingredients

1 cup red beans
2 tbsp vegetable oil
½ cup rice
½ tbsp cayenne pepper
1 ½ cup vegetable broth
1 onion, diced

1 garlic clove
1 red bell pepper, diced
1 stalk celery, diced
1 tbsp fresh thyme leaves
Salt and black pepper to taste

## Directions

Add beans and water to cover about 1-inch. Seal the lid and cook for 1 minute on High Pressure. Release the pressure quickly. Drain the beans and set aside. Rinse and pat dry the inner pot.

Return inner pot to the cooker, add oil to the pot and press Sauté. Add onion to the oil and Sauté for 3 minutes until soft. Add celery and bell pepper and cook for 1 to 2 minutes until fragrant.

Add garlic and cook for 30 seconds until soft. Add rice, transfer the beans back to the pot and top with broth. Stir black pepper, thyme, cayenne pepper, and salt into the mixture. Seal the lid and cook for 15 minutes on High Pressure. Release the pressure quickly. Season with more thyme, black pepper and salt.

# Classic Palak Paneer Dip

Serving Size: 4 | Total Time: 20 minutes

## Ingredients

¼ cup milk
2 tsp butter
1 tsp cumin seeds
1 tsp coriander seeds
1 tomato, chopped
1 tsp minced fresh ginger
1 tsp minced fresh garlic

1 red onion, chopped
1 pound spinach, chopped
1 cup water
1 tsp salt
2 cups paneer, cubed
1 tsp chili powder

## Directions

Warm butter on Sauté. Add in garlic, cumin seeds, coriander, chili powder, ginger, and fry for 1 minute until fragrant. Add onion and cook for 2 minutes until crispy. Add in salt, water and spinach.

Seal the lid and cook for 1 minute on High Pressure. Release the pressure quickly. Add spinach mixture to a blender and blend to obtain a smooth paste. Mix paneer, milk, and tomato with spinach mixture.

# Grandma's Asparagus with Feta & Lemon

Serving Size: 4 | Total Time: 15 minutes

## Ingredients

1 cup water
1 lb asparagus spears, ends trimmed
1 tbsp olive oil

Salt and black pepper to taste
1 lemon, cut into wedges
1 cup feta cheese, cubed

## Directions

Into the pot, add water and set trivet over the water. Place steamer basket on the trivet. Place the asparagus into the steamer basket. Seal the lid and cook on High Pressure for 1 minute. Release the Pressure quickly. Add olive oil in a bowl and toss in asparagus until well coated. Season with pepper and salt. Serve alongside feta cheese and lemon wedges.

# Delicious Thai Vegetable Stew

Serving Size: 4 | Total Time: 30 minutes

## Ingredients

1 tbsp coconut oil
1 cup onion, chopped
1 tbsp fresh ginger, minced
2 garlic cloves, minced
3 carrots, peeled and chopped
1 red bell pepper, chopped

1 orange bell pepper, chopped
1 (14-ounce) can coconut milk
1 cup bok choy, chopped
½ cup water
2 tbsp red curry paste
Salt and black pepper to taste

## Directions

Melt coconut oil on Sauté. Add in onion and cook for 3 to 4 minutes until soft; add garlic and ginger and cook for 30 more seconds until soft. Mix in orange bell pepper, red bell pepper and carrots; cook for 3 to 4 minutes until the peppers become soft and tender.

Add curry paste, bok choy, coconut milk, and water and stir well to obtain a consistent color of the sauce. Press Cancel and seal lid. Cook for 1 minute on High Pressure. Release the pressure quickly. Adjust the seasoning and serve hot.

# Parmesan Topped Vegetable Mash

Serving Size: 6 | Total Time: 15 minutes

## Ingredients

3 pounds yukon gold potatoes, chopped
1 ½ cups cauliflower, broken into florets
1 carrot, chopped
1 cup Parmesan cheese, shredded
¼ cup butter, melted

¼ cup milk
1 tsp salt
1 garlic clove, minced
Fresh parsley for garnish

## Directions

Into the pot, add veggies, salt and cover with enough water. Seal the lid and cook on High Pressure for 10 minutes. Release the pressure quickly. Drain the vegetables and mash them with a potato masher.

Add garlic, butter and milk, and whisk until everything is well incorporated. Serve topped with Parmesan cheese and chopped parsley.

# Steamed Artichokes & Green Beans with Mayo Dip

Serving Size: 4 | Total Time: 20 minutes

## Ingredients

4 artichokes, trimmed
½ pound green beans, trimmed
1 lemon, halved
1 tbsp lemon zest
1 tbsp lemon juice

3 cloves garlic, crushed
½ cup mayonnaise
1 cup water
Salt to taste
1 handful of parsley, chopped

## Directions

Rub the artichokes and green beans with lemon. Add water into the pot. Set steamer rack over water and set steamer basket on top. Place artichokes and green beans into the basket and sprinkle with salt.

Seal lid and cook on high Pressure for 10 minutes. Release the pressure quickly. In a mixing bowl, combine mayonnaise, garlic, lemon juice, and lemon zest. Season to taste with salt. Serve with warm steamed artichokes and green beans sprinkled with parsley.

# Cauliflower Rice with Peas & Chili

Serving Size: 2 | Total Time: 15 minutes

## Ingredients

1 head cauliflower, cut into florets
1 cup water
2 tbsp olive oil
Salt to taste

1 tsp chili powder
¼ cup green peas
1 tbsp chopped fresh parsley

## Directions

Add water, set rack over water and place the steamer basket onto the rack. Add cauliflower into the steamer basket. Seal the lid and cook on High Pressure for 1 minute. Release the pressure quickly. Remove rack and steamer basket. Drain water from the pot, pat dry, and return to pressure cooker base.

Set on Sauté mode and warm oil. Add in cauliflower and stir to break into smaller pieces like rice. Stir in chili powder, peas and salt. Place the cauliflower rice into plates and add parsley for garnishing.

# Vegetarian Chili with Lentils & Quinoa

Serving Size: 12 | Total Time: 45 minutes

## Ingredients

1 (28-ounce) can diced tomatoes
2 cups cashews, chopped
1 cup onion, chopped
1 cup red lentils
1 cup red quinoa
3 chipotle peppers, chopped
3 garlic cloves, minced

2 tbsp chili powder
1 tsp salt
4 ½ cups water
2 cups carrots, chopped
1 (15-ounce) can black beans, rinsed and drained
¼ cup fresh parsley, chopped

## Directions

In the pot, mix tomatoes, onion, chipotle peppers, chili powder, lentils, cashews, carrots, quinoa, garlic, and salt. Stir in more water. Seal the lid, Press Soup/Stew and cook for 30 minutes on High Pressure.

Release the pressure quickly. Into the chili, add black beans; simmer on Sauté until heated through. Add ¼ cup to 1 cup water if you want a thinner consistency. Top with a garnish of parsley.

# Homemade Coconut Milk Yogurt with Lime & Honey

Serving Size: 6 | Total Time: 15 hours

## Ingredients

2 cans coconut milk
1 tbsp gelatin
1 tbsp honey

1 tbsp probiotic powder
Zest from 1 lime

## Directions

Into the pot, stir in gelatin and coconut milk until well dissolved. Seal the lid, Press Yogurt button until the display is reading "Boil". Once done, the screen will then display "Yogurt". Ensure milk temperature is at 180°F. Remove steel pot from Pressure cooker base and place into a large ice bath to cool milk for 5 minutes to reach 112°F.

Remove pot from ice bath and wipe the outside dry. Into the coconut milk mixture, add probiotic powder, honey, and Lime zest, and stir to combine. Return steel pot to the base of the instant pot. Seal the lid, press Yogurt and cook for 10 hours. Once complete, spoon yogurt into clean glass canning jars with rings and lids; place in the refrigerator to chill for 4 hrs to thicken.

# Tofu with Noodles & Peanuts

Serving Size: 4 | Total Time: 20 minutes

## Ingredients

1 package tofu, cubed
8 ounces egg noodles
2 bell peppers, chopped
¼ cup soy sauce
¼ cup orange juice
1 tbsp fresh ginger, minced

2 tbsp vinegar
1 tbsp sesame oil
1 tbsp sriracha
¼ cup roasted peanuts
3 scallions, chopped

## Directions

In the instant pot, mix tofu, bell peppers, orange juice, sesame oil, ginger, egg noodles, soy sauce, vinegar, and sriracha. Cover with enough water. Seal the lid and cook for 2 minutes on High Pressure.

Release the pressure quickly. Place the mixture into 4 plates; top with scallions and peanuts to serve.

# Speedy Mac & Goat Cheese

Serving Size: 4 | Total Time: 20 minutes

## Ingredients

1 lb elbow macaroni
2 oz goat's cheese, crumbled
½ cup skim milk
1 tsp Dijon mustard
1 tsp dried oregano, ground

1 tsp salt
1 tsp Italian seasoning mix
2 tbsp extra virgin olive oil
1 tbsp vegetable oil
5 oz olives

## Directions

Add macaroni in the instant pot and Pour in 4 cups of water. Add 1 tablespoon of oil. Seal the lid and cook on High Pressure for 3 minutes. Do a quick release.

Drain the macaroni in a colander and set aside. Press Sauté, add olive oil, mustard, milk, oregano, salt, and Italian seasoning mix. Stir-fry for 5 minutes.

Stir in macaroni and cook for 2 more minutes. Top with some fresh goat's cheese and olives and serve immediately.

# Elegant Farro with Greens & Pine Nuts

Serving Size: 6 | Total Time: 15 minutes

## Ingredients

6 oz kale, chopped
6 oz spinach, chopped
6 oz collard greens, chopped
3 oz Swiss chard, chopped
3 oz parsley leaves, chopped
1 medium-sized leek, chopped

1 ½ cups farro
4 tbsp olive oil
5 cups vegetable broth
1 tbsp salt
½ cup toasted pine nuts

## Directions

Add farro and vegetable broth to the Instant Pot. Season with salt and seal the lid. Cook on Rice mode for 9 minutes on High. Do a quick release and open the lid. Remove farro and wipe the instant pot clean. Pour two cups of water, insert the steamer basket and place the chopped collard greens on the basket. Seal the lid.

Cook on Steam mode for 2 minutes on High. Do a quick release and remove the greens to a large bowl. Toss in the farro, drizzle with olive oil and sprinkle with pine nuts to serve.

# Acorn Squash with Sweet Glaze

Serving Size: 4 | Total Time: 25 minutes

## Ingredients

½ cup water
3 tbsp honey
1 lb acorn squash, cut into 2-inch chunks
2 tbsp butter

1 tbsp dark brown sugar
1 tbsp cinnamon
Salt and black pepper to taste

## Directions

In a small bowl, mix 1 tbsp honey, butter and water. Pour into the pot. Add in acorn squash, seal the lid and cook on High Pressure for 4 minutes. Release the pressure quickly.

Transfer the squash to a serving dish. Set on Sauté. Mix sugar, cinnamon, the remaining 2 tbsp honey and the liquid in the pot. Cook as you stir for 4 minutes to obtain a thick consistency and starts to turn caramelized and golden. Spread honey glaze over squash; add pepper and salt to taste.

# Power Green Soup with Lasagna Noodles

Serving Size: 4 | Total Time: 30 minutes

## Ingredients

1 tsp olive oil
1 cup leeks, chopped
2 garlic cloves minced
1 cup tomato paste
1 cup tomatoes, chopped
1 carrot, chopped

½ pound broccoli, chopped
¼ cup dried green lentils
2 tsp Italian seasoning
Salt to taste
2 cups vegetable broth
3 lasagna noodles

## Directions

Warm olive oil on Sauté mode. Add garlic and leeks and cook for 2 minutes until soft; add tomato paste, carrot, Italian seasoning, broccoli, tomatoes, lentils, and salt. Stir in vegetable broth and lasagna noodles.

Seal the lid and cook on High Pressure for 3 minutes. Release pressure naturally for 10 minutes, then release the remaining pressure quickly. Divide soup into serving bowls and serve.

# Stuffed with Rice Grape Leaves

Serving Size: 4 | Total Time: 60 minutes

## Ingredients

32 wine leaves, fresh or in jar
1 cup long grain rice, rinsed
½ cup olive oil
2 garlic cloves, crushed

¼ cup freshly squeezed lemon juice
2 tbsp fresh mint
Salt and black pepper to taste

## Directions

In a bowl, mix rice with 3 tbsp of olive oil, garlic, mint, salt, and pepper. Place 1 wine leaf at a time on a working surface and add 1 tbsp of filling at the bottom.

Fold the leaves over the filling towards the center. Bring the 2 sides in towards the center and roll them up tightly. Grease the instant pot with 2 tbsp olive oil.

Make a layer of wine leaves and then Transfer the previously prepared rolls. Add the remaining olive oil, 2 cups of water, and lemon juice. Seal the lid and cook on High Pressure for to 30 minutes.

Do a natural release, for about 10 minutes. Remove the dolmades from the pot and chill overnight.

# Mushroom & Gouda Cheese Pizza

Serving Size: 4 | Total Time: 25 minutes

## Ingredients

1 pizza crust
½ cup tomato paste
¼ cup water
1 tbsp sugar
1 tbsp dried oregano

4 oz button mushrooms, chopped
½ cup grated gouda cheese
2 tbsp extra virgin olive oil
12 olives
1 cup arugula for serving

## Directions

Grease the bottom of a baking dish with one tbsp of olive oil. Line some parchment paper. Flour the working surface and roll out the pizza crust to the approximate size of your instant pot gently fit the dough in the previously prepared baking dish.

In a bowl, combine tomato paste, water, sugar, and dried oregano. Spread the mixture over crust, make a layer with button mushrooms and grated gouda.

Add a trivet inside the pot and pour in 1 cup of water. Seal the lid, and cook for 15 minutes on High Pressure. Do a quick release. Remove the pizza from your pot using a parchment paper. Sprinkle with the remaining olive oil and top with olives and arugula. Cut and serve.

# Sweet Potato Medallions with Garlic & Rosemary

Serving Size: 4 | Total Time: 25 minutes

## Ingredients

1 cup water
1 tbsp fresh rosemary
1 tbsp garlic powder

4 sweet potatoes
2 tbsp butter
Salt to taste

## Directions

Add water and place steamer rack over the water. Use a fork to prick sweet potatoes all over and set onto steamer rack. Seal the lid and cook on High Pressure for 12 minutes. Release the pressure quickly. Transfer sweet potatoes to a cutting board and slice into ½-inch medallions and ensure they are peeled.

Melt butter in the on Sauté mode. Add in the medallions and cook each side for 2 to 3 minutes until browned. Season with salt and garlic powder. Serve topped with fresh rosemary.

# Parsnip & Cauliflower Mash with Chives

Serving Size: 8 | Total Time: 15 minutes

## Ingredients

1 ½ lb parsnips, peeled and cubed
1 head cauliflower, cut into florets
2 garlic cloves
Salt and black pepper to taste
2 cups water

¼ cup sour cream
¼ cup grated Parmesan cheese
1 tbsp butter
2 tbsp minced chives

## Directions

In the pot, mix parsnips, garlic, water, salt, cauliflower, and pepper. Seal the lid and cook on High Pressure for 4 minutes. Release the pressure quickly. Drain parsnips and cauliflower and return to pot.

Add Parmesan, butter, and sour cream. Use a potato masher to mash until desired consistency is attained. Into the mashed parsnip, add 1 tbsp chives; place to a serving plate and garnish with remaining chives.

# Mozzarella & Eggplant Lasagna

Serving Size: 2 | Total Time: 35 minutes

## Ingredients

1 large eggplant, chopped
4 oz mozzarella, chopped
3 oz mascarpone cheese, at room temperature
2 tomatoes, sliced

¼ cup olive oil
Salt and black pepper to taste
1 tsp oregano, dried

## Directions

Grease a baking dish with olive oil. Slice the eggplant and make a layer in the dish. Cover with mozzarella and tomato slices. Top with mascarpone cheese.

Repeat the process until you run out of ingredients. Meanwhile, in a bowl, mix olive oil, salt, pepper, and dried oregano. Pour the mixture over the lasagna, and add ½ cup of water. In your inner pot, Pour 1 ½ cups of water and insert a trivet.

Lower the baking dish on the trivet, Seal the lid and cook on High Pressure for 4 minutes. When ready, do a natural release, for 10 minutes.

# Chickpea Stew with Red Onion & Tomatoes

Serving Size: 4 | Total Time: 45 minutes

## Ingredients

6 oz chickpeas, soaked overnight
2 tomatoes, peeled and chopped
1 red onion, chopped
1 tbsp cumin seeds
2 cups vegetable broth

2 tbsp olive oil
2 tbsp butter
2 tbsp fresh parsley, chopped
Salt and black pepper to taste

## Directions

To the instant pot, add in the olive oil, tomatoes, onion, cumin seeds, chickpeas, and pour in the broth. Seal the lid and set the steam handle. Cook on Soup/Broth for 30 minutes on High. Do a quick release and set aside to cool for a while.

Transfer the soup to a food processor and season with salt and pepper. Process until pureed and ladle to a serving dish. Stir in 2 tbsp of butter. Top freshly chopped parsley.

# Spanish-Style "Tortilla de Patatas"

Serving Size: 3 | Total Time: 30 minutes

## Ingredients

5 eggs, beaten
1 cup spinach, torn, rinsed
1 potato, chopped
1 cup heavy cream

Salt and black pepper to taste
¼ tsp dried thyme
1 tbsp olive oil

## Directions

In a bowl, mix eggs, heavy cream, and potato. Sprinkle with salt and black pepper, and stir to combine.Heat olive oil on Sauté and cook the spinach and thyme for 3 minutes, or until wilted. Remove the spinach from the pot.

Stir in the spinach in the previously prepared mixture. Transfer all to an oven-safe dish, that fits in the instant pot. Add 1 cup of water, insert the trivet, pour 1 cup of water, and place the oven-safe dish on top. Seal the lid and cook on High Pressure for 20 minutes. Release the steam naturally, for 5 minutes.

# English Vegetable Potage

Serving Size: 4 | Total Time: 50 minutes

## Ingredients

1 lb potatoes, peeled, cut into bite-sized pieces
2 carrots, peeled, chopped
3 celery stalks, chopped
2 onions, peeled, chopped
1 zucchini, chopped into ½ -inch thick slices
A handful of fresh celery leaves

2 tbsp butter, unsalted
3 tbsp olive oil
2 cups vegetable broth
1 tbsp paprika
Salt and black pepper to taste
2 bay leaves

## Directions

Warm olive oil on Sauté and stir-fry the onions for 3-4 minutes, until translucent. Add carrots, celery, zucchini, and ¼ cup of broth. Continue to cook for 10 more minutes, stirring constantly.

Stir in potatoes, paprika, salt, pepper, bay leaves, remaining broth, and celery leaves. Seal the lid and cook on Meat/Stew mode for 30 minutes on High. Do a quick release and stir in butter.

# Corn & Lentil Hummus with Parmesan

Serving Size: 6 | Total Time: 45 minutes

## Ingredients

1 lb lentils, cooked
1 cup sweet corn
2 tomatoes, diced
3 tbsp tomato paste
½ tbsp dried oregano, ground
2 tbsp Parmesan cheese

1 tbsp salt
½ tbsp red pepper flakes
3 tbsp olive oil
1 cup water
¼ cup red wine

## Directions

Heat olive oil on Sauté and add tomatoes, tomato paste, and ½ cup of water. Sprinkle with salt, pepper flakes, and oregano and stir-fry for 5 minutes. Press Cancel and add lentils, sweet corn, and red wine.

Pour in the remaining water and seal the lid. Cook on High Pressure for 2 minutes. Do a quick release. Set aside to cool completely and refrigerate for 30 minutes. Sprinkle with Parmesan Cheese before serving.

# Spinach, Mushrooms & Ricotta Cheese Manicotti

Serving Size: 4 | Total Time: 40 minutes

## Ingredients

1 (8 oz) pack manicotti pasta
12 oz spinach, torn
6 oz button mushrooms, chopped
3 oz ricotta cheese

¼ cup milk
3 oz butter
¼ tbsp salt
1 tbsp sour cream

## Directions

Melt butter on Sauté and add mushrooms. Stir well and cook until soft. Add spinach and milk, and continue to cook for 6 minutes, stirring constantly. Stir in the cheese, season with salt, to taste and Press Cancel.

Line a baking dish with parchment paper. Fill manicotti with spinach mixture. gently place them on the baking sheet. Pour 2 cups of water in the instant pot and insert a trivet.

Lay the baking sheet on the trivet. Seal the lid, and cook on High Pressure for 20 minutes. Do a quick release. Remove and chill for a while. Top with sour cream and serve.

# Carrot & Chickpea Boil with Cherry Tomatoes

Serving Size: 4 | Total Time: 20 minutes

## Ingredients

1 cup chickpeas, cooked
1 onion, peeled, chopped
A handful of string beans, trimmed
1 apple, chopped into 1-inch cubes
½ cup raisins
½ tbsp button mushrooms, chopped
2 carrots, chopped

2 garlic cloves, crushed
4 cherry tomatoes
A handful of fresh mint
1 tbsp grated ginger
½ cup freshly squeezed orange juice
½ tbsp salt

## Directions

Place all ingredients in the instant pot. Pour enough water to cover. Cook on High Pressure for 8 minutes. Do a natural release, for 10 minutes.

# Amazing Vegetable Paella

Serving Size: 4 | Total Time: 30 minutes

## Ingredients

½ cup frozen green peas
2 carrots, finely chopped
1 cup fire-roasted tomatoes
1 cup zucchini, finely chopped
½ tbsp celery root, finely chopped

6 saffron threads
1 tbsp turmeric, ground
Salt and black pepper to taste
2 cup vegetable broth
1 cup long grain rice

## Directions

Place all ingredients, except rice, in the instant pot. Stir well and seal the lid. Cook on Rice mode for 8 minutes, on High. Do a quick release, open the lid and stir in the rice. Seal the lid and cook on High pressure for 3 minutes. When ready, release the pressure naturally, for about 10 minutes.

# One-Pot Swiss Chard & Potatoes

Serving Size: 4 | Total Time: 15 minutes

## Ingredients

1 lb Swiss chard, torn, chopped, with stems
2 potatoes, peeled, chopped
¼ tsp oregano

1 tsp salt
1 tsp Italian seasoning

## Directions

Add Swiss chard and potatoes to the pot. Pour water to cover all and sprinkle with salt. Seal the lid and select Manual/Pressure Cook. Cook for 3 minutes on High. Release the steam naturally, for 5 minutes. Transfer to a serving plate. Sprinkle with oregano and Italian seasoning, to serve.

# Sautéed Spinach & Leeks with Blue Cheese

Serving Size: 2 | Total Time: 10 minutes

## Ingredients

9 oz fresh spinach
2 leeks, chopped
2 red onions, chopped
2 garlic cloves, crushed

½ cup blue cheese, crumbled
3 tbsp olive oil
1 tbsp salt

### Directions

Grease the inner pot with oil. Stir-fry leeks, garlic, and onions, for about 5 minutes, on Sauté mode. Add spinach and give it a good stir.

Season with salt and cook for 3 more minutes, stirring constantly. Press Cancel, Transfer to a serving dish and sprinkle with blue cheese. Serve right away.

# Warm Green Beans Salad with Cheese & Pine Nuts

Serving Size: 6 | Total Time: 15 minutes

### Ingredients

Juice from 1 lemon
1 ½ cups water
2 pounds green beans, trimmed
1 cup chopped toasted pine nuts

1 cup feta cheese, crumbled
6 tbsp olive oil
Salt and black pepper to taste

### Directions

Add water and set rack over the water and the steamer basket on the rack. Loosely heap green beans into the steamer basket. Seal lid and cook on High Pressure for 5 minutes. Release pressure quickly. Drop green beans into a salad bowl. Top with the olive oil, feta cheese, salt, lemon juice, black pepper, and pine nuts.

# Stuffed Potatoes with Feta Cheese & Rosemary

Serving Size: 3 | Total Time: 45 minutes

### Ingredients

6 potatoes, whole, rinsed, drained
¼ cup olive oil
3 garlic cloves, crushed
¼ cup feta cheese

1 tsp fresh rosemary, chopped
½ tsp dried thyme
2 oz button mushrooms, chopped
1 tsp salt

### Directions

Rub the potatoes with salt and place them in the instant pot. Add enough water to cover and seal the lid. Cook on High Pressure for 30 minutes. Do a quick release and remove the potatoes. Let chill for a while.

Meanwhile, in the pot, mix olive oil, garlic, rosemary, thyme, and mushrooms. Sauté until the mushrooms soften, about 5 minutes, on Sauté. Remove from the cooker and stir in feta. Cut the top of each potato and spoon out the middle. Fill with cheese mixture and serve immediately.

# Delicious Mushroom Goulash

Serving Size: 4 | Total Time: 45 minutes

### Ingredients

6 oz portobello mushrooms, sliced
1 cup green peas
1 cup pearl onions, minced
2 carrots, chopped
½ cup celery stalks, chopped
2 garlic cloves, crushed

2 potatoes, chopped
1 tbsp apple cider vinegar
1 tbsp rosemary
Salt and black pepper to taste
2 tbsp butter
4 cups vegetable stock

### Directions

Melt butter on Sauté and stir fry onions, carrots, celery stalks, and garlic, for 2-3 minutes. Season with salt, pepper, and rosemary. Add the remaining ingredients and seal the lid. Cook on High Pressure for 30 minutes. When ready, release the pressure naturally, for about 5 minutes.

# Vegan Lentil & Quinoa Stew

Serving Size: 4 | Total Time: 25 minutes

### Ingredients

1 cup quinoa, soaked overnight
1 cup tomatoes, diced
1 cup lentils, soaked overnight
¼ cup sun-dried tomatoes, chopped

1 tsp garlic, minced
4 cups vegetable broth
1 tsp salt
1 tsp red pepper flakes

### Directions

Add all ingredients in your instant pot. Seal the lid and adjust the steam release handle. Cook on High Pressure for 20 minutes. Release the steam naturally, for about 5 minutes.

# Roman Beans Stewed with Carrot & Tomatoes

Serving Size: 6 | Total Time: 30 minutes

### Ingredients

2 cups cranberry beans, soaked, rinsed
2 onions, chopped
3 carrots, chopped
3 tomatoes, peeled, diced

3 tbsp olive oil
A handful of fresh parsley
2 cups water
Salt and black pepper to taste

### Directions

Heat olive oil on Sauté, and stir-fry the onions, for 3-4 minutes, until translucent. Add in carrots and tomatoes. Stir well and cook for 5 minutes. Stir in beans, salt, black pepper and water, and seal the lid. Cook on High Pressure for 15 minutes. Do a quick release and serve hot sprinkled with fresh parsley.

# Mixed Vegetables Medley

Serving Size: 4 | Total Time: 15 minutes

### Ingredients

1 small head broccoli, broken into florets
16 asparagus, trimmed
1 small head cauliflower, broken into florets

5 ounces green beans
2 carrots, peeled and cut on bias
Salt to taste

### Directions

Add 1 cup of water and set trivet on top of water and place steamer basket on top. In an even layer, spread green beans, broccoli, cauliflower, asparagus, and carrots in the steamer basket. Seal the lid and cook on Steam for 3 minutes on High. Release the pressure quickly. Remove basket from the pot and season with salt.

# Creamy Spinach Tagliatelle with Mushrooms

Serving Size: 4 | Total Time: 25 minutes

### Ingredients

8 oz spinach tagliatelle
6 oz frozen mixed mushrooms
3 tbsp butter, unsalted
¼ cup feta cheese

¼ cup grated Parmesan cheese
2 garlic cloves, crushed
¼ cup heavy cream
1 tbsp Italian seasoning mix

### Directions

Melt butter on Sauté, and stir-fry the garlic for a minute. Stir in feta, Italian seasoning, and mushrooms. Add tagliatelle, 2 cups of water and heavy cream. Cook on High Pressure for 4 minutes. Quick release the pressure and top with Parmesan cheese.

# Stuffed Bell Peppers with Rice & Mushrooms

Serving Size: 4 | Total Time: 35 minutes

## Ingredients

4 bell peppers, seeds and stems removed
1 onion, peeled, chopped
6 oz button mushrooms, chopped
2 garlic cloves, peeled, crushed
2 tbsp olive oil

Salt and black pepper to taste
½ cup rice
½ tbsp of paprika
2 cups vegetable stock

## Directions

Warm the olive oil on Sauté. Add onion, garlic, and mushrooms, and stir-fry until tender, for about 5 minutes. Press Cancel and set aside. In a bowl, combine rice and mushrooms with the mixture from the pot. Season with salt, pepper, and paprika, and stuff each bell pepper with this mixture.

Place them in the instant pot, filled side up, and pour in stock. Seal the lid and cook on High Pressure for 15 minutes. Release the pressure naturally, for about 5 minutes.

# Celery & Red Bean Stew

Serving Size: 4 | Total Time: 30 minutes

## Ingredients

6 oz red beans, cooked
2 carrots, chopped
2 celery stalks, cut into pieces
1 onion, peeled, chopped
2 tbsp tomato paste
1 bay leaf

2 cups vegetable broth
3 tbsp olive oil
1 tbsp salt
A handful of fresh parsley
1 tbsp of flour

## Directions

Warm olive oil on Sauté and stir-fry the onion, for 3 minutes, until soft. Add celery and carrots. Cook for 5 more minutes, adding 1 tbsp of broth at the time. Add red beans, bay leaf, salt, parsley, and tomato paste.

Stir in 1 tbsp of flour and pour in the remaining broth. Seal the lid and cook on High pressure for 5 minutes on. Do a natural release, for about 10 minutes. Sprinkle with some fresh parsley and serve warm.

# Cannellini Beans with Garlic & Leeks

Serving Size: 4 | Total Time: 45 minutes

## Ingredients

1 lb cannellini beans, soaked overnight
1 onion, peeled, chopped
2 large leeks, finely chopped

3 garlic cloves, whole
Salt and black pepper to taste

*Topping:*
4 tbsp vegetable oil
2 tbsp flour

1 tbsp cayenne pepper

## Directions

Add all ingredients, except for the topping ones, in the instant pot. Press Manual/Pressure Cook and cook for 20 minutes on High. Meanwhile, heat 4 tbsp of oil in a skillet. Add flour and cayenne pepper.

Stir-fry for 2 minutes and set aside. When you hear the cooker's end signal, do a quick release. Pour in the cayenne mixture and give it a good stir. Let it sit for 15 minutes before serving.

# Traditional Italian Pesto

Serving Size: 4 | Total Time: 25 minutes

## Ingredients

3 zucchini, peeled, chopped
1 eggplant, peeled, chopped
3 red bell peppers, chopped
½ cup fresh tomato juice

2 tbsp oregano, chopped
½ tbsp salt
2 tbsp olive oil

## Directions

Add all ingredients in the pot and give it a good stir. Pour 1 cup of water. Seal the lid and cook on High pressure for 15 minutes. Do a quick release. Set aside to cool completely. Serve as a cold salad or a side dish.

# Paprika Garbanzo Stew with Onions & Tomatoes

Serving Size: 5 | Total Time: 35 minutes

## Ingredients

1 lb chickpeas, soaked
3 purple onions, chopped
2 tomatoes, roughly chopped
2 oz fresh parsley, chopped
3 cups vegetable broth

1 tbsp paprika
3 tbsp butter
2 tbsp olive oil
Salt and black pepper to taste

## Directions

Warm olive oil on Sauté and stir-fry the onions for 3 minutes. Add the rest of the ingredients. Seal the lid and cook on the Meat/Stew for 30 minutes on High. Do a quick release and serve warm.

# Spicy Shiitake Mushrooms with Potatoes & Zucchini

Serving Size: 4 | Total Time: 45 minutes

## Ingredients

1 lb shiitake mushrooms
2 potatoes, chopped
3 garlic cloves, crushed
2 tbsp oil
1 tsp garlic powder
1 tbsp cumin seeds

½ tbsp chili powder
1 large zucchini, chopped
1 cup onions
2 cups vegetable stock
1 cup tomato sauce

## Directions

Warm olive oil on Sauté. Stir-fry cumin seeds for one minute. Add onions, chili powder, garlic, and garlic powder. Cook for 3 minutes, stirring constantly.

Add mushrooms and continue to cook on Sauté mode for 3 more minutes. Add the remaining ingredients and seal the lid. Cook on High Pressure for 20 minutes. When done, release the Pressure naturally.

# Pasta Orecchiette with Broccoli & Tofu

Serving Size: 4 | Total Time: 25 minutes

## Ingredients

1 (9 oz) pack orecchiette
16 oz broccoli, roughly chopped
2 garlic cloves

3 tbsp olive oil
1 tbsp grated tofu
Salt and black pepper to taste

### Directions

Place the orecchiette and broccoli in your instant pot. Cover with water and seal the lid. Cook on High Pressure for 10 minutes. Do a quick release.

Drain the broccoli and orecchiette. Set aside. Heat the olive oil on Sauté mode. Stir-fry garlic for 2 minutes. Stir in broccoli, orecchiette, salt, and pepper. Cook for 2 more minutes. Press Cancel and Stir in grated tofu, to serve.

# Spicy Split Pea Stew

Serving Size: 4 | Total Time: 40 minutes

### Ingredients

2 cups split yellow peas
1 cup onion, chopped
1 carrot, chopped
2 potatoes, chopped
2 tbsp butter

¼ cup lemon juice
2 garlic cloves, crushed
1 tbsp chili pepper
½ tbsp salt
4 cups vegetable stock

### Directions

Melt butter on Sauté, and stir-fry the onion, for 1 minute. Add the remaining vegetables and cook for 5-6 minutes, until tender. Stir in chili pepper and season with salt. Pour in the stock and seal the lid.

Cook on High on Meat/Stew for 25 minutes. Do a quick release, drizzle with lemon juice and serve.

# Penne Pasta with Shiitake & Vegetables

Serving Size: 4 | Total Time: 25 minutes

### Ingredients

6 oz penne pasta
6 oz shiitake mushrooms, chopped
2 garlic cloves, crushed
1 small carrot, chopped into strips
6 oz zucchini cut into strips
6 oz finely chopped leek

4 oz baby spinach, finely chopped
3 tbsp oil
2 tbsp soy sauce
1 tbsp ground ginger
½ tbsp salt

### Directions

Heat oil on Sauté and stir-fry carrot and garlic for 3-4 minutes. Add the remaining ingredients and pour in 2 cup of water. Cook on High Pressure for 4 minutes. Quick release the pressure and serve.

# Carrot & Sweet Potato Thick Soup

Serving Size: 5 | Total Time: 40 minutes

### Ingredients

3 sweet potatoes, cut into bite-sized pieces
2 carrots, chopped
1 onion, peeled, chopped
6 tbsp olive oil
2 tbsp tomato sauce

4 cups water
1 tbsp celery, finely chopped
1 tbsp parsley, finely chopped
Salt and black pepper to taste

### Directions

Heat olive oil on Sauté mode. Add onion, carrots, celery, and potatoes. Stir-fry for 2 minutes.

Stir in water, tomato sauce, and the potatoes. Seal the lid and cook for 25 minutes on High Pressure. Do a quick release. Open the pot and add the other ingredients. Seal again, and cook for 5 minutes on High. Do a quick release.

# Turmeric Stew with Green Peas

Serving Size: 4 | Total Time: 35 minutes

## Ingredients

2 cups green peas, frozen
1 large onion, chopped
4 cloves garlic, chopped
3 oz of olives, pitted
1 tbsp ginger, shredded

1 tbsp turmeric
1 tbsp salt
4 cups vegetable stock
3 tbsp olive oil

## Directions

Heat olive oil on Sauté. Stir-fry the onion and garlic for 2-3 minutes, stirring a few times.

Add the remaining ingredients and press Cancel. Seal the lid, select manual and cook on High Pressure for 20 minutes.

Once the timer goes off, do a quick release before opening the lid. Serve with dollop of natural yoghurt.

# Indian Dhal with Veggies

Serving Size: 4 | Total Time: 35 minutes

## Ingredients

10 oz lentils, soaked overnight
2 tbsp almond butter
1 carrot, peeled, chopped
1 potato, peeled, chopped
1 bay leaf
¼ tbsp parsley, chopped

½ tbsp chili powder
2 tbsp ground cumin
1 tbsp garam masala
3 cups vegetable stock
Salt to taste

## Directions

Melt almond butter on Sauté. Add carrots, potatoes, and parsley. Give it a good stir and cook for 10 minutes.

Add the remaining ingredients, except for the parsley and press Cancel. If the mixture is very thick, add a bit of water. Seal the lid, select manual and cook on High Pressure for 15 minutes.

Once the timer goes off, do a quick release. Serve hot sprinkled with parsley.

# Stuffed Avocado Bake

Serving Size: 2 | Total Time: 20 minutes

## Ingredients

1 avocado, halved
2 eggs
3 tbsp butter, melted

1 tbsp dried oregano
Salt and black pepper to taste
1 tomato, chopped

## Directions

Grease a baking dish with butter. With a spoon, remove some of the avocado flesh to create more space for the egg. Reserve the flesh for garnish.

Place the avocado halves the baking dish. Crack an egg into each avocado half. Season with salt and oregano. Add 1 ½ cups of water and place the trivet inside the pot. Lower the baking dish on top. Seal the lid, select Manual and cook on High Pressure for 10 minutes.

When done, do a quick release before opening the lid. Mix the reserved avocado flesh with the tomato, season with salt and pepper and serve with the baked avocado halves.

# Pasta, Beans & Grains

## Fusilli with Chicken Bolognese Sauce

Serving Size: 8 | Total Time: 50 minutes

### Ingredients

2 tbsp olive oil

6 ounces bacon, cubed

1 onion, minced

1 carrot, minced

1 celery stalk, minced

2 garlic cloves, crushed

¼ cup tomato paste

¼ tbsp crushed red pepper flakes

1 ½ pounds ground chicken

½ cup white wine

1 cup milk

1 cup chicken broth

Salt to taste

1 pound fusilli pasta

### Directions

Warm olive oil on Sauté. Add in bacon and fry for 5 minutes until crispy. Add celery, carrot, garlic and onion and cook for 5 minutes until fragrant.

Mix in red pepper flakes and tomato paste, and cook for 2 minutes. Break chicken into small pieces and place in the pot.

Cook for 10 minutes, as you stir, until browned. Pour in wine and simmer for 2 minutes. Add in chicken broth, salt, and milk. Seal the lid and cook for 15 minutes on High Pressure. Release the pressure quickly.

Add in the fusilli and stir. Seal the lid, and cook on High Pressure for another 5 minutes. Release the Pressure quickly. Check the pasta for doneness. Taste, adjust the seasoning and serve.

## Parmesan-Coated Yellow Squash with Linguine

Serving Size: 4 | Total Time: 45 minutes

### Ingredients

1 cup flour

Salt and black pepper to taste

2 eggs

4 cups water

1 cup breadcrumbs

½ cup grated Parmesan cheese + more for garnish

1 yellow squash, peeled and sliced

1 pound linguine pasta

24 ounces canned tomato sauce

2 tbsp olive oil

1 cup shredded mozzarella cheese

Minced fresh basil, for garnish

### Directions

Break the linguine in half. Put it in the pot and add water and salt. Seal the lid and cook on High Pressure for 5 minutes. Quickly release the pressure.

Combine the flour and 1 tbsp of salt in a bowl. In another bowl, whisk the eggs and 2 tbsp of water. In a third bowl, mix the breadcrumbs and mozzarella cheese.

Coat each yellow squash slice in the flour. Shake off excess flour, dip in the egg wash, and dredge in the breadcrumbs.

Heat oil on Sauté and fry breaded squash until crispy.

Remove linguine to a serving bowl and mix in the tomato sauce and sprinkle with fresh basil.

Serve the squash with the linguine on the side.

# Chili Mac & Cheese

Serving Size: 6 | Total Time: 15 minutes

## Ingredients

12 ounces macaroni
4 cups cold water
Salt and black pepper to taste
2 eggs
1 tbsp chili powder

4 tbsp butter
1 ½ cups milk
4 cups sharp cheddar cheese, grated
2 cups Pecorino Romano cheese, grated

## Directions

Add salt, water and macaroni. Seal the lid and cook for 4 minutes on High Pressure.

Take a bowl and beat eggs, chili powder, and black pepper, to mix well. Release the pressure quickly. Add butter to the pasta and stir until melts. Stir in milk and egg mixture. Pour in Pecorino Romano and cheddar cheeses until melted. Cook in batches, if needed. Season to taste.

# Four-Cheese Traditional Italian Pasta

Serving Size: 6 | Total Time: 15 minutes

## Ingredients

¼ cup goat cheese, chopped
¼ cup grated Pecorino cheese
½ cup grated Parmesan
1 cup heavy cream
½ cup grated gouda cheese

¼ cup butter, softened
1 tbsp Italian seasoning mix
1 cup vegetable broth
1 lb tagliatelle pasta

## Directions

In a bowl, mix goat cheese, pecorino, parmesan, and heavy cream. Stir in Italian seasoning. Transfer to your instant pot. Stir in the broth and butter.

Seal the lid and cook on High Pressure for 4 minutes. Do a quick release. Meanwhile, drop the tagliatelle in boiling water and cook for 6 minutes. Remove the instant pot lid and stir in the tagliatelle. Top with grated gouda and let simmer for about 10 minutes on Sauté mode.

# Tomato & Spinach Sausage Spaghetti

Serving Size: 4 | Total Time: 35 minutes

## Ingredients

2 tbsp olive oil
½ cup onion, chopped
1 garlic clove, minced
1 pound pork sausage meat
2 cups water
1 (14-ounce) can diced tomatoes, drained
½ cup sun-dried tomatoes

1 tbsp dried oregano
1 tbsp Italian seasoning
1 fresh jalapeño pepper, stemmed, seeded, minced
1 tbsp salt
8 ounces spaghetti, halved
1 cup spinach

## Directions

Warm olive oil on Sauté. Add in onion and garlic and cook for 2 minutes until softened. Stir in sausage meat and cook for 5 minutes. Stir in jalapeño pepper, water, sun-dried tomatoes, Italian seasoning, oregano, diced tomatoes, and salt; Mix spaghetti and press to submerge into the sauce.

Seal the lid and cook on High Pressure for 9 minutes. Release the Pressure quickly. Stir in spinach, seal the lid again, and simmer on Keep Warm for 5 minutes until spinach is wilted.

# Ziti Green Minestrone

Serving Size: 4 | Total Time: 15 minutes

## Ingredients

3 tbsp olive oil
1 onion, diced
1 celery stalk, diced
1 large carrot, peeled and diced
14 ounces canned chopped tomatoes
4 ounces ziti pasta
3 cups water
1 cup chopped zucchini

1 bay leaf
1 tbsp mixed herbs
¼ tbsp cayenne pepper
Salt and black pepper to taste
¼ cup shredded, Pecorino Romano cheese
1 garlic clove, minced
1/3 cup olive pesto pasta

## Directions

Heat olive oil on Sauté and cook onion, celery, garlic, and carrot for 3 minutes, stirring occasionally until the vegetables are softened. Stir in ziti pasta, tomatoes, water, zucchini, bay leaf, mixed herbs, cayenne, black pepper, and salt.

Seal the lid and cook on High for 4 minutes. Do a natural pressure release for 5 minutes. Adjust the taste and remove the bay leaf. Ladle the soup into serving bowls and drizzle the pesto over. Serve with the garlic toasts.

# Tri-Color Rotini with Kale & Spicy Pomodoro Sauce

Serving Size: 6 | Total Time: 15 minutes

## Ingredients

1 pound tri-color rotini pasta
15 ounces canned tomato sauce
3 garlic cloves, minced
1 tsp chili flakes
2 tsp salt

2 tsp extra-virgin olive oil
1 handful fresh basil, minced
1 cup kale, chopped
¼ cup Parmesan cheese

## Directions

Add tomato sauce, salt, pasta, chili flakes, and garlic and mix well in the pot. Cover with water. Seal lid and cook for 5 minutes on High Pressure. Release the Pressure quickly. Stir in kale until wilted. Plate the pasta and top with the Parmesan cheese and basil. Drizzle extra-virgin olive oil over the pasta to serve.

# Primavera Egg Noodles

Serving Size: 4 | Total Time: 20 minutes

## Ingredients

1 bunch asparagus, trimmed
2 cups broccoli florets
3 tbsp olive oil
Salt to taste
10 ounces egg noodles
3 garlic cloves, minced

2 ½ cups vegetable stock
½ cup heavy cream
1 cup small tomatoes, halved
¼ cup chopped basil
½ cup grated Parmesan cheese

## Directions

Pour 2 cups of water, add the noodles, 2 tbsp of olive oil, garlic and salt. Place a trivet over the water. Combine asparagus, broccoli, remaining olive oil, stock, and salt in a bowl. Place the vegetables on the trivet. Seal the lid and cook on Steam for 12 minutes on High. Do a quick release. Remove the vegetables to a plate.

Stir the heavy cream and tomatoes in the pasta. Press Sauté and simmer the cream until desired consistency. gently mix in the asparagus and broccoli. Garnish with basil and Parmesan, to serve.

# Roasted Mushrooms and Swiss-Style Garganelli

Serving Size: 4 | Total Time: 10 minutes

## Ingredients

8 ounces garganelli
2 cups water
1 tbsp salt
1 large egg
8 ounces Gruyère cheese, shredded

2 cups mushrooms, sliced
2 tbsp chopped fresh cilantro
3 tbsp sour cream
3 tbsp butter
3 tbsp cheddar cheese, grated

## Directions

Put the garganelli with water, butter, and salt into the pot. Seal lid and cook on High Pressure for 4 minutes. Do a quick pressure release. Set aside.

Melt butter on Sauté and cook mushrooms for 5-6 minutes until tender.

In a bowl, whisk egg, Gruyère cheese, and sour cream. Add in garganelli to melt the cheese and stir in the mushrooms. Serve sprinkled with cheddar cheese and fresh cilantro.

# Sausage, Spinach & Tomato Rigatoni

Serving Size: 4 | Total Time: 45 minutes

## Ingredients

1 tbsp butter
½ cup diced red bell pepper
1 onion, chopped
3 cups vegetable broth
¼ cup tomato purée
4 sausage links, chopped

½ cup milk
2 tbsp chili powder
Salt and black pepper to taste
12 ounces rigatoni pasta
1 cup baby spinach
½ cup Parmesan cheese

## Directions

Warm butter on Sauté. Add red bell pepper, onion, and sausage, and cook for 5 minutes. Mix in broth, chili, tomato pureé, milk, salt, and pepper. Stir in rigatoni pasta.

Seal the lid and cook on High Pressure for 12 minutes. Naturally release Pressure for 20 minutes. Stir in spinach and let simmer until wilted. Sprinkle with Parmesan and serve.

# Pasta Caprese with Ricotta & Basil

Serving Size: 3 | Total Time: 15 minutes

## Ingredients

1 tbsp olive oil
1 onion, chopped
6 garlic cloves, minced
1 tbsp red pepper flakes
2 ½ cups fusilli pasta
1 (15-ounce) can tomato sauce

1 cup cherry tomatoes, halved
1 cup water
¼ cup basil leaves
1 tbsp salt
1 cup Ricotta cheese, crumbled
2 tbsp chopped fresh basil

## Directions

Warm olive oil on Sauté. Add in red pepper flakes, garlic and onion and cook for 3 minutes until soft.

Mix in fusilli, tomatoes, half of the basil leaves, water, tomato sauce, and salt. Seal the lid, and cook on High Pressure for 4 minutes. Release the pressure quickly. Transfer the pasta to a serving platter and top with the crumbled cheese and remaining chopped basil.

# Quinoa Bowls with Broccoli & Pesto

Serving Size: 2 | Total Time: 30 minutes

## Ingredients

1 cup quinoa, rinsed and drained
2 cups vegetable broth
Salt and black pepper to taste
1 potato, peeled, cubed
1 head broccoli, cut into small florets
1 bunch baby heirloom carrots, peeled

¼ cabbage, chopped
2 eggs
1 avocado, sliced
¼ cup pesto sauce
Lemon wedges, for serving

## Directions

In the pot, mix broth, pepper, quinoa and salt. Set trivet to the inner pot on top of quinoa and add a steamer basket to the top of the trivet. Mix carrots, potato, eggs and broccoli in the steamer basket. Add pepper and salt.

Seal the lid and cook for 1 minute on High Pressure. Quick-release the pressure.

Take away the trivet and steamer basket from the pot. Set the eggs in a bowl of ice water. Then peel and halve the eggs. Use a fork to fluff quinoa. Adjust the seasonings. In two bowls, equally divide avocado, quinoa, broccoli, eggs, carrots, potato, cabbage and a dollop of pesto. Serve alongside a lemon wedge.

# Pancetta with Garbanzo Beans

Serving Size: 6 | Total Time: 50 minutes

## Ingredients

3 strips pancetta
1 onion, diced
15 oz canned garbanzo beans
2 cups water
1 cup apple cider
2 garlic cloves, minced

½ cup ketchup
¼ cup sugar
1 tbsp ground mustard powder
Salt and black pepper to taste
Fresh parsley to garnish

## Directions

Cook pancetta for 5 minutes, until crispy, on Sauté mode. Add onion and garlic, and cook for 3 minutes until soft. Mix in garbanzo beans, ketchup, sugar, salt, apple cider, mustard powder, water, and black pepper.

Seal the lid, press Bean/Chili and cook on High Pressure for 30 minutes. Release Pressure naturally for 10 minutes. Serve in bowls garnished with parsley.

# Homemade Veggie Quinoa

Serving Size: 6 | Total Time: 15 minutes

## Ingredients

1 cup quinoa, rinsed
2 cups water
2 carrots, cut into sticks
1 large onion, chopped

2 tbsp olive oil
Salt to taste
Fresh cilantro, chopped for garnish

## Directions

Heat olive oil on Sauté. Add in onion and carrots and stir-fry for about 10 minutes until tender and crispy. Remove to a plate and set aside. Add water, salt and quinoa in the instant pot.

Seal the lid and cook on High Pressure for 1 minute. Do a quick release. Fluff the cooked quinoa with a fork. Transfer to a serving plate and top with the carrots and onion. Serve scattered with cilantro.

# Beef Garam Masala with Rice

Serving Size: 5 | Total Time: 40 minutes

## Ingredients

¼ cup yogurt
2 cloves garlic, smashed
1 tbsp olive oil
1 lime, juiced
Salt and black pepper to taste
2 pounds beef stew meat, cubed
1 tbsp garam masala
1 tbsp fresh ginger, grated
1 ½ tbsp smoked paprika
1 tsp ground cumin

¼ tbsp cayenne pepper
3 tbsp butter
1 onion, chopped
1 (14-ounce) can puréed tomatoes
½ cup beef broth
2 cups basmati rice, rinsed
2 cups water
½ cup heavy cream
½ bunch fresh cilantro, chopped

## Directions

In a bowl, mix garlic, lime juice, olive oil, pepper, salt and yogurt. Stir in the beef to coat. In a different bowl, thoroughly mix paprika, garam masala, cumin, ginger, and cayenne pepper.

Melt butter on Sauté and stir-fry the onion for 7 to 9 minutes, until translucent. Sprinkle spice mixture over onion; cook for about 30 seconds until soft.

To the onion, add in the beef-yogurt mixture; Sauté for 3 to 4 minutes until meat is slightly cooked. Mix in broth and puréed tomatoes. Set trivet over beef in the Pressure cooker's inner pot.

In an oven-proof bowl, mix water and rice. Set the bowl onto the trivet. Seal the lid and cook on High Pressure for 10 minutes. Release pressure quickly. Remove the bowl with rice and trivet. Add pepper, salt and heavy cream into beef and stir. Use a fork to fluff rice and divide into serving plates; apply a topping of beef. Use cilantro to garnish.

# Chickpea & Jalapeño Chicken Stew

Serving Size: 6 | Total Time: 40 minutes

## Ingredients

1 pound boneless, skinless chicken legs
2 tbsp ground cumin
½ tbsp cayenne pepper
2 tbsp olive oil
1 onion, minced
2 jalapeño peppers, deseeded and minced
3 garlic cloves, crushed
2 tbsp freshly grated ginger

¼ cup chicken stock
1 (24 oz) can crushed tomatoes
2 (14 oz) cans chickpeas, drained and rinsed
Salt to taste
½ cup coconut milk
¼ cup fresh parsley, chopped
2 cups hot cooked basmati rice

## Directions

Season the chicken with 1 tbsp salt, cayenne pepper, and cumin. Set on Sauté and warm the oil. Add in jalapeño peppers, and onion, and cook for 5 minutes until soft. Mix in ginger and garlic, and cook for 3 minutes until tender.

Add ¼ cup chicken stock into the cooker to ensure the pan is deglazed, from the pan's bottom scrape any browned bits of food.

Mix the onion mixture with, chickpeas, tomatoes, and salt. Stir in seasoned chicken to coat in sauce. Seal the lid and cook on High Pressure for 20 minutes. Release the pressure quickly.

Remove the chicken and slice into chunks. Into the remaining sauce, mix in coconut milk; simmer for 5 minutes on Keep Warm. Split rice into 4 bowls. Top with chicken, then sauce and add parsley for garnish.

# Kale & Parmesan Pearl Barley

Serving Size: 2 | Total Time: 35 minutes

## Ingredients

1 tbsp butter
1 small onion, diced
1 cup pearl barley, rinsed and drained
2 garlic cloves, smashed
2 cups vegetable broth

½ cup grated Parmesan cheese + 1 tbsp for topping
1 cup kale, chopped
juice of ½ lemon, juiced
Salt and black pepper to taste

## Directions

Warm butter on Sauté. Add in onion and cook for 3 minutes until soft. Stir in garlic and barley and continue cooking for 1 to 2 minutes until barley is toasted. Mix in broth.

Seal the lid and cook for 9 minutes on High Pressure. Release Pressure naturally for 10 minutes, then quick-release the remaining Pressure. Add Parmesan cheese into barley mixture and stir until fully melted.

Just before serving, add lemon juice and kale into barley mixture. Add pepper and salt to taste.

# Stewed Spinach with Kidney Beans

Serving Size: 4 | Total Time: 45 minutes

## Ingredients

2 tbsp olive oil
1 onion, chopped
2 cloves garlic, minced
2 carrots, peeled and chopped
1 cup celery, chopped
4 cups vegetable broth

1 cup white kidney beans, soaked, drained, rinsed
1 tsp dried thyme
1 tsp dried rosemary
1 bay leaf
1 cup spinach, torn into pieces
Salt and black pepper to taste

## Directions

Warm olive oil on Sauté. Stir in garlic and onion, and cook for 3 minutes until tender and fragrant. Mix in celery and carrots and cook for 2 to 3 minutes more until they start to soften. Add broth, bay leaf, thyme, rosemary, kidney beans, and salt.

Seal the lid and cook for 30 minutes on High Pressure. Quick release the pressure and stir in spinach. Allow to sitting for 2 to 4 minutes until the spinach wilts, and season with pepper and salt.

# Lime Bulgur with Olives

Serving Size: 4 | Total Time: 30 minutes

## Ingredients

1 tbsp olive oil
1 small onion, chopped
2 cloves garlic, minced
1 tbsp cilantro
1 cup bulgur

2 ½ cups vegetable broth
1 tbsp lime juice, or more to taste
1 handful fresh parsley, roughly chopped
10 black olives to garnish
Salt and black pepper to taste

## Directions

Heat oil on Sauté. Stir in garlic and onion and cook for 10 to 13 minutes until golden brown. Add in cilantro, bulgur, and salt. Place 1 tbsp of lime juice and broth into the cooker. Seal the lid and cook on High Pressure for 1 minute. Do a quick release.

Use a fork to fluff bulgur. Add fresh parsley as you stir. Serve in bowls topped with black olives.

# Risotto with Spring Vegetables & Shrimp

Serving Size: 4 | Total Time: 1 hour 15 minutes

## Ingredients

1 tbsp avocado oil
1 pound asparagus, trimmed and roughly chopped
1 cup spinach, chopped
1 ½ cups mushrooms, sliced
1 cup rice, rinsed and drained
1 ¼ cups chicken broth

¾ cup coconut milk
1 tbsp coconut oil
16 shrimp, cleaned and deveined
Salt and black pepper to taste
¾ cup Parmesan cheese, shredded

## Directions

Warm the avocado oil on Sauté. Add spinach, mushrooms and asparagus and Sauté for 10 minutes until cooked through. Press Cancel. Add rice, coconut milk and chicken broth to the pot as you stir.

Seal the lid, press Multigrain and cook for 40 minutes on High Pressure. Do a quick release, open the lid and put the rice on a serving plate.

Take back the empty pot to the pressure cooker, add coconut oil and press Sauté. Add shrimp and cook each side taking 4 minutes until cooked through and turns pink. Set shrimp over rice, add pepper and salt. Serve topped with shredded Parmesan cheese.

# Mexican Frijoles Chili

Serving Size: 8 | Total Time: 45 minutes

## Ingredients

1 tsp olive oil
1 onion, chopped
3 cloves garlic, minced
6 cups vegetable broth
2 cups black beans, soaked, drained and rinsed
1 jalapeño pepper, deseeded and diced

1 tsp dried oregano
1 tsp dried chili flakes
Salt to taste
Cotija cheese, crumbled for garnish
Fresh cilantro for garnish

## Directions

Warm oil on Sauté. Add in garlic and onion and cook for 3 to 4 minutes until fragrant. Add beans, vegetable broth, oregano, chili flakes, salt and jalapeño pepper. Seal the lid and cook for 35 minutes on High Pressure. quick release the pressure. Divide into serving plates. Top with cilantro and Cotija cheese, to serve.

# Colorful Quinoa with Red Salsa

Serving Size: 5 | Total Time: 30 minutes

## Ingredients

1 tsp olive oil
1 green bell pepper, diced
1 red onion, diced
1 tsp ground cumin
½ tsp salt

14 oz canned pinto beans, drained and rinsed
1 cup organic tri-color quinoa, rinsed
1 cup red salsa
1 cup vegetable broth

## Directions

Warm oil on Sauté mode. Add red onion and green bell pepper as you stir. Add salt and cumin, and cook for 7-8 minutes until fragrant. To the vegetable mixture, add quinoa, broth, red salsa, and pinto beans.

Seal the lid and cook on High Pressure for 12 minutes. Do a quick Pressure release. Use a fork to fluff quinoa and divide between serving bowls to serve.

# Chorizo & Lentil Stew

Serving Size: 10 | Total Time: 50 minutes

## Ingredients

2 cups lentils, drained and rinsed
7 ounces chorizo, chopped
1 onion, diced
2 garlic cloves, crushed
2 cups tomato sauce
2 cups vegetable broth
½ cup mustard
½ cup cider vinegar
3 tbsp Worcestershire sauce

2 tbsp maple syrup
2 tbsp liquid smoke
1 tbsp lime juice
2 cups brown sugar
Salt and black pepper to taste
1 tsp chili powder
1 tsp paprika
¼ tsp cayenne pepper

## Directions

Set on Sauté mode, add in chorizo and cook for 3 minutes as you stir until crisp. Add garlic and onion and cook for 2 minutes until translucent.

Mix tomato sauce, broth, cider vinegar, liquid smoke, Worcestershire sauce, lime juice, mustard, and maple syrup in a mixing bowl. Pour the mixture in the Pressure cooker to deglaze the pan, scrape the bottom of the pan to do away with any browned bits of food.

Add pepper, chili, sugar, paprika, salt, and cayenne into the sauce mixture as you stir to mix. Stir in lentils to coat. Seal the lid and cook on High Pressure for 30 minutes. Release pressure naturally for 10 minutes.

# Vegetarian Wild Rice with Carrots

Serving Size: 6 | Total Time: 20 minutes

## Ingredients

4 cups vegetable broth
2 carrots, chopped
2 cups wild rice, rinsed and drained

3 tbsp butter
Zest and juice from 1 lemon
Salt and black pepper to taste

## Directions

Add rice, lemon zest, butter, and broth. Stir, seal the lid and cook on High Pressure for 3 minutes.

Release Pressure naturally for 10 minutes. Sprinkle salt, lemon juice, and black pepper over the rice and use a fork to gently fluff.

# Tasty Tacos with Black Beans & Avocado

Serving Size: 6 | Total Time: 1 hour 30 minutes

## Ingredients

2 cups black beans, soaked overnight
1 cup shallots, chopped
4 cups water
1 tbsp dried oregano
1 tsp chili powder

6 soft taco tortillas
1 avocado, sliced
Salt to taste
Fresh cilantro for garnish

## Directions

Drain the beans and add to the cooker. Mix in the shallots, oregano, salt and chili powder. Top with water.

Seal the lid and cook on High Pressure for 60 minutes. Do a quick release, and allow to cool for a few minutes. Serve with taco tortillas, avocado slices and cilantro for garnish.

# Delicious Millet with Herbs & Cherry Tomatoes

Serving Size: 8 | Total Time: 35 minutes

## Ingredients

2 cups millet, rinsed and drained
4 cups vegetable stock
½ sweet onion, chopped
1 cup cherry tomatoes, halved

1 tbsp fresh sage, chopped
1 tsp fresh thyme, chopped
1 tsp fresh parsley, chopped
Salt and black pepper to taste

## Directions

Add millet, onion, and vegetable stock. Seal the lid and cook for 10 minutes on High Pressure. Release Pressure quickly. Fluff the millet with a fork, add in herbs and tomatoes and season with pepper and salt.

# Easy Red Lentil Dhal with Spinach

Serving Size: 6 | Total Time: 35 minutes

## Ingredients

2 tbsp olive oil
1 red jalapeño, seeded and minced
1 cup spinach, chopped
4 cloves garlic, minced
1 tsp fresh ginger, peeled and grated
1 tbsp cumin seeds
1 tbsp coriander seeds
1 tsp ground turmeric

¼ tsp cayenne pepper
3 cups water
1 ½ cups red lentils
1 tomato, diced
¼ cup lemon juice
Salt to taste
Fresh cilantro, chopped for garnish
Natural yogurt for garnish

## Directions

Heat oil on Sauté, add cayenne, red jalapeño, ginger, turmeric, cumin, and garlic, and coriander and cook for 2 to 3 minutes until seeds become fragrant and begin to pop.

Pour in water, tomato, and lentils into the pot and stir. Seal the lid and cook on High Pressure for 10 minutes.

Release Pressure naturally for 10 minutes, then release the remaining pressure quickly. Stir in spinach until wilted. Add lemon juice and Season to taste. Divide lentils between bowls and garnish with yogurt and cilantro.

# Risotto with Broccoli & Grana Padano

Serving Size: 6 | Total Time: 25 minutes

## Ingredients

2 tbsp olive oil
1 head broccoli, cut into florets
1 onion, chopped
3 tbsp butter
2 cups carnaroli rice, rinsed

¼ cup dry white wine
4 cups chicken stock
Salt and white pepper to taste
2 tbsp Grana Padano cheese, grated
¼ tbsp Grana Padano cheese, flakes

## Directions

Warm oil on Sauté. stir-fry onion for 3 minutes until soft and translucent. Add in butter, broccoli, and rice and cook for 5 minutes stirring occasionally.

Pour wine into the pot to deglaze, scrape away any browned bits of food from the pan.

Stir in stock, white pepper, and salt to the pot. Seal the lid, press Rice and cook on High for 15 minutes. Release the Pressure quickly.

Sprinkle with grated Padano cheese and stir well. Top with flaked Padano cheese for garnish before serving.

# Mom's Black-Eyed Peas with Garlic & Kale

Serving Size: 6 | Total Time: 30 minutes

## Ingredients

1 tsp olive oil
1 onion, chopped
2 garlic cloves, minced
1 cup fire-roasted red peppers, diced
½ tsp ground allspice
½ tsp red pepper, crushed

Salt to taste
1 ½ cups black-eyed peas, soaked and rinsed
1 ½ cups vegetable broth
1 bay leaf
1 (15-ounce) can fire roasted tomatoes
2 cups chopped kale

## Directions

Warm oil on Sauté mode. Add onion and cook for 5 minutes until fragrant; add garlic and fire roasted red peppers and cook for 1 more minute until softened. Season with salt, crushed red pepper, and allspice.

Add broth, bay leaf, and black-eyed peas to the pot. Seal the lid and cook on High Pressure for 5 minutes. Do a quick Pressure release. Remove the bay leaf and discard. Mix the peas with kale and tomatoes.

Seal the lid and cook on High for 1 minute. Release the Pressure quickly. Adjust the seasoning to serve.

# Cilantro Stuffed Mushrooms with Rice & Cheese

Serving Size: 4 | Total Time: 30 minutes

## Ingredients

4 portobello mushrooms, stems and gills removed
2 tbsp melted butter
½ cup brown rice, cooked
1 tomato, seed removed and chopped
¼ cup black olives, pitted and chopped
1 green bell pepper, seeded and diced

½ cup feta cheese, crumbled
Juice of 1 lemon
Salt and black pepper to taste
Minced fresh cilantro, for garnish
1 cup vegetable broth

## Directions

Brush the mushrooms with butter. Arrange the mushrooms in a single layer in an oiled baking pan. In a bowl, mix the rice, tomato, olives, bell pepper, feta cheese, lemon juice, salt, and black pepper.

Spoon the rice mixture into the mushrooms. Pour in the broth, seal the lid and cook on High Pressure for 10 minutes. Do a quick release. Garnish with fresh cilantro and serve immediately.

# Pearl Barley Sloppy Joes

Serving Size: 6 | Total Time: 35 minutes

## Ingredients

2 cups water
1 cup pearl barley, rinsed
1 cup green onion, chopped
1 clove garlic, minced
2 cups tomato sauce
2 tbsp brown sugar
2 tbsp Worcestershire sauce

1 tsp Dijon mustard
1 tsp smoked paprika
1 tsp chili powder
Salt and black pepper to taste
6 brioche buns
Dill pickles for garnish

## Directions

In the pot, mix Worcestershire sauce, water, onion, garlic, brown sugar, barley, tomato sauce, and spices. Season with salt and pepper. Seal the lid and cook for 25 minutes on High Pressure. Release the pressure quickly. Press Sauté and cook until the mixture becomes thick. Transfer the sloppy joe mixture to the brioche buns and top with dill pickles.

# Spinach & Cheese Filled Conchiglie Shells

Serving Size: 6 | Total Time: 1 hour

## Ingredients

2 cups onions, chopped
1 cup carrots, chopped
3 garlic cloves, minced
3 ½ tbsp olive oil
1 (28-ounce) canned tomatoes, crushed
12 ounces conchiglie pasta
1 tbsp olive oil for greasing
2 cups ricotta cheese, crumbled

1 ½ cups feta cheese, crumbled
2 cups spinach, chopped
¾ cup grated Pecorino Romano cheese
2 tbsp chopped fresh chives
1 tbsp chopped fresh dill
Salt and black pepper to taste
1 cup shredded cheddar cheese

## Directions

Warm olive oil on Sauté. Add in onions, carrots, and garlic, and cook for 5 minutes until tender. Stir in tomatoes and cook for another 10 minutes. Remove to a bowl and set aside.

Wipe the pot with a damp cloth, add pasta and cover with enough water. Seal the lid and cook for 5 minutes on High Pressure. Do a quick release and drain the pasta. Lightly grease olive oil to a baking sheet.

In a bowl, combine feta and ricotta cheese. Add in spinach, Pecorino Romano cheese, dill, and chives, salt, black pepper, and stir well. Adjust the seasonings. Using a spoon, fill the shells with the mixture.

Spread 4 cups tomato sauce on the baking sheet. Place the stuffed shells over with seam-sides down and sprinkle cheddar cheese on the top. Use aluminum foil to the cover the baking dish.

Pour 1 cup of water in the pot of the Pressure cooker and insert the trivet. Lower the baking dish onto the trivet. Seal the lid, and cook for 15 minutes on High Pressure. Do a quick release. Take away the foil. Place the stuffed shells to serving plates and top with tomato sauce before serving.

# Colorful Turkey Fajitas with Rotini Pasta

Serving Size: 6 | Total Time: 35 minutes

## Ingredients

2 tsp chili powder
1 tsp salt
1 tsp cumin
1 tsp onion powder
1 tsp garlic powder
½ tsp thyme
1 ½ lb turkey breast, cut into strips
1 tbsp olive oil
1 red onion, cut into wedges
4 garlic cloves, minced

3 cups chicken broth
1 cup pasta sauce
16 ounces rotini pasta
1 red bell pepper, chopped diagonally
1 yellow bell pepper, chopped diagonally
1 green bell pepper, chopped diagonally
1 cup shredded Gouda cheese
½ cup sour cream
½ cup chopped parsley

## Directions

In a bowl, mix chili powder, cumin, garlic powder, onion powder, salt, and thyme. Reserve 1 tsp of seasoning. Coat turkey with the remaining seasoning.

Warm oil on Sauté. Add in turkey strips and Sauté for 4 to 5 minutes until browned. Place the turkey in a bowl. Sauté the red onion and garlic cloves for 1 minute in the cooker until soft. Press Cancel.

Mix in salsa, broth, and scrape the bottom of any brown bits. Into the broth mixture, stir in rotini pasta and cover with bell peppers and chicken. Seal the lid and cook for 5 minutes on High Pressure. Do a quick Pressure release.

Open the lid and sprinkle with shredded Gouda cheese and reserved seasoning, and stir well. Divide into plates and top with sour cream. Add parsley for garnishing and serve.

# Spicy Three-Bean Vegetable Chili

Serving Size: 8 | Total Time: 40 minutes

## Ingredients

1 tbsp canola oil
1 onion, chopped
3 stalks of celery, chopped
1 green bell pepper, chopped
1 head broccoli, chopped into florets
2 tbsp minced garlic
2 tbsp chili powder
2 tsp ground cumin

4 cups vegetable broth
1 (28-ounce) can tomatoes, crushed
½ cup pinto beans, soaked, drained and rinsed
½ cup black beans, soaked, drained and rinsed
½ cup cannellini beans, soaked, drained and rinsed
1 bay leaf
Salt to taste
Fresh parsley, chopped for garnish

## Directions

Warm oil on Sauté. Add onion and bell pepper, broccoli, and celery, and cook for about 8 minutes until softened. Mix in cumin, chili powder, and garlic and cook for another 1 minute.

Add vegetable broth, tomatoes, black beans, salt, cannellini beans, pinto beans, and bay leaf to the pot. Seal the lid and cook for 25 minutes on High Pressure. Do a quick Pressure release. Dispose of the bay leaf. Taste and adjust the seasonings. Sprinkle with fresh parsley and serve.

# Bell Pepper & Pinto Bean Stew

Serving Size: 6 | Total Time: 1 hour 5 minutes

## Ingredients

2 tbsp olive oil
1 onion, chopped
1 red bell pepper, chopped
1 tbsp dried oregano
1 tbsp ground cumin
1 tsp red pepper flakes
3 cups vegetable stock

2 cups dried pinto beans, rinsed
14 ounces canned tomatoes, chopped
1 tsp salt
1 tbsp white wine vinegar
½ cup fresh chives, chopped
¼ cup fresh corn kernels

## Directions

Set on Sauté, stir in oil, bell pepper, pepper flakes, oregano, onion, and cumin. Cook for 3 minutes until soft. Mix in pinto beans, vegetable stock, and tomatoes.

Seal the lid, select Bean/Chili and cook for 30 minutes on High Pressure. Release the pressure naturally for 20 minutes. Add in salt and vinegar. Divide among serving plates and top with corn and fresh chives.

# Spinach, Garlic & Mushroom Pilaf

Serving Size: 6 | Total Time: 35 minutes

## Ingredients

1 tbsp olive oil
2 cloves garlic, minced
1 onion, chopped
2 cups button mushrooms, sliced
1 cup spinach, chopped

4 cups vegetable stock
2 cups white rice
1 tsp salt
2 sprigs parsley, chopped

## Directions

Select Sauté mode and heat oil. Add mushrooms, onion, and garlic, and stir-fry for 5 minutes until tender. Mix in rice, stock, spinach, and salt. Seal the lid and cook on High Pressure for 20 minutes. Release Pressure naturally for 10 minutes. Use a fork to fluff the rice and add parsley for garnishing before serving.

# Traditional Indian Lentil Soup

Serving Size: 6 | Total Time: 30 minutes

## Ingredients

1 tbsp ghee
2 tsp cumin seeds
1 onion, chopped
4 garlic cloves, minced
1-inch piece of ginger, peeled, minced
Salt to taste
1 tomato, chopped

2 cups split yellow lentils, soaked
2 tbsp garam masala
½ tsp ground turmeric
½ tsp cayenne pepper
6 cups water
1 tbsp fresh cilantro, finely chopped

## Directions

Warm ghee on Sauté. Add cumin seeds and cook for 10 seconds until they begin to pop. Stir in onion and cook for 2 to 3 minutes until softened. Mix in ginger, salt and garlic and cook for 1 minute as you stir.

Mix in tomato and cook for 3 to 5 minutes until the mixture breaks down. Stir in turmeric, lentils, garam masala, and cayenne and cover with water. Seal the lid and cook for 8 minutes on High Pressure. Release the pressure quickly. Serve in bowls sprinkled with fresh cilantro.

# Bulgur Pilaf with Roasted Red Bell Peppers

Serving Size: 4 | Total Time: 25 minutes

## Ingredients

2 tbsp olive oil
1 garlic clove, minced
1 onion, chopped
2 cups vegetable stock
¼ cup lemon juice

1 tsp grated lemon zest
1 cup bulgur
Salt and black pepper to taste
6 ounces roasted bell peppers

## Directions

In a bowl, toss bell peppers with the remaining oil, salt, and black pepper. Set aside.

Warm half of the oil on Sauté and cook onion and garlic until soft, about 3 minutes. Stir in stock, lemon juice, lemon zest, salt, and bulgur. Seal the lid and cook on High Pressure for 5 minutes.

Do a natural pressure release for 10 minutes. Fluff the rice with a fork and transfer to a plate. Top with roasted peppers to serve.

# Bean & Rice Stuffed Zucchini Boats

Serving Size: 4 | Total Time: 20 minutes

## Ingredients

2 small zucchinis, halved lengthwise
½ cup cooked rice
½ cup canned white beans, drained and rinsed
½ cup chopped tomatoes

½ cup chopped toasted cashew nuts
½ cup grated Parmesan cheese
2 tbsp melted butter
Salt and black pepper to taste

## Directions

Pour 1 cup of water in the instant pot and insert a trivet. Scoop out the pulp of zucchinis and chop roughly.

In a bowl, mix the zucchini pulp, rice, tomatoes, cashew nuts, beans, Parmesan cheese, melted butter, salt, and black pepper. Fill the zucchini boats with the mixture, and arrange the stuffed boats in a single layer on the trivet. Seal the lid and cook for 15 minutes on Steam on High. Do a quick release and serve.

# Arugula & Wild Mushroom Risotto

Serving Size: 4 | Total Time: 30 minutes

## Ingredients

3 tbsp olive oil
1 onion, chopped
2 cups arugula, chopped
1 cup arborio rice
1/3 cup white wine

3 cups vegetable stock
Salt and black pepper to taste
½ cup wild mushrooms, chopped
4 tbsp pumpkin seeds, toasted
1/3 cup grated Pecorino Romano cheese

## Directions

Heat oil on Sauté, and cook onion and mushrooms for 5 minutes, until tender. Add the rice and cook for a minute. Stir in white wine and cook for 2 to 3 minutes until almost evaporated.

Pour in stock and season with salt and black pepper. Seal the lid and cook on High Pressure for 10 minutes. Do a quick release. Stir in arugula until wilted, mix in Pecorino Romano cheese to melt, and serve scattered with pumpkin seeds.

# Butternut Squash with Jasmine Rice & Feta Cheese

Serving Size: 4 | Total Time: 30 minutes

## Ingredients

½ cup water
2 cups vegetable broth
1 small butternut squash, sliced
2 tablespoons melted butter, divided
Salt and black pepper to taste

1 cup feta cheese, cubed
1 tbsp coconut aminos
2 tsp arrowroot starch
1 cup jasmine rice, cooked

## Directions

Pour the rice and broth in the pot and stir to combine. In a bowl, toss butternut squash with 1 tbsp of melted butter and season with salt and black pepper. Mix in the pot with the rice.

In another bowl, mix the remaining butter, water and coconut aminos. Toss feta in the mixture, add the arrowroot starch, and toss again to combine well. Transfer to a greased baking dish. Lay a trivet over the rice butternut squash and place the baking dish on the trivet. Seal the lid and cook on High for 15 minutes. Do a quick pressure release. Fluff the rice with a fork and serve with feta cheese.

# Yummy Mexican-Style Rice & Pinto Beans

Serving Size: 4 | Total Time: 30 minutes

## Ingredients

3 tbsp olive oil
1 small onion, chopped
2 garlic cloves, minced
1 serrano pepper, seeded and chopped
1 cup rice
1/3 cup red salsa

¼ cup tomato sauce
½ cup vegetable broth
1 tsp Mexican seasoning mix
16 ounces canned pinto beans, drained and rinsed
1 tsp salt
1 tbsp chopped fresh parsley

## Directions

Warm oil on Sauté and cook onion, garlic, and serrano pepper for 2 minutes, stirring occasionally until fragrant. Stir in rice, salsa, tomato sauce, vegetable broth, Mexican seasoning, beans, and salt.

Seal the lid and cook on High Pressure for 10 minutes. Do a natural pressure release for 10 minutes. Sprinkle with fresh parsley and serve.

# Creamy Fettuccine with Ground Beef

Serving Size: 6 | Total Time: 20 minutes

## Ingredients

10 oz ground beef
1 lb fettuccine pasta
1 cup cheddar cheese, shredded
1 cup fresh spinach, torn

1 medium onion, chopped
2 cups tomatoes, diced
1 tbsp butter
Salt and black pepper to taste

## Directions

Melt butter on Sauté. Stir-fry the beef and onion for 5 minutes. Add the pasta. Pour water enough to cover and season with salt and pepper. Cook on High Pressure for 5 minutes. Do a quick release. Press Sauté and stir in the tomatoes and spinach. Cook for 5 minutes. Top with shredded cheddar and serve.

# Chinese Shrimp with Green Beans

Serving Size: 2 | Total Time: 20 minutes

## Ingredients

1 tbsp sesame oil
1 lb shrimp, peeled and deveined
½ cup diced onion
2 cloves garlic, minced
1 cup carrots, cut into strips
1 cup green beans, washed

2 cups vegetable stock
3 tbsp soy sauce
2 tbsp rice wine vinegar
10 ounces lo mein egg noodles
½ tsp toasted sesame seeds
Sea salt and black pepper to taste

## Directions

Warm oil on Sauté. Stir-fry the shrimp for 5 minutes. Remove to a plate and set aside.

Add in garlic and onion, and cook for 3 minutes until fragrant. Mix in soy sauce, carrots, stock, beans, and rice wine vinegar. Add noodles into the mixture and ensure they are covered. Season with pepper and salt. Seal the lid and cook on High Pressure for 5 minutes. Release the pressure quickly.

Place the main in 2 plates, add the reserved shrimp, sprinkle with sesame seeds, and serve.

# Spicy Linguine with Cherry Tomato & Basil

Serving Size: 4 | Total Time: 22 minutes

## Ingredients

2 tbsp olive oil
1 small onion, diced
2 garlic cloves, minced
1 cup cherry tomatoes, halved
1 ½ cups vegetable stock
¼ cup julienned basil leaves

Salt and black pepper to taste
¼ tsp red chili flakes
1 pound linguine noodles, halved
Fresh basil leaves for garnish
½ cup Parmigiano-Reggiano cheese, grated

## Directions

Warm oil on Sauté. Add onion and Sauté for 2 minutes until soft. Mix garlic and tomatoes and Sauté for 4 minutes. To the pot, add vegetable stock, salt, julienned basil, red chili flakes and pepper.

Add linguine to the tomato mixture until covered. Seal the lid and cook on High Pressure for 5 minutes. Naturally release the pressure for 5 minutes. Stir the mixture to ensure it is broken down.

Divide into plates. Top with basil and Parmigiano-Reggiano cheese and serve.

# Pasta Tortiglioni with Beef & Black Beans

Serving Size: 4 | Total Time: 35 minutes

## Ingredients

2 tbsp olive oil
1 pound ground beef
16 ounces tortiglioni pasta
2 cups water
15 ounces tomato sauce
15-ounce canned black beans, drained and rinsed
15-ounces canned corn, drained

10 ounces red enchilada sauce
4 ounces diced green chiles
1 cup shredded mozzarella cheese
Salt and black pepper to taste
Additional cheese for topping
Finely chopped parsley for garnish

## Directions

Heat oil on Sauté. Add ground beef and cook for 7 minutes until it starts to brown. Mix in pasta, tomato sauce, enchilada sauce, black beans, water, corn, and green chiles and stir to coat well.

Seal the lid and cook on High Pressure for 10 minutes. Do a quick Pressure release. Into the pasta mixture, mix in mozzarella cheese until melted; add black pepper and salt. Garnish with parsley to serve.

# Spicy Rice Noodles with Tofu & Chives

Serving Size: 6 | Total Time: 20 minutes

## Ingredients

2 cups water
1 tbsp olive oil
½ cup soy sauce
2 tbsp brown sugar
2 tbsp rice vinegar
1 tbsp sweet chili sauce

1 tbsp sesame oil
1 tsp fresh minced garlic
20 oz extra firm tofu, pressed and cubed
8 ounces rice noodles
¼ cup chopped fresh chives, for garnish

## Directions

Heat the oil on Sauté and fry the tofu for 5 minutes until golden brown. Set aside.

To the pot, add water, garlic, olive oil, vinegar, sugar, soy sauce, and chili sauce and mix well until smooth. Stir in rice noodles. Seal the lid and cook on High Pressure for 3 minutes.

Release the Pressure quickly. Split the noodles between bowls. Top with fried tofu and sprinkle with fresh chives before serving.

# Easy Brown Rice with Sunflower Seeds

Serving Size: 6 | Total Time: 30 minutes

## Ingredients

1 ½ cups brown rice
3 cups chicken broth
2 tsp lemon juice

2 tsp olive oil
1 tbsp toasted sunflower seeds
Salt and black pepper to taste

## Directions

Add broth and brown rice. Season with salt and black pepper. Seal the lid, press Multigrain and cook on High for 15 minutes.

Release the pressure quickly. Do not open the lid for 5 minutes. Use a fork to fluff rice. Add lemon juice, sunflower seeds and drizzle of olive oil to serve.

# Soups and Side Dishes

## Mushroom-Spinach Cream Soup

Serving Size: 4 | Total Time: 25 minutes

### Ingredients

1 tbsp olive oil
8 button mushrooms, sliced
1 cup spinach, chopped
1 red onion, chopped
4 cups vegetable stock

2 sweet potatoes, peeled and chopped
2 tbsp white wine
1 tbsp dry porcini mushrooms, soaked and drained
Salt and black pepper to taste
1 cup creme fraiche

### Directions

Set on Sauté and add in olive oil and mushrooms. Sauté for 3 to 5 minutes until browning on stock sides; Set aside. Add onion and spinach, and cook for 3 to 5 minutes until the onion becomes translucent. Stir in chopped mushrooms, and cook for a further 5 minutes, stirring occasionally, until golden brown.

Pour in wine to deglaze the bottom of the pot, scrape to remove browned bits. Cook for 5 minutes until wine evaporates. Mix in the remaining mushrooms, potatoes, soaked mushrooms, stock, and salt.

Seal the lid and cook on High Pressure for 5 minutes. Quick release the pressure. Add in pepper and creme fraiche to mix. Using an immersion blender, whizz the mixture until smooth. Stir in the Sautéed mushrooms. Add reserved mushrooms for garnish before serving.

## Grilled Cheese Croutons and Tomato Soup

Serving Size: 6 | Total Time: 1hour

### Ingredients

2 tbsp olive oil
1 onion, chopped
1 carrot, peeled and chopped
1 garlic clove, minced
Salt and black pepper to taste
1 cup vegetable stock
28 ounces canned tomatoes

1 cup heavy cream
4 slices Monterey Jack cheese
4 slices bread
2 slices gouda cheese
4 tbsp butter, at room temperature
2 tbsp parsley, finely chopped

### Directions

Warm oil on Sauté. Stir-fry garlic, onion, carrot, pepper and salt for 6 minutes until soft. In the pot, add vegetable stock to deglaze. Scrape any brown bits from the pot. Mix the stock with tomatoes. Seal the lid and cook on High Pressure for 30 minutes.

Allow for a natural release, for about 10 minutes. Transfer soup to a blender and process until smooth. Add in heavy cream and stir; add pepper and salt for seasoning.

Place 2 slices Monterey Jack cheese onto 1 bread slice and cover with 1 Gouda cheese slice, and the second slice of bread. Spread a tablespoon of butter and parsley over the top. Do the same with the rest of the cheese, bread, parsley, and butter.

Over medium heat, heat a skillet. With butter sides down, place the sandwiches on the skillet. Spread 1 tbsp butter on top of each sandwich. Cook each side for 3 to 5 minutes until browned and all cheese melt. Transfer sandwiches to a cutting board and chop into bite-sized pieces. Divide the soup into serving plates and apply a top with parsley cheese croutons before serving.

# Full-Flavor Vegetable Soup

Serving Size: 8 | Total Time: 42minutes

## Ingredients

2 tbsp olive oil
1 cup leeks, chopped
2 garlic cloves, minced
4 cups vegetable stock
1 carrot, diced
1 parsnip, diced
1 celery stalk, diced
1 cup mushrooms
1 cup broccoli florets

1 cup cauliflower florets
½ red bell pepper, diced
¼ head green cabbage, chopped
½ cup green beans
2 tbsp nutritional yeast
½ tsp dried thyme
Salt and black pepper to taste
½ cup fresh parsley, chopped

## Directions

Heat oil on Sauté. Add in garlic and leeks and cook for 6 minutes until slightly browned. Add in stock, carrot, celery, broccoli, bell pepper, green beans, salt, nutritional yeast, cabbage, cauliflower, mushrooms, parsnip, thyme, and pepper.

Seal the lid and cook on High Pressure for 6 minutes. Release pressure naturally. Stir in parsley and serve.

# Spicy Tomato Soup with Rice

Serving Size: 4 | Total Time: 40 minutes

## Ingredients

1 cup tomato puree
1 onion, chopped
1 garlic clove, minced
¼ cup rice
Salt and black pepper to taste

2 tbsp olive oil
4 cups vegetable broth
¼ tsp cayenne pepper
1 tsp basil, chopped

## Directions

Heat oil on Sauté and cook garlic and onion 3 minutes until soft. Add in tomato puree, ice, vegetable broth, and cayenne pepper. Season with salt and black pepper. Seal the lid and cook on Soup/Broth mode for 30 minutes on High Pressure. Release the pressure naturally, for about 10 minutes. Serve in bowls sprinkled with basil.

# Homemade Vichyssoise Soup with Chives

Serving Size: 5 | Total Time: 30 minutes

## Ingredients

2 tbsp butter
3 leeks, white part only, chopped
2 cloves garlic, minced
4 cups vegetable broth
3 potatoes, peeled and cubed

½ cup sour cream
2 tbsp rosemary
2 bay leaves
Salt and black pepper to taste
2 tbsp fresh chives, to garnish

## Directions

Melt butter on Sauté mode. Stir in garlic and leeks and cook for 3 to 4 minutes, until soft. Stir in bay leaves, potatoes, rosemary, and broth. Seal the lid and cook on High Pressure for 15 minutes. Release pressure quickly. Remove the bay leaves and cobs and discard.

Transfer soup to immersion blender and puree soup to obtain a smooth consistency. Season with salt and pepper. Top with fresh chives and sour cream.

# Celery & Cauliflower Soup with Blue Cheese

Serving Size: 5 | Total Time: 20 minutes

## Ingredients

2 tbsp butter
½ tbsp olive oil
1 onion, chopped
2 stalks celery, chopped
1 large head cauliflower, cut into florets
1 potato, peeled and finely diced

3 cups vegetable broth
Salt and black pepper to taste
2 cups milk
1 bay leaf
4 ounces blue cheese

## Directions

Warm oil and butter on Sauté mode. Add celery and onion and Sauté for 3-5 minutes, until fragrant. Stir in half the cauliflower and cook for 5 minutes until golden brown. Add in broth, bay leaf, potato and the remaining cauliflower.

Seal the lid and cook on High Pressure for 5 minutes. Release the Pressure quickly. Remove the bay leaf. Place the soup in an immersion blender, add in the milk and puree until smooth. Adjust the seasoning. Spoon the soup into serving bowls and top with blue cheese before serving.

# Traditional Italian Vegetable Soup

Serving Size: 6 | Total Time: 25 minutes

## Ingredients

2 tbsp olive oil
1 onion, diced
1 cup celery, chopped
1 carrot, peeled and diced
1 green bell pepper, chopped
2 cloves garlic, minced
3 cups chicken broth
½ tsp dried parsley
½ tsp dried thyme

½ tsp dried oregano
Salt and black pepper to taste
2 bay leaves
28 ounces canned diced tomatoes
6 ounces canned tomato paste
2 cups kale
14 oz canned navy beans, rinsed, drained
½ cup rice
¼ cup Parmesan cheese, shredded

## Directions

Warm olive oil on Sauté. Stir in carrot, celery and onion and cook for 5 to 6 minutes until soft. Add garlic and bell pepper and cook for 2 minutes as you stir until aromatic. Stir in pepper, thyme, broth, salt, parsley, oregano, tomatoes, bay leaves, and tomato paste to dissolve. Mix in rice.

Seal the lid and cook on High Pressure for 15 minutes. Do a quick release. Add kale and stir. Use residual heat in slightly wilting the greens. Discard bay leaves. Stir in navy beans and serve topped with Parmesan cheese.

# Asian Pork and Noodle Soup

Serving Size: 4 | Total Time: 1 hour 10 minutes

## Ingredients

2 tbsp olive oil
2 yellow onions, halved
1 piece fresh ginger, halved lengthwise
2 tsp fennel seeds
1 tsp red pepper flakes
½ tsp coriander seeds
10 black peppercorns

2-star anise
8 cups water
1 pound pork tenderloin, cut into strips
Salt and black pepper to taste
8 ounces rice noodles
1 Lime, cut into wedges
A handful of fresh cilantro leaves

### Directions

Warm oil on Sauté mode. Add ginger and onions and cook for 4 minutes. Add in flakes, fennel, anise, peppercorns and coriander and cook for 1 minute as you stir. Add water, salt, pepper and pork into the pot.

Seal the lid and cook on High Pressure for 60 minutes. Release the Pressure naturally for 10 minutes.

As the pork continues to cook, soak rice noodles in hot water for 8 minutes until softened and pliable; stop the cooking process by draining and rinsing with cold water. Separate the noodles into 4 soup plates.

Remove the pork from the cooker and ladle among bowls. Strain the broth to get rid of solids. Pour it over the pork and noodles; Season with red pepper flakes. Garnish with lime wedges and cilantro leaves.

# Noodle & Turkey Soup

Serving Size: 6 | Total Time: 40 minutes

### Ingredients

1 tbsp olive oil
1 onion, minced
3 cloves garlic, minced
1 turnip, chopped
1 cup celery rib, chopped
1 tbsp dry basil

1 bay leaf
6 cups vegetable broth
1 lb turkey breasts, bone-in, skin on, cubed
8 ounces dry egg noodles
Salt and black pepper to taste

### Directions

Warm olive oil on Sauté. Stir-fry in garlic and onion, for 3 minutes until soft. Mix in celery, bay leaf, basil, and turnip. Pour in 3 cups of broth and deglaze. Scrape any brown bits from the pan's bottom and add turkey. Seal the lid and cook on High Pressure for 10 minutes.

Naturally release the pressure for about 8 minutes. Transfer turkey breasts to another bowl. Do away with the skin and bones. Using two forks, shred the meat.

Set the cooker on Sauté. Transfer the turkey to the pot; add noodles and the remaining broth. Simmer for 10 minutes until noodles are done. Season to taste and serve.

# Simple Chicken Soup with Fennel & Celery

Serving Size: 8 | Total Time: 1 hour 10 minutes

### Ingredients

1 ½ pounds chicken drumsticks, boneless
4 celery stalks
1 cup fennel bulb, chopped
2 onions, diced
2 carrots, diced
2 garlic cloves

3 parsley, chopped
2 bay leaves
Salt and black pepper to taste
½ cup matzo meal
2 eggs, beaten
2 tbsp canola oil

### Directions

In the pot, add drumsticks, bay leaves, onions, carrots, pepper, garlic, parsley, salt, and fennel. Add enough water such that ingredients are covered by 2 inches.

Seal the lid and cook for 30 minutes on High Pressure. Release pressure naturally, for about 10 minutes. Meanwhile, mix eggs, oil, black pepper, salt and matzo meal, in a bowl. Use a plastic wrap to close the bowl and place in a fridge for 10 minutes.

Get rid of celery stalks. Transfer chicken to a cutting board, strip and shred it from the bones. Take back to pot. Select Sauté and boil the soup. Roll matzo mixture into 1 inch balls and place in the boiling soup. Cook for 3 mins to heat through as you gently stir.

# Chipotle Pumpkin Soup

Serving Size: 4 | Total Time: 25 minutes

## Ingredients

1 tbsp olive oil
1 onion, chopped
2 chipotle peppers, seeded and minced
1 tsp ground black pepper
¼ tsp grated nutmeg
¼ tsp ground cloves

A pinch of ground cinnamon
1 butternut pumpkin, cubed
4 cups vegetable broth
1 tsp salt
1 cup half-and-half

## Directions

Warm oil on Sauté and cook nutmeg, pepper, cloves, cinnamon, and onion for 3 to 5 minutes, until translucent. Add pumpkin and cook for 5 minutes, stirring infrequently. Pour in broth and add chipotle peppers and any remaining pumpkin. Seal the lid and cook on High Pressure for 10 minutes. Release pressure quickly.

Stir in half-and-half and transfer to a blender to purée until you obtain a smooth consistency.

# Black Bean & Corn Chicken Soup

Serving Size: 5 | Total Time: 35 minutes

## Ingredients

5 boneless, skinless chicken thighs
5 cups chicken broth
Salt and black pepper to taste
14 ounces canned whole tomatoes, chopped
2 jalapeño peppers, stemmed, cored, chopped
2 tbsp tomato puree
3 cloves garlic, minced
1 tbsp chili powder

1 tbsp ground cumin
½ tsp dried oregano
1 (14.5-ounce) can black beans, rinsed and drained
2 cups frozen corn kernels, thawed
Crushed tortilla chips for garnish
¼ cup cheddar cheese, shredded for garnish
Fresh cilantro, chopped for garnish

## Directions

Add chicken, oregano, garlic, tomato puree, broth, cumin, tomatoes, chili, and jalapeño peppers.

Seal the lid and cook on High Pressure for 10 minutes.

Once cooking is done, release the pressure quickly. Transfer the chicken to a plate. On Sauté mode; cook corn and black beans. Shred the chicken with a pair of forks, and return to the pot, stirring well.

Select Keep Warm and simmer the soup for 5 minutes until heated through. Adjust the seasoning and divide among serving plates. Garnish with cilantro, shredded cheese and crushed tortilla chips to serve.

# Green Immune-Boosting Soup

Serving Size: 3 | Total Time: 35 minutes

## Ingredients

1 lb fresh brussels sprouts, rinsed, halved
6 oz baby spinach, torn, chopped
1 tsp salt
1 tbsp whole milk

3 tbsp sour cream
¼ cup celery, chopped
3 cups water
1 tbsp butter

## Directions

Add all ingredients to the instant pot. Seal the lid and set the steam release. Press Soup/Broth and cook for 30 minutes on High. Do a quick release. Transfer to a food processor, and blend well to combine.

# Simple Chowder with Broccoli, Carrot & Tofu

Serving Size: 4 | Total Time: 35 minutes

## Ingredients

1 head broccoli, finely chopped
1 carrot, chopped
2 tbsp sesame oil
1 onion, peeled, chopped
2 garlic cloves

1 cup soy milk
2 cups vegetable broth
¼ cup tofu, crumbled
A pinch of salt

## Directions

Heat oil on Sauté. Add onion, garlic and stir-fry for 2 minutes, or until translucent. Pour in broth, a cup of water, broccoli, salt and carrot. Seal the lid and cook on Manual/Pressure mode for 5 minutes on High.

Do a quick release. Let chill for a while, and transfer to a food processor. Pulse until creamy. Serve with crumbled tofu.

# Chili Cream of Acorn Squash Soup

Serving Size: 4 | Total Time: 25 minutes

## Ingredients

4 cups vegetable broth
2 tbsp butter
1 onion, diced
1 acorn squash, chopped
2 carrots, peeled and diced

½ tsp ground cinnamon
¼ tsp chili pepper
A pinch of salt
½ cup coconut milk
1/3 cup sour cream

## Directions

Melt butter on Sauté. Add onion and cook for 3 minutes until soft. Add in carrots, cinnamon, squash, salt, and chili pepper and stir-fry for 2 minutes until fragrant.

Add the broth to the vegetable mixture. Seal the lid and cook for 12 minutes on High Pressure. Quick-release the Pressure. Add soup to a food processor and puree to obtain a smooth consistency. Take the soup back to the cooker, stir in coconut milk until you get a consistent color. Serve hot with a dollop of sour cream.

# Kimchi Ramen Noodle Soup

Serving Size: 4 | Total Time: 20 minutes

## Ingredients

1 tbsp olive oil
½ tsp ground ginger
2 tbsp garlic, minced
6 cups chicken broth stock
2 tbsp soy sauce
½ tbsp kimchi paste

1 cup mushrooms, chopped
10 ounces ramen noodles
1 (1-pound) package fresh collard greens, trimmed
A bunch of fresh cilantro, chopped to serve
1 red chili, chopped to serve

## Directions

On Sauté, warm oil, stir in garlic and ginger, and cook for 2 minutes until soft. Add in stock, mix in kimchi paste, ramen noodles and soy sauce.

Seal the lid and cook on High Pressure for 10 minutes. Release pressure quickly. Stir in collard greens until wilted. Ladle the soup into serving bowls and add red chili and cilantro to serve.

# Delicious Pork & Vegetables Soup

Serving Size: 4 | Total Time: 60 minutes

## Ingredients

2 (8-ounce) pork chops, with bones
1 tbsp cayenne pepper
1 tsp chili powder
½ tsp garlic powder
2 bay leaves
4 cups beef broth
2 tbsp oil

2 large carrots, chopped
2 celery stalks, diced
2 onions, diced
2 tbsp flour
2 tbsp soy sauce
3 tbsp butter

## Directions

Grease the stainless steel pot with oil and stir-fry the onions, until translucent on Sauté mode. Add celery stalks, carrots, cayenne, and chili pepper. Give it a good stir and continue to cook for 6-7 minutes.

Press Cancel, and add pork chops, garlic, bay leaves, and soy sauce. Pour in the broth and seal the lid. Cook on Manual/Pressure Cook mode for 35 minutes on High. Do a quick release. Let chill for 5 minutes.

# Green Soup with Navy & Pinto Beans

Serving Size: 5 | Total Time: 35 minutes

## Ingredients

1 tbsp olive oil
1 onion, chopped
2 cloves garlic, minced
5 cups vegetable broth
½ cup pinto beans, soaked overnight
½ cup navy beans, soaked overnight

3 carrots, chopped
1 large celery stalk, chopped
1 tsp dried thyme
16 oz zucchini noodles
Salt and black pepper, to taste

## Directions

Warm oil on Sauté. Stir in garlic and onion and cook for 5 minutes. Mix in pepper, broth, carrots, salt, celery, beans, and thyme. Seal the lid and cook for 15 minutes on High Pressure. Release the pressure naturally. Mix zucchini noodles into the soup and stir until wilted. Taste and adjust the seasoning.

# White Cabbage and Beetroot Borscht Soup

Serving Size: 4 | Total Time: 30 minutes

## Ingredients

2 tbsp olive oil
1 cup leeks, chopped
1 tsp garlic, smashed
2 beets, peeled and diced
1 tbsp cayenne pepper, finely minced
1 dried habanero pepper, crushed

4 cups beef stock
3 cups white cabbage, shredded
1 tsp salt
2 tsp red wine apple cider vinegar
¼ tsp paprika
Greek yogurt for garnish

## Directions

Warm oil on Sauté. Stir in garlic and leeks and cook for 5 minutes until soft. Mix in, stock, paprika, salt, peppers, vinegar, beets, white cabbage, cayenne pepper, and crushed habanero pepper.

Seal the lid and cook on High Pressure for 20 minutes. Do a quick release. Place in serving bowls and top with Greek yogurt to serve.

# Spicy Pumpkin Curry

Serving Size: 5 | Total Time: 30 minutes

## Ingredients

1 ½ pounds butternut squash, chopped
4 cups chicken stock
½ cup buttermilk
4 spring onions, chopped into lengths
2 tbsp curry powder
1 ½ tsp ground turmeric

1 ½ tsp ground cumin
¼ tsp cayenne pepper
2 bay leaves
Salt and black pepper, to taste
A bunch of cilantro leaves, chopped

## Directions

In the pot, stir in squash, buttermilk, curry, turmeric, spring onions, stock, cumin, and cayenne. Season with pepper and salt. Add bay leaves to the liquid and ensure they are submerged.

Seal the lid, press Soup/Broth and cook for 10 minutes on High. Naturally release the pressure for 10 minutes. Discard bay leaves. Transfer the soup to a blender and process until smooth. Use a fine-mesh strainer to strain the soup. Divide into plates and garnish with cilantro before serving.

# Fall Vegetable Soup

Serving Size: 5 | Total Time: 30 minutes

## Ingredients

2 tbsp olive oil
1 onion, chopped
2 carrots, peeled and chopped
1 cup celery, chopped
2 cloves garlic, minced
5 cups vegetable broth
2 turnips, peeled and chopped

28 ounces canned tomatoes
15 oz canned garbanzo beans, rinsed and drained
1 cup frozen green peas
2 bay leaves
1 sprig fresh sage
Salt and black pepper to taste
¼ cup Parmesan cheese, grated

## Directions

On Sauté, warm oil, stir in celery, carrots, and onion and cook for 4 minutes until soft. Add in garlic and cook for 30 seconds until crispy. Add vegetable broth, turnips, garbanzo beans, bay leaves, tomatoes, pepper, salt, peas, and sage. Seal the lid and cook on High Pressure for 12 minutes.

Allow natural pressure release, for about 5 minutes. Serve topped with Parmesan cheese.

# Vegetarian Lentil Soup with Nachos

Serving Size: 6 | Total Time: 40 minutes

## Ingredients

2 ½ cups vegetable broth
1 ½ cups tomato sauce
1 onion, chopped
1 cup dry red lentils
½ cup prepared salsa verde
2 garlic cloves, minced

1 tbsp smoked paprika
2 tsp ground cumin
1 tsp chili powder
¼ tsp cayenne pepper
Salt and black pepper to taste
Crushed tortilla chips for garnish

## Directions

Add in tomato sauce, broth, onion, salsa verde, cumin, cayenne pepper, chili powder, garlic, lentils, paprika, salt and pepper. Seal the lid and cook for 20 minutes on High Pressure. Release Pressure naturally, for 10 minutes. Divide into serving bowls and add crushed tortilla chips for garnish.

# Quick Mushroom-Quinoa Soup

Serving Size: 4 | Total Time: 20 minutes

## Ingredients

4 cups vegetable broth
1 carrot, peeled and chopped
1 stalk celery, diced
2 cups quinoa, rinsed
1 cup mushrooms, sliced
1 onion, chopped

2 garlic cloves, smashed
1 tsp salt
½ tsp dried thyme
3 tbsp butter
½ cup heavy cream

## Directions

Melt the butter on Sauté. Add onion, garlic, celery, and carrot, and cook for 8 minutes until tender. Mix in broth, thyme, quinoa, mushrooms, and salt.

Seal the lid and cook on High Pressure for 10 minutes. Release pressure quickly. Stir in heavy cream. Cook for 2 minutes to obtain a creamy consistency. Serve warm.

# Carrot & Squash Soup with Yogurt & Cilantro

Serving Size: 6 | Total Time: 1hour

## Ingredients

1 tbsp olive oil
1 onion, diced
1 stalk celery, diced
1 large carrot, diced
2 garlic cloves, minced
1 lb acorn squash, peeled diced

6 cups chicken stock
Juice from 1 lemon
1 cup coconut milk
Salt and black pepper to taste
2 tbsp cilantro leaves, chopped
Yogurt for garnish

## Directions

Heat oil on Sauté and stir-fry carrot, celery, garlic, salt and onion, for 4 to 5 minutes until soft. Mix acorn squash with the vegetables; cook for 1 more minute until tender.

Add stock and seal the lid and cook on High Pressure for 20 minutes. Release pressure naturally, for about 10 minutes.

Add in lemon juice and coconut milk and stir. Transfer the soup to a blender and process until smooth. Divide soup into serving plates. Garnish with cilantro, black pepper and yogurt.

# Chicken & Vegetable Rice Soup

Serving Size: 4 | Total Time: 20 minutes

## Ingredients

1 lb chicken breast, boneless, skinless, cubed
1 large carrot, chopped
1 onion, chopped
¼ cup rice
1 potato, finely chopped

½ tsp salt
1 tsp cayenne pepper
A handful of parsley, finely chopped
3 tbsp olive oil
4 cups chicken broth

## Directions

Add all ingredients, except parsley, to the pot, and seal the lid. Cook on Soup/Broth for 15 minutes on High. Do a quick pressure release. Stir in fresh parsley and serve.

# Simple Vegan Black Bean Soup

Serving Size: 6 | Total Time: 30 minutes

## Ingredients

1 tsp olive oil
1 onion, chopped
2 celery stalks, chopped
3 carrots, chopped
2 serrano peppers, deseeded, chopped
5 cups vegetable broth

30 ounces canned diced tomatoes
1 (14 oz) can black beans, rinsed and drained
¼ cup chopped fresh cilantro
2 tsp ground cumin
Salt and black pepper to taste

## Directions

Warm oil on Sauté. Add in carrots, onion, serrano peppers, and celery and cook for 6 to 7 minutes. Mix in broth, sea salt, black beans, cumin, tomatoes, cilantro, and black pepper. Seal lid and cook for 8 minutes on High Pressure. Release pressure naturally.

# Traditional Cheesy Onion Soup

Serving Size: 8 | Total Time: 45 minutes

## Ingredients

2 tbsp butter
8 cups thinly chopped onions
½ cup water
2 tsp sugar
Salt and black pepper to taste
½ cup dry white wine

4 cups beef stock
2 sprigs fresh thyme
2 bay leaves
4 baguette slices
1 cup Swiss cheese, shredded

## Directions

Melt butter on Sauté. Add in onions and cook for 3 to 5 minutes until soft. Add water, sugar, and salt, and pepper as you stir. Seal the lid, press Poultry, and cook for 15 minutes on High.

Do a quick release. Add beef stock, wine, bay leaves and thyme sprigs into the pot. Seal the lid cook for 4 minutes on High Pressure. Quick-release Pressure. Discard the bay leaves and thyme. Preheat the oven's broiler.

Divide into four soup bowls. Top with ¼ cup Swiss cheese and 1 baguette slice.

Transfer the bowls to a baking sheet and cook for 2-4 minutes under broiler until golden brown.

# Garden Vegetable Soup

Serving Size: 4 | Total Time: 22 minutes

## Ingredients

1 carrot, finely chopped
2 spring onions, finely chopped
1 red bell pepper, chopped, seeds removed
2 celery stalks, finely chopped
½ cup celery leaves, chopped
½ tsp dried thyme

2 tbsp butter
1 tsp vegetable oil
4 cups vegetable broth
1 cup milk
Salt and black pepper to taste

## Directions

Melt butter on Sauté. Add carrot, onions, bell pepper, and celery. Cook for 5 minutes, stirring constantly. Pour in vegetable broth, seal the lid and cook on Manual/Pressure Cook mode for 5 minutes on High.

Do a quick release. Stir in all remaining ingredients and cook for 2-3 minutes, on Sauté. Serve warm.

# Farro & Vegetable Chicken Soup

Serving Size: 6 | Total Time: 50 minutes

## Ingredients

1 tbsp olive oil
4 boneless, skinless chicken thighs
¼ cup white wine
1 cup farro
1 large onion, chopped
2 celery stalks, cut into squares

3 large carrots, chopped
1 tsp garlic powder
1 tsp ground cumin
1 bay leaf
6 cups chicken broth
2 tsp fresh parsley leaves to garnish

## Directions

Warm oil on Sauté. Brown the chicken on all sides, for 6 minutes. Transfer the chicken to a bowl. Into the pot, add wine to deglaze, scraping any brown bits present at the bottom of the cooker.

Mix the wine with farro, cumin, broth, onion, carrots, celery, garlic powder, and bay leaf. Seal the lid, press Meat/Stew and cook on High for 20 minutes.

Release pressure naturally for about 10 minutes. Divide into serving plates and add parsley for garnish.

# Chorizo Sausage Soup with Roasted Tomatoes & Basil

Serving Size: 6 | Total Time: 30 minutes

## Ingredients

1 tbsp olive oil
2 shallots, chopped
3 cloves garlic, minced
Salt and black pepper to taste
4 cups beef broth
28 ounces fire-roasted diced tomatoes

½ cup fresh ripe tomatoes
½ cup raw cashews
1 tbsp red wine vinegar
3 chorizo sausage, chopped
½ cup thinly chopped fresh basil

## Directions

Warn oil on Sauté and cook chorizo until crispy. Remove to a plate lined with paper towel.

Add in garlic, shallots and cook for 5 minutes until soft. Season with salt. Stir in red wine vinegar, broth, diced tomatoes, cashews, fresh ripe tomatoes, and black pepper into the cooker.

Seal the lid and cook on High Pressure for 8 minutes. Release the pressure quickly. Pour the soup into a blender and process until smooth. Divide into bowls. Top with chorizo and decorate with basil.

# Mediterranean Carrot & Chickpea Soup

Serving Size: 6 | Total Time: 15 minutes

## Ingredients

14 oz chickpeas, soaked, rinsed, drained
2 carrots, chopped
2 onions, peeled, chopped
2 tomatoes, peeled, chopped
3 tbsp tomato paste

A handful of fresh chopped parsley
2 cups vegetable broth
2 tbsp olive oil
1 tsp salt

## Directions

Add in chickpeas, oil, onions, carrots, and tomatoes. Pour in the broth and sprinkle salt. Stir in the paste and seal the lid. Cook on High Pressure for 6 minutes. Do a quick release and remove to a serving place. Sprinkle with freshly chopped parsley, to serve.

# Garam Masala Parsnip & Red Onion Soup

Serving Size: 4 | Total Time: 15 minutes

## Ingredients

2 tbsp vegetable oil
1 red onion, finely chopped
3 parsnips, chopped
2 garlic cloves, crushed
2 tsp garam masala
½ tsp chili powder

1 tbsp plain flour
4 cups vegetable stock
1 whole lemon, juiced
Salt and black pepper to taste
Strips of lemon rind, to garnish

## Directions

Heat oil on Sauté, and stir-fry onion, parsnips and garlic for 5 minutes, or until soft but not changed color. Stir in garam masala and chili powder and cook for 30 seconds. Stir in flour, for another 30 seconds.

Pour in the stock, lemon rind and lemon juice, and seal the lid. Cook on Manual/Pressure Cook for 5 minutes on High. Do a quick release, remove a third of the vegetable pieces with a slotted spoon and reserve.

Process the remaining soup and vegetables in a food processor for about 1 minute, to a smooth puree. Return to the pot, and stir in the reserved vegetables. Press Keep Warm and heat the soup for 2 minutes until piping hot. Season with salt and pepper, then ladle into bowls. Garnish with strips of lemon, to serve.

# Potato-Leek Soup with Tofu

Serving Size: 4 | Total Time: 25 minutes

## Ingredients

3 large leeks
3 tbsp butter
1 onion, chopped
1 lb potatoes, chopped
5 cups vegetable stock
2 tsp lemon juice

¼ tsp nutmeg
¼ tsp ground coriander
1 bay leaf
5 oz silken tofu
Salt and white pepper to taste
Chopped chives, to garnish

## Directions

Remove most of the green parts of the leeks. Slice the white parts very finely. Melt butter on Sauté, and stir-fry leeks and onion for 5 minutes without browning. Add potatoes, stock, lemon juice, nutmeg, coriander and bay leaf. Season to taste with salt and white pepper, and seal the lid.

Press Manual and set the timer to 10 minutes. Cook on High. Do a quick release and discard the bay leaf. Process the soup in a food processor until smooth. Season to taste, add silken tofu. Sprinkle with chives to serve.

# Delicious Chicken & Potato Soup

Serving Size: 4 | Total Time: 35 minutes

## Ingredients

1 lb chicken breast, boneless, skinless, chopped
1 onion, chopped
1 carrot, chopped
2 small potatoes, peeled, chopped
1 tsp cayenne pepper

2 egg yolks
1 tsp salt
3 tbsp lemon juice
3 tbsp olive oil
4 cups water

## Directions

Add all ingredients to the pot, and seal the lid. Set the steam release handle and cook on Soup/Broth mode for 20 minutes on High. Release the pressure naturally, for 10 minutes, open the lid and serve.

# Awesome Pork & Celery Soup

Serving Size: 4 | Total Time: 45 minutes

### Ingredients

1.5 lb pork ribs
1 large leek, chopped into bite-sized pieces
1 onion, chopped
1 cup celery root, diced
½ cup parsley, chopped
4 cups beef broth

1 tsp salt
¼ tsp chili flakes
2 bay leaves
A handful of fresh basil, torn
3 tbsp oil

### Directions

Heat oil on Sauté. Add the ribs in batches and brown on all sides, for 5-6 minutes. Add the remaining ingredients. Seal the lid and cook on Meat/Stew mode on High for 30 minutes. Do a quick release.

# Rustic Soup with Turkey Balls & Carrots

Serving Size: 4 | Total Time: 35 minutes

### Ingredients

2 tbsp olive oil
6 oz turkey balls
4 cups chicken broth
1 onion, chopped

1 garlic clove, minced
3 large carrots, chopped
Salt and white pepper to taste
1 tbsp cilantro, finely chopped

### Directions

Heat olive oil on Sauté, and stir-fry onion, carrots and garlic for 5 minutes until soft. Add the rest of the ingredients, except for the cilantro in the pot. Seal the lid and press Manual/Pressure Cook. Cook for 25 minutes on HIgh. Release the pressure naturally for 10 minutes and serve sprinkle with cilantro.

# Cauliflower & Potato Cream Soup with Parsley

Serving Size: 4 | Total Time: 35 minutes

### Ingredients

1 lb cauliflower, chopped into florets
2 potatoes, chopped
4 cups chicken broth
A handful of fresh parsley, finely chopped

Salt and black pepper to taste
¼ cup heavy cream
¼ cup sour cream
1 cup milk

### Directions

Add all ingredients to the pot. Seal the lid and set the steam release handle. Cook on High pressure for 20 minutes. Do a quick release. Let chill and transfer to a blender. Pulse until well- combined.

# Simple Carrot & Oregano Soup

Serving Size: 3 | Total Time: 22 minutes

### Ingredients

4 carrots, chopped
3 cups vegetable broth
1 tbsp butter

½ tsp dried oregano
½ tsp salt

### Directions

Add all ingredients to the pot. Seal the lid and cook on Manual/Pressure Cook for 12 minutes on High. Do a natural release, for 10 minutes. Transfer to a food processor and pulse until creamy. Serve warm.

# Potato & Broccoli Soup with Rosemary

Serving Size: 4 | Total Time: 30 minutes

## Ingredients

1 lb broccoli, cut into florets
2 potatoes, peeled, chopped
4 cups vegetable broth

½ tsp dried rosemary
½ tsp salt
½ cup sour cream

## Directions

Place broccoli and potatoes in the pot. Pour the broth, rosemary, and seal the lid. Cook on Soup/Broth for 20 minutes on High. Do a quick release and remove to a blender. Pulse to combine. Stir in sour cream and add salt.

# Homemade Winter Soup

Serving Size: 4 | Total Time: 30 minutes

## Ingredients

3 sweet potatoes, chopped
1 tsp salt
2 fennel bulbs, chopped
16 oz pureed pumpkin

1 large onion, chopped
1 tbsp coconut oil
4 cups water
1 tbsp sour cream

## Directions

Heat the oil on Sauté, and add onion and fennel bulbs. Cook for 3-5 minutes until tender. Add the remaining ingredients, and seal the lid. Cook on High pressure for 25 minutes. Do a quick release, transfer the soup to a blender and blend for 20 seconds until creamy. Top with sour cream and serve.

# Vegetable Beef Soup

Serving Size: 4 | Total Time: 40 minutes

## Ingredients

1.5 lb lean beef, cut into bite-sized pieces
1 onion, peeled and chopped
2 carrots, chopped
1 tsp cayenne pepper

Salt and black pepper to taste
1 garlic clove, crushed
1 tbsp butter
4 cups water

## Directions

Melt butter on Sauté. Add onion and garlic, and stir-fry for 3 minutes, or until translucent. Add carrots and spices. Cook for 2 more minutes. Add the meat and pour in water. Seal the lid and cook on Manual/Pressure Cook for 35 minutes on High. Release the pressure quickly.

# Vegetarian Soup with White Beans

Serving Size: 4 | Total Time: 15 minutes

## Ingredients

1 cup green peas
1 carrot, peeled, chopped
2 red bell peppers, seeds removed, chopped
1 cup white beans, cut into bite-sized pieces
1 tomato, roughly chopped

2 cups vegetable broth
2 cups water
2 tbsp olive oil
Salt and black pepper to taste
¼ tsp dried oregano, ground

## Directions

Stir in all ingredients in the pot. Seal the lid. Cook on High pressure for 8 minutes. Do a quick release.

# Parsley Noodle Soup with Chicken

Serving Size: 4 | Total Time: 40 minutes

## Ingredients

1 lb chicken breasts, chopped
½ cup egg noodles
4 cups chicken broth

A handful of fresh parsley
Salt and black pepper to taste

## Directions

Season the fillets with salt and place in the pot. Pour the broth and seal the lid. Cook on Soup/Broth for 20 minutes on High. Do a quick release. Add in the noodles and seal the lid again.

Press the Manual/Pressure Cook and cook for 5 minutes on High Pressure. Release the pressure quickly, and sprinkle with freshly ground black pepper and parsley. Serve warm.

# Spicy Red Kidney Bean Soup

Serving Size: 4 | Total Time: 45 minutes

## Ingredients

14.5 oz canned red kidney beans, rinsed
14.5 oz canned tomatoes
2 tbsp oil
1 onion, chopped
4 cups water

2 cloves garlic, crushed
2 small fresh red chilies, finely chopped
1 green bell pepper, diced
½ cup tomato sauce

## Directions

Heat oil on Sauté, and stir-fry garlic, chili, and onion for 3 minutes, or until translucent. Add the remaining ingredients and seal the lid. Cook on Manual/Pressure Cook mode for 25 minutes on High Pressure. Release the steam naturally for 10 minutes and serve immediately.

# Turmeric Butternut Squash Soup

Serving Size: 4 | Total Time: 35 minutes

## Ingredients

1.5 lb butternut squash, pureed
1 onion, peeled and chopped
4 cups vegetable broth
1 tbsp ground turmeric

½ tbsp heavy cream
Salt and black pepper to taste
A handful of fresh parsley
3 tbsp olive oil

## Directions

Add onion, butternut squash, turmeric, salt, and oil to your instant pot. Pour in broth and stir well. Seal the lid and adjust the steam release handle. Press Soup/Broth and cook for 30 minutes on High. Do a quick release.

With an immersion blender, blend until smooth. Stir in heavy cream and top with freshly chopped parsley.

# Creamy Broccoli-Gorgonzola Soup

Serving Size: 4 | Total Time: 35 minutes

## Ingredients

8 oz Gorgonzola cheese, crumbled
1 cup broccoli, finely chopped
4 cups water
1 tbsp olive oil

½ cup full-fat milk
1 tbsp fresh parsley, finely chopped
Salt and black pepper to taste

**Directions**

Add all ingredients to the pot, seal the lid and cook on Soup/Broth mode for 30 minutes on High Pressure. Do a quick release. Remove the lid and sprinkle with fresh parsley. Serve warm.

# Delicious Creamy Celery & Green Pea Soup

Serving Size: 4 | Total Time: 15 minutes

**Ingredients**

3 oz carrots, finely chopped
3 oz celery root, finely chopped
A handful of green peas, soaked
2 tbsp butter
2 tbsp fresh parsley, finely chopped

1 egg yolk
2 tbsp cream cheese
¼ cup freshly squeezed lemon juice
Salt and black pepper to taste
4 cups beef broth

**Directions**

Add all ingredients to the instant pot and seal the lid. Cook on High Pressure for 5 minutes. When done, release the steam naturally, for 10 minutes. Serve warm.

# Tasty Asparagus Soup

Serving Size: 4 | Total Time: 40 minutes

**Ingredients**

2 lb fresh asparagus, trimmed
2 onions, chopped
1 cup heavy cream
4 cups vegetable broth
2 tbsp butter

1 tbsp vegetable oil
½ tsp salt
½ tsp dried oregano
½ tsp paprika

**Directions**

Melt butter on Sauté, and add 1 tbsp of oil. Stir-fry the onions for 2 minutes, until translucent. Add asparagus, oregano, salt, and paprika. Stir well and cook until asparagus soften, for a few minutes.

Pour the broth and mix well to combine. Seal the lid and cook on Soup/Broth for 20 minutes on High. Do a quick release and whisk in 1 cup of heavy cream. Serve chilled or warm.

# Parsley Creamy Tomato Soup

Serving Size: 4 | Total Time: 45 minutes

**Ingredients**

2 lb tomatoes, diced
1 cup white beans, pre-cooked
1 small onion, diced
2 garlic cloves, crushed
1 cup heavy cream

1 cup vegetable broth
2 tbsp fresh parsley, finely chopped
Salt and black pepper to taste
2 tbsp olive oil
½ tsp sugar

**Directions**

Warm oil on Sauté mode. Stir-fry onion and garlic on Sauté, for 2 minutes. Add tomatoes, beans, broth, 3 cups of water, parsley, salt, pepper, and a little bit of sugar to balance the bitterness.

Seal the lid and cook on Soup/Broth for 30 minutes on High Pressure. Release the pressure naturally, for 10 minutes.

Top with a dollop of heavy cream and chopped parsley, to serve.

# Effortless Tomato-Lentil Soup

Serving Size: 4 | Total Time: 17 minutes

## Ingredients

2 cups red lentils, soaked overnight
1 carrot, cut into thin slices
3 tbsp tomato paste
3 garlic cloves, crushed
4 cups vegetable broth

2 tomatoes, wedged
1 onion, diced
½ tsp dried thyme, ground
½ tsp cumin, ground
Salt and black pepper to taste

## Directions

Add all ingredients to the pot. Seal the lid and cook on High pressure for 7 minutes. Do a quick release.

# Spicy Sweet Potato Soup

Serving Size: 2 | Total Time: 20 minutes

## Ingredients

2 sweet potatoes, chopped
1 carrot, chopped
1 onion, chopped
2 cups chicken broth

2 garlic cloves, chopped
Salt and black pepper to taste
1 tbsp chili flakes
1 tbsp olive oil

## Directions

Warm oil on Sauté, and stir-fry potatoes, onion, and garlic for 3-4 minutes. Stir in the remaining ingredients, seal the lid and cook on High pressure for 7 minutes. Do a natural release, for 10 minutes.

# Gingery Squash & Leek Soup

Serving Size: 4 | Total Time: 35 minutes

## Ingredients

4 leeks, washed and trimmed
2 cups butternut squash, chopped
Salt and black pepper to taste
1 tsp ginger, grated

4 cups vegetable broth
2 tbsp olive oil
1 tsp cumin
1 tsp ginger powder

## Directions

Heat the oil on Sauté, add stir-fry leeks for about 5 minutes, on Sauté. Add ginger powder and cumin. Give it a good stir and continue to cook for 1 more minute. Pour in the remaining ingredients and seal the lid. Cook on Soup/Broth mode for 10 minutes on High. Release the pressure naturally, for about 10 minutes.

# Lentil and Carrot Soup

Serving Size: 4 | Total Time: 35 minutes

## Ingredients

1 cup red lentils, soaked overnight
1 red bell pepper, seeded and chopped
1 onion, peeled, chopped
½ cup carrot puree

Salt and black pepper to taste
½ tsp cumin, ground
2 tbsp olive oil
A handful of parsley, to garnish

## Directions

Heat the oil on Sauté, add stir-fry the onion, for 4 minutes. Add the remaining ingredients and pour in 4 cups of water. Seal the lid and cook on Soup/Broth for 30 minutes on High. Do a quick Pressure release. Sprinkle with fresh parsley and serve warm.

# Creamy Bean & Potato Soup

Serving Size: 3 | Total Time: 20 minutes

## Ingredients

½ cup canned beans, pre-cooked
3 cups beef broth
1 potato, chopped

½ cup heavy cream
Salt and white pepper to taste
1 tsp garlic powder

## Directions

Add all ingredients to the pot, seal the lid and cook on Manual/Pressure mode for 10 minutes on High. Release the steam naturally, for 10 minutes. Transfer the ingredients to a blender. Pulse until smooth.

Return the soup to the clean stainless steel insert. Press Sauté and add a half cup of water. Cook for 5 more minutes, or until desired thickness. Let it chill uncovered for a while before serving.

# Chili Soup with Avocado & Corn

Serving Size: 3 | Total Time: 25 minutes

## Ingredients

1 large, ripe avocado
2 tbsp lemon juice
1 tbsp vegetable oil
4 oz canned sweet corn, drained
2 tomatoes, skinned and deseeded
1 garlic clove, crushed

1 leek, chopped
1 red chili, chopped
14 oz vegetable stock
4 oz soy milk
Chopped leeks, to garnish

## Directions

Peel the avocado and mash the flesh with a fork. Stir in the lemon juice and reserve until required. Heat the oil on Sauté and add corn, tomatoes, garlic, leek and chili. Stir-fry for 4-5 minutes, until softened.

Put half of the vegetable mixture in a food processor, add the mashed avocado and process until smooth. Transfer the contents to the instant pot. Pour in the stock, soy milk, and reserved vegetables, and seal the lid.

Cook on Manual/Pressure Cook mode for 4 minutes on High. Once ready, press Cancel and release the steam naturally, for about 5 minutes. Garnish with chopped leeks and serve immediately.

# Hot Beef Chili

Serving Size: 4 | Total Time: 40 minutes

## Ingredients:

2 lb ground beef
2 tbsp olive oil
1 red bell pepper, seeded and chopped
1 large yellow bell pepper, seeded and chopped
1 onion, chopped
2 cups tomatoes, chopped
2 carrots, chopped

5 tsp chili powder
2 tbsp Worcestershire sauce
2 tsp paprika
½ tsp cumin powder
2 tbsp parsley, chopped
Salt and black pepper to taste

## Directions:

Select Sauté and add the olive oil and minced beef. Cook the beef until it browns while stirring occasionally for about 8 minutes. Top it with the onion, bell peppers, tomatoes, carrots, chili powder, Worcestershire sauce, paprika, cumin powder, salt, and pepper. Stir the ingredients well.

Seal the lid, and select Soup/Broth on High Pressure and cook for 20 minutes. Once the timer has ended, do a quick pressure release, and open the lid. Sprinkle with parsley to serve.

# Arugula Salad with Sweet Potatoes & Eggs

Serving Size: 8 | Total Time: 20 minutes

## Ingredients

1 ½ cups water
6 sweet potatoes, peeled and diced
4 large eggs
2 ½ cups mayonnaise

¼ cup dill, chopped
1/3 cup Greek yogurt
Salt and black pepper to taste
½ cup arugula

## Directions

Pour water. Place eggs and potatoes into the steamer basket; Transfer to the pot and seal the lid. Cook for 4 minutes on High Pressure. Do a quick release.

Take out the eggs and place in a bowl of ice-cold water for purposes of cooling. In a bowl, combine yogurt, mayonnaise, and dill.

In a separate bowl, mash potatoes using a potato masher; mix with mayonnaise mixture to coat. Skin and dice the eggs. Transfer to the potato salad and mix. Season with salt and pepper to taste and serve with arugula.

# Potatoes & Tuna Salad with Pickles

Serving Size: 4 | Total Time: 15 minutes

## Ingredients

1 ½ pounds potatoes, quartered
2 eggs
3 tbsp melted butter
Salt and black pepper to taste
6 pickles, chopped

2 tbsp red wine vinegar
½ cup pimento stuffed green olives
½ cup chopped roasted red peppers
2 tbsp chopped fresh parsley
10 ounces canned tuna, drained

## Directions

Pour 2 cups of water into the pot and add potatoes. Place a trivet over the potatoes. Lay the eggs on the trivet. Seal the lid and cook for 8 minutes on High Pressure. Do a quick release.

Drain and remove potatoes to a bowl. Transfer the eggs in filled with an ice water bowl. Drizzle melted butter over the potatoes and season with salt and pepper. Peel and chop the chilled eggs.

Add pickles, eggs, peppers, tuna, vinegar to the potatoes and mix to coat. Serve topped with olives.

# Authentic German Salad with Smoked Bacon

Serving Size: 6 | Total Time: 20 minutes

## Ingredients

6 slices smoked bacon, chopped
½ cup apple cider vinegar
½ cup water
3 tbsp sugar
2 tsp mustard

Salt and black pepper to serve
6 red potatoes, peeled and quartered
2 red onions, chopped
A handful of parsley for garnishing

## Directions

On Sauté, briefly brown the bacon for 2 minutes per side. Set aside. In a bowl, mix sugar, salt, mustard, vinegar, water, and black pepper. In the pot, add potatoes, chopped bacon, and onions, and top with the vinegar mixture.

Seal the lid and cook for 6 minutes on High Pressure. Release pressure naturally for 10 minutes. Place on serving plate and add fresh parsley for garnishing.

# Feta & Potato Salad

Serving Size: 12 | Total Time: 30 minutes

## Ingredients

3 pounds potatoes, chopped
3 cups water
1 cup mayonnaise
¼ cup mustard

¼ cup pickles
¼ cup white onion, chopped
Salt to taste
1 cup feta cheese, crumbled

## Directions

In the pot, mix salt, water and potatoes. Seal the lid and cook for 6 minutes on High Pressure. Once ready, do a natural release for 10 minutes. Drain the potatoes and allow to cool. Chop into smaller pieces.

In a bowl, mix salt, pickles, mayonnaise, potatoes, mustard, and onion to get a desired consistency. Chill for one hour while covered. Top with feta cheese to serve.

# Warm Spinach Salad With Eggs & Nuts

Serving Size: 4 | Total Time: 25 minutes

## Ingredients

1 lb spinach, rinsed, chopped
3 tbsp olive oil
1 tbsp butter
1 tbsp almonds, crushed

1 tbsp peanuts, crushed
4 eggs
½ tsp chili flakes
½ tsp salt

## Directions

Pour 1 ½ cups of water into the inner pot and insert a steamer basket. Place the eggs onto the basket. Seal the lid and cook on High Pressure for 5 minutes.

Do a quick release. Remove the eggs to an ice bath. Wipe the pot clean, and heat oil on Sauté. Add spinach and cook for 2-3 minutes, stirring occasionally.

Stir in 1 tbsp of butter and Season with salt and chili flakes. Mix well and cook for 1 more minute. Press Cancel and sprinkle with nuts. Peel and slice each egg in half, lengthwise. Transfer to a serving plate and pour over spinach mixture.

# Goat Cheese & Beef Steak Salad

Serving Size: 4 | Total Time: 60 minutes

## Ingredients

1 lb rib-eye steak, boneless
4 oz fresh arugula
1 large tomato, sliced
¼ cup fresh goat's cheese
4 almonds
4 walnuts

4 hazelnuts
3 tbsp olive oil
2 cups beef broth
2 tbsp red wine vinegar
1 tbsp Italian seasoning mix

## Directions

Whisk together vinegar, Italian mix, and olive oil. Brush each steak with this mixture and place in your instant pot. Pour in the broth and seal the lid. Cook on Meat/Stew for 25 minutes on High Pressure. Release the Pressure naturally, for about 10 minutes, and remove the steaks along with the broth.

Grease the inner pot with oil and hit Sauté. Brown the steaks on both sides for 5-6 minutes. Remove from the pot and chill for 5 minutes before slicing. In a bowl, mix arugula, tomato, cheese, almonds, walnuts, and hazelnuts. Top with steaks and drizzle with red wine mixture.

# Chili Poached Eggs with Leeks

Serving Size: 3 | Total Time: 15 minutes

## Ingredients

1 cup leeks, chopped into 1-inch pieces
6 eggs
2 tbsp oil
1 tbsp butter

1 tsp mustard seeds
1 tbsp dried rosemary
¼ tsp chili flakes
¼ tsp salt

## Directions

Heat oil on Sauté and add mustard seeds. Stir-fry for 2-3 minutes. Add leeks and butter. Cook for 5 minutes, stirring occasionally. Crack eggs and season with dried rosemary, chili flakes, and salt. Cook until set, for about 4 minutes. Press Cancel and serve immediately.

# Scrambled Eggs with Cranberries & Mint

Serving Size: 2 | Total Time: 10 minutes

## Ingredients

4 large eggs, beaten
¼ tsp cranberry extract, sugar-free
2 tbsp butter
¼ tsp salt

1 tbsp skim milk
4-5 cranberries, to garnish
Fresh mint, to garnish

## Directions

In a bowl, whisk eggs, cranberry extract, salt, and milk. Melt butter on Sauté. Pour the egg mixture and pull the eggs across the pot with a spatula.

Do not stir constantly. Cook for 2 minutes, or until thickened and no visible liquid egg lumps. When done, press Cancel and transfer to a serving plate. Top with cranberries and garnish with fresh mint.

# Healthy Kale & Egg Muffins

Serving Size: 3 | Total Time: 10 minutes

## Ingredients

6 eggs
½ cup cheddar cheese, crumbled
1 small onion, finely chopped
½ tsp Italian seasoning mix

Salt and black pepper to taste
2 tbsp heavy cream
1 ½ cups of water

## Directions

In a bowl, mix eggs, salt, pepper, and heavy cream. Whisk until well combined and add the remaining ingredients.

Add 1 ½ cups of water and lay the steam rack. Lower the ramekins on the steam rack and seal the lid. Cook on High Pressure for 6 minutes. When ready, do a quick release. Serve hot.

# Grandma's Egg Salad

Serving Size: 6 | Total Time: 15 minutes

## Ingredients

2 cups water
6 eggs
¼ cup crème frâiche
2 large spring onions, minced
1 tbsp dill, minced

1 tbsp curry paste
2 tsp mustard
Salt and black pepper to taste

**Directions**

Grease a cake pan with cooking spray. Carefully crack in the eggs.

To the inner pot, add water. Set the pan with the eggs on a trivet. Seal the lid and cook for 5 minutes on High Pressure. Do a quick release. Drain any water from the eggs in the pan. Loosen the eggs on the edges with a knife. Transfer to a cutting board and chop into smaller sizes.

Transfer the chopped eggs to a bowl. Add in onions, mustard, salt, dill, crème frâiche, curry paste and pepper.

# Egg Pancake with Spinach & Herbs

Serving Size: 2 | Total Time: 15 minutes

**Ingredients**

6 oz spinach, chopped
2 eggs
3 tbsp oil
½ tsp garlic powder

¼ tsp dried oregano
¼ tsp dried rosemary
½ tsp salt
Kalamata olives and red bell peppers, for garnishing

**Directions**

Heat the oil on Sauté and add chopped spinach. Season with salt and garlic powder. Give it a good stir and cook for 5 minutes, until soft.

Crack eggs and season with oregano, rosemary, and salt. Cook until completely set, for about 5 more minutes. Transfer to a serving plate and serve with kalamata olives or chopped red bell peppers.

# Delicious Broccoli & Cauliflower Salad

Serving Size: 4 | Total Time: 10 minutes

**Ingredients**

1 lb cauliflower florets
1 lb broccoli, into florets
3 garlic cloves, crushed

¼ tbsp olive oil
1 tsp salt
1 tbsp dry rosemary, crushed

**Directions**

Cut the veggies into bite-sized pieces and place them in the pot. Add olive oil and 1 cup of water. Season with salt, garlic and rosemary. Seal the lid. Cook on High Pressure for 3 minutes. When ready, do a quick release.

# Egg Bites with Mushrooms & Arugula

Serving Size: 4 | Total Time: 15 minutes

**Ingredients**

12 oz button mushrooms, sliced
8 oz fresh arugula, chopped
4 eggs

2 tbsp butter, melted
Chili flakes, for seasoning
3 ounces asiago cheese, shredded

**Directions**

Place a trivet in the Instant Pot and pour in a cup of water. Grease 4 heatproof cups with the butter.

In a mixing bowl, whisk the eggs with salt and black pepper and stir in the mushrooms and arugula. Pour the mixture into the cups. Top with the cheese and chili flakes.

Arrange the cups on top of the trivet. Seal the lid and cook on Manual for 7 minutes on High. Do a quick release.

Allow cooling slightly, then pop egg bites out of the cups to serve.

# *Poultry*

## Chicken & Pineapple Salad The "Hawaiian Style"

Serving Size: 12 | Total Time: 1 hour 55 minutes

### Ingredients

*Pineapple salad:*

¼ cup apple cider vinegar
¼ cup canola oil
1 pineapple, chopped
½ head red cabbage, shredded

4 cups arugula
¼ cup chopped fresh cilantro
4 green onions, chopped

*Hawaiian-Style Chicken:*

1 cup brown sugar
½ cup chicken broth
½ cup soy sauce
½ cup honey
¼ cup orange juice
2 garlic cloves, minced

2 tbsp grated fresh ginger
1 tsp freshly ground black pepper
6 skinless, boneless chicken breasts, halved
2 tbsp cornstarch
2 tbsp water
12 Hawaiian bread rolls

### Directions

In a bowl, mix oil and vinegar; add pineapple, green onions, cilantro, cabbage, and arugula and toss well to coat. Refrigerate for 1 hour while the bowl is covered.

In the pot, mix in sugar, soy sauce, garlic, black pepper, ginger, honey, chicken broth, and orange juice. Press Sauté. Allow to a simmer. Cook until the honey and sugar dissolve. Arrange chicken into the sauce and toss to coat. Seal the lid and cook on High for 16 minutes. Release the Pressure quickly. Shred chicken with 2 forks.

Preheat your oven's broiler. In a small bowl, mix water and cornstarch; stir into the sauce in the cooker. Set the cooker to Sauté mode and cook the sauce for 2 to 3 minutes until it begins to thicken. Stir in the shredded chicken. Halve the loaf of Hawaiian rolls. Set the halves, cut-side up, onto a baking sheet. Under the preheated broiler, toast the rolls for 3 minutes until golden brown.

Transfer the shredded chicken to the bottom half of the rolls and apply a topping of salad. Replace the top half of the rolls and cut into individual sliders before serving.

## Pancetta, Cabbage & Chicken Thighs

Serving Size: 4 | Total Time: 35 minutes

### Ingredients

1 tbsp lard
4 slices pancetta, diced
4 chicken thighs, boneless skinless
Salt and black pepper to taste

1 cup chicken broth
1 tbsp Dijon mustard
1 pound green cabbage, shredded
Fresh parsley, chopped

### Directions

Warm lard on Sauté. Fry pancetta for 5 minutes until crisp. Set aside. Season chicken with pepper and salt. Sear in the pressure cooker for 2 minutes each side until browned. In a bowl, mix mustard and chicken broth.

In your Pressure cooker, add pancetta, mustard, and chicken broth mixture. Seal the lid and cook on High Pressure for 6 minutes. Release the Pressure quickly.

Open the lid, mix in green cabbage, Seal again, and cook on High Pressure for 2 minutes. Release the pressure quickly. Serve with sprinkled parsley.

# Honey-Lemon Chicken with Vegetables

Serving Size: 4 | Total Time: 40 minutes

## Ingredients

4 skin-on, bone-in chicken legs
2 tbsp olive oil
Salt and black pepper to taste
4 cloves garlic, minced
1 tsp fresh chopped thyme
½ cup dry white wine
1 ¼ cups chicken stock

1 cup carrots, chopped
1 cup parsnip, chopped
3 tomatoes, chopped
1 tbsp honey
4 slices lemon
Fresh thyme, chopped for garnish

## Directions

Season the chicken with pepper and salt. Warm oil on Sauté mode. Arrange chicken legs into the hot oil; cook for 3 to 5 minutes each side until browned. Place in a bowl and set aside.

Sauté thyme and garlic in the chicken fat for 1 minute until soft and lightly golden.

Add wine into the pot to deglaze, scrape the pot's bottom to get rid of any brown bits of food. Simmer the wine for 2 to 3 minutes until slightly reduced in volume. Add stock, carrots, parsnip, tomatoes, pepper and salt into the pot. Lay steam rack onto veggies.

Into the pressure cooker's steamer basket, arrange chicken legs. Set the steamer basket onto the rack. Drizzle the chicken with honey then top with lemon slices.

Seal the lid and cook on High Pressure for 12 minutes. Release Pressure naturally for 10 minutes.

Place the chicken to a bowl. Drain the veggies and place them around the chicken. Garnish with fresh thyme before serving.

# Chicken Drumsticks with Potatoes & Veggies

Serving Size: 4 | Total Time: 40 minutes

## Ingredients

4 potatoes, peeled and quartered
4 cups water
2 lemons, zested and juiced
1 tbsp olive oil
2 tsp fresh oregano
1 tsp red pepper flakes
Salt and black pepper to taste
2 serrano peppers, stemmed, cored, chopped
4 boneless skinless chicken drumsticks

3 tbsp finely chopped parsley
1 cup packed watercress
1 cucumber, sliced
½ cup cherry tomatoes, quartered
¼ cup kalamata olives, pitted
¼ cup hummus
¼ cup feta cheese, crumbled
Lemon wedges, for serving

## Directions

In the cooker, add water and potatoes. Set trivet over them. In a baking bowl, mix lemon juice, olive oil, black pepper, oregano, zest, salt, and red pepper flakes. Add chicken drumsticks in the marinade and stir to coat.

Set the bowl with chicken on the trivet in the inner pot. Seal the lid, select Poultry and cook on High for 15 minutes. Do a quick release.

Take out the bowl with chicken and the trivet from the pot. Drain potatoes and add parsley and salt.

Divide the potatoes between four serving plates and top with watercress, cucumber slices, hummus, cherry tomatoes, chicken, olives, and feta cheese.

Garnish with lemon wedges to serve.

# Lebanese-Style Chicken with Fresh Couscous

Serving Size: 4 | Total Time: 40 minutes

## Ingredients

4 chicken thighs
2 tbsp za'atar mix
1 tbsp ground sumac
Salt and black pepper to taste
2 tbsp butter
2 ½ cups chicken stock, divided

1 onion, chopped
1 garlic clove, minced
1 ½ cups couscous
Juice from 1 lemon
Fresh parsley, chopped

## Directions

Season the chicken with salt, sumac, za'atar, and pepper.

Melt butter on Sauté and sear the chicken in batches for 5 minutes per batch until lightly browned. Set aside. Into the cooker, add ¼ cup chicken stock to deglaze the pan, scrape the bottom to get rid of any browned bits of food. Add garlic and onion to the stock; cook for 3 minutes until soft.

Add the remaining chicken stock into the pan; add lemon juice and couscous. Add in chicken. Seal the lid and cook on High Pressure for 5 minutes. Naturally release the pressure for 5 minutes. Transfer the couscous and chicken to a serving plate; and garnish with parsley.

# Sweet & Citrusy Chicken Breasts

Serving Size: 4 | Total Time: 30 minutes

## Ingredients

2 chicken breasts, cubed
½ cup honey
½ cup orange juice
1/3 cup soy sauce
1/3 cup chicken stock
1/3 cup hoisin sauce

1 garlic clove, minced
2 tsp cornstarch
2 tsp water
1 cup diced orange
3 cups hot cooked quinoa

## Directions

Arrange the chicken at the bottom of the pot. In a bowl, mix honey, soy sauce, garlic, hoisin sauce, chicken stock, and orange juice, until the honey is dissolved. Pour the mixture over the chicken.

Seal the lid and cook on High Pressure for 7 minutes. Release the pressure quickly. Take the chicken from the pot and set to a bowl. Press Sauté. In a small bowl, mix water with cornstarch. Pour into the liquid within the pot and cook for 3 minutes until thick. Stir diced orange and chicken into the sauce until well coated. Serve with quinoa.

# Tasty Chicken Breasts with Barbeque Sauce

Serving Size: 6 | Total Time: 20 minutes

## Ingredients

2 pounds boneless skinless chicken breasts
1 tsp salt
1 ½ cups barbecue sauce

1 small onion, minced
1 cup carrots, chopped
4 garlic cloves

## Directions

Rub salt onto chicken and place inside the instant pot. Add onion, carrots, garlic and barbeque sauce. Toss the chicken to coat. Seal the lid, press Poultry and cook on High for 15 minutes. Do a quick release. Use two forks to shred chicken and stir into the sauce.

# Savory Orange Chicken

Serving Size: 6 | Total Time: 50 minutes

## Ingredients

2 tbsp olive oil
6 chicken breasts, boneless, skinless, cubed
1/3 cup chicken stock
¼ cup soy sauce
2 tbsp brown sugar
1 tbsp lemon juice

1 tbsp garlic powder
1 tsp chili sauce
1 cup orange juice
Salt and black pepper to taste
2 cups cooked gnocchi

## Directions

Warm oil on Sauté. In batches, sear chicken in the oil for 5 minutes until browned. Set aside in a bowl.

In your pot, mix orange juice, chicken stock, sugar, chili sauce, garlic powder, lemon juice, and soy sauce; Stir in chicken to coat. Seal the lid and cook on High Pressure for 7 minutes. Release the Pressure quickly.

Take ¼ cup liquid from the pot to a bowl; stir in cornstarch to dissolve; mix into sauce in the pot until the color is consistent. Press Sauté and cook sauce for 5 minutes until thickened. Season with pepper and salt. Serve the chicken with gnocchi.

# Friday Chicken & Avocado Fajitas

Serving Size: 4 | Total Time: 30 minutes

## Ingredients

4 chicken breasts, boneless and skinless
1 taco seasoning
1 tbsp olive oil
1 (24-ounce) can diced tomatoes
3 bell peppers, julienned
1 shallot, chopped

4 garlic cloves, minced
juice of 1 lemon
Salt and pepper to taste
4 flour tortillas
2 tbsp cilantro, chopped
1 avocado, sliced

## Directions

In a bowl, mix taco seasoning and chicken until evenly coated. Warm oil on Sauté mode.

Sear chicken for 2 minutes per side until browned. To the chicken, add tomatoes, cilantro, shallot, lemon juice, garlic, and bell peppers; Season with pepper and salt.

Seal the lid, press Poultry and cook for 4 minutes on High Pressure. Release the Pressure quickly. Move the bell peppers and chicken to tortillas. Add avocado slices and serve.

# White Wine Chicken Breasts with Fresh Herbs

Serving Size: 4 | Total Time: 15 minutes

## Ingredients

4 boneless, skinless chicken breasts
½ tsp salt
1 cup water
¼ cup dry white wine

½ tsp rosemary, chopped
½ tsp mint, chopped
½ tsp marjoram, chopped
½ tsp sage, chopped

## Directions

Sprinkle salt over the chicken and set in the pot. Mix in mint, rosemary, marjoram, and sage. Pour wine and water around the chicken. Seal the lid, and cook for 6 minutes on High Pressure. Release the pressure naturally for 10 minutes.

# Crispy Bacon & Bean Chicken

Serving Size: 4 | Total Time: 45 minutes

## Ingredients

1 tbsp olive oil
4 slices bacon, crumbled
4 boneless, skinless chicken thighs
1 onion, diced
4 garlic cloves, minced
1 tbsp tomato paste
1 tbsp oregano
1 tbsp ground cumin
1 tsp chili powder
½ tsp cayenne pepper

1 (14.5-ounce) can whole tomatoes
1 cup chicken broth
1 tsp salt
1 cup cooked corn
1 red bell pepper, chopped
15 oz red kidney beans, drained and rinsed
1 cup shredded Monterey Jack cheese
1 cup chopped red onion
¼ cup chopped cilantro

## Directions

Warm oil on Sauté. Sear the chicken for 3 minutes for each side until browned. Set the chicken on a plate. In the same oil, fry bacon until crispy, about 5 minutes and set aside.

Add in onion, red onion, and cook for 3 minutes until fragrant. Stir in garlic, oregano, cayenne, cumin, tomato paste, bell pepper, and chili, and cook for 30 more seconds. Pour the chicken broth, salt, and tomatoes and bring to a boil. Take back the chicken and bacon to the pot and ensure it is submerged in the braising liquid.

Seal the lid and cook on High Pressure for 15 minutes. Release the Pressure quickly. Pour the corn and kidney beans in the cooker, Press Sauté and bring the liquid to a boil; cook for 10 minutes. Serve topped with shredded cheese and chopped cilantro.

# Delicious Pulled Chicken with Peach Sauce

Serving Size: 4 | Total Time: 40 minutes

## Ingredients

15 ounces canned peach chunks
4 boneless, skinless chicken thighs
14 ounces canned diced tomatoes
2 cloves garlic, minced

½ tsp cumin
½ tsp salt
Cheddar shredded cheese
Fresh chopped mint leaves

## Directions

Strain canned peach chunks. Reserve the juice and set aside. In your instant pot, add chicken, tomatoes, cumin, garlic, peach juice (about 1 cup), and salt. Seal the lid, press Poultry and cook on High for 15 minutes. Do a quick Pressure release. Shred chicken with the use of two forks.

Transfer to a serving plate. Add peach chunks to the cooking juices and mix until well combined. Pour the peach salsa over the chicken, top with chopped mint leaves and shredded cheese. Serve immediately.

# Chicken & Quinoa Soup

Serving Size: 6 | Total Time: 30 minutes

## Ingredients

2 tbsp butter
1 cup red onion, chopped
1 cup carrots, chopped
1 cup celery, chopped
2 boneless, skinless chicken breasts, cubed
4 cups chicken broth

6 ounces quinoa, rinsed
1 tbsp fresh parsley, chopped
Salt and black pepper to taste
4 oz mascarpone cheese, at room temperature
1 cup milk
1 cup heavy cream

## Directions

Melt butter on Sauté. Add carrots, onion, and celery and cook for 5 minutes until tender.

Add broth, mix in parsley, quinoa and chicken. Season with pepper and salt.

Seal the lid and cook on High Pressure for 5 minutes. Release the pressure quickly. Press Sauté.

Add mascarpone cheese to the soup and stir well to melt completely; mix in heavy cream and milk. Simmer the soup for 3 to 4 minutes until thickened and creamy.

# Okra & Rice Chicken with Spring Onions

Serving Size: 4 | Total Time: 25 minutes

## Ingredients

6 garlic cloves, grated
¼ cup tomato puree
½ cup soy sauce
1/3 cup honey
2 tbsp rice vinegar
1 tbsp olive oil
4 boneless, skinless chicken breasts, chopped
1 cup rice, rinsed

½ tsp salt
2 cups water
2 cups frozen okra
1 tbsp cornstarch
1 tbsp water
2 tsp toasted sesame seeds
4 spring onions, chopped

## Directions

In the pot, mix garlic, tomato puree, vinegar, soy sauce, honey, and oil; toss in chicken to coat. In an ovenproof bowl that can fit in the instant pot, mix water, salt and rice.

Set the steamer rack on top of chicken. Lower the bowl onto the rack. Seal the lid and cook on High Pressure for 10 minutes. Release the pressure quickly. Use a fork to fluff the rice. Lay okra onto the rice. Allow the okra steam in the residual heat for 3 minutes.

Take the trivet and bowl from the pot. Set the chicken to a plate. Press Sauté. In a small bowl, mix 1 tablespoon of water and cornstarch until smooth. Stir into the sauce and cook for 3 to 4 minutes until thickened. Divide the rice, chicken, and okra between 4 bowls. Drizzle sauce over each portion; garnish with spring onions and sesame seeds.

# Macaroni with Chicken & Pesto Sauce

Serving Size: 8 | Total Time: 30 minutes

## Ingredients

3 ½ cups water
4 chicken breast, boneless, skinless, cubed
8 oz macaroni pasta
1 tbsp butter
Salt and black pepper to taste
2 cups fresh collard greens, trimmed

1 cup cherry tomatoes, halved
½ cup basil pesto sauce
¼ cup cream cheese, at room temperature
1 garlic clove, minced
¼ cup asiago cheese, grated
Freshly chopped basil for garnish

## Directions

Add water, chicken, 2 tsp salt, butter, and macaroni, and stir well to mix and be submerged in water. Seal the lid and cook for 2 minutes on High Pressure. Release the Pressure quickly. Press Cancel, open the lid, get rid of ¼ cup water from the pot.

Set on Sauté mode. Into the pot, mix in collard greens, pesto sauce, garlic, remaining 1 teaspoon salt, cream cheese, cherry tomatoes, and black pepper. Cook for 1 to 2 minutes as you stir, until sauce is creamy. Place the pasta into serving plates. Top with asiago cheese and basil before serving.

# Mouthwatering Green Salsa on Chicken Breasts

Serving Size: 4 | Total Time: 40 minutes

## Ingredients

*Salsa Verde:*

1 jalapeño pepper, deveined and chopped
½ cup capers
¼ cup parsley

1 lime, juiced
1 tsp salt
¼ cup extra virgin olive oil

*Chicken:*

4 boneless skinless chicken breasts
2 cups water

1 cup quinoa, rinsed

## Directions

In a blender, mix olive oil, salt, lime juice, jalapeño pepper, capers, and parsley and blend until smooth. Arrange chicken breasts at the bottom of the cooker. Over the chicken, add salsa verde mixture.

In a bowl that can fit in the cooker, mix quinoa and water. Set a steamer rack onto chicken and sauce. Set the bowl onto the rack. Seal the lid and cook on High Pressure for 20 minutes. Release the Pressure quickly.

Remove the quinoa bowl and rack. Using two forks, shred chicken into the sauce; stir to coat. Divide the quinoa, between plates. Top with chicken and salsa verde before serving.

# Sweet Chicken Carnitas in Lettuce Wraps

Serving Size: 6 | Total Time: 40 minutes

## Ingredients

2 tbsp canola oil
2 lb chicken thighs, boneless, skinless
1 cup pineapple juice
1/3 cup water
¼ cup soy sauce
2 tbsp maple syrup

1 tbsp rice vinegar
1 tsp chili-garlic sauce
3 tbsp cornstarch
Salt and black pepper to taste
12 lettuce large leaves
2 cups canned pinto beans, rinsed and drained

## Directions

Warm oil on Sauté. In batches, stir chicken in the oil for 5 minutes until browned. Set aside in a bowl.

Into your pot, mix chili-garlic sauce, pineapple juice, soy sauce, vinegar, maple syrup, and water; Stir in chicken to coat.

Seal the lid and cook on High Pressure for 7 minutes. Release Pressure naturally for 10 minutes. Shred the chicken with two forks. Take ¼ cup liquid from the pot to a bowl; Stir in cornstarch to dissolve.

Mix the cornstarch mixture with the mixture in the pot and return the chicken. Select Sauté and cook for 5 minutes until the sauce thickens; add pepper and salt for seasoning. Transfer beans into lettuce leaves, top with chicken carnitas and serve.

# Buttered Chicken with Artichokes & Rosemary

Serving Size: 3 | Total Time: 35 minutes

## Ingredients

1 lb chicken breasts, boneless, skinless, chopped
2 artichokes, trimmed, halved
2 tbsp butter, melted
2 tbsp olive oil

1 lemon, juiced
Salt and black pepper to taste
1 tbsp rosemary, chopped
1 cup water

Heat oil on Sauté and cook the chicken for a minute per side, until slightly golden. Pour in 1 cup of water, seal the lid, and cook on High pressure for 13 minutes. Do a quick release. Set aside.

Place the trivet and pour water. Rub the artichoke halves with half of the lemon juice, and arrange on top of the trivet. Seal the lid and cook on Steam for 3 minutes on High. Do a quick release. Combine artichoke and chicken in a large bowl. Stir in salt, pepper, and lemon juice. Drizzle butter over and sprinkle with rosemary to serve.

# Pumpkin & Wild Rice Cajun Chicken

Serving Size: 6 | Total Time: 45 minutes

## Ingredients

6 chicken thighs, skinless
Salt and white pepper to taste
½ tsp ground red pepper
½ tsp onion powder
1 tsp cajun seasoning
1/8 tsp smoked paprika
2 tbsp olive oil

1 cup pumpkin, peeled and cubed
2 celery stalks, diced
2 onions, diced
2 garlic cloves, crushed
3 cups chicken broth
1 ½ cups wild rice

## Directions

Season the chicken with salt, onion powder, cajun seasoning, white pepper, red pepper, and paprika. Warm oil on Sauté. Stir in celery and pumpkin and cook for 5 minutes until tender; set the vegetables on a plate. In batches, sear chicken in oil for 3 minutes each side until golden brown; set on a plate.

Into the cooker, add ¼ cup chicken stock to deglaze the pan, scrape away any browned bits from the bottom; add garlic and onion and cook for 2 minutes until fragrant.

Take back the celery and pumpkin the cooker; add the wild rice and remaining chicken stock. Place the chicken over the rice mixture.

Seal the lid and cook for 10 minutes on High Pressure. Release the Pressure quickly. Place rice and chicken pieces in serving plates and serve.

# Savory Chicken Chili with Chickpeas & Cilantro

Serving Size: 4 | Total Time: 25 minutes

## Ingredients

1 tbsp olive oil
3 large serrano peppers, diced
1 onion, diced
1 jalapeño pepper, diced
1 pound boneless, skinless chicken breast, cubed
1 tsp ground cumin
1 tsp minced fresh garlic

1 tsp salt
2 (14.5 oz) cans chickpeas, drained and rinsed
2 ½ cups water,
2 tbsp chili powder
½ cup chopped fresh cilantro
½ cup shredded Monterey Jack cheese
1 lime, cut into six wedges

## Directions

Warm oil on Sauté. Add in onion, serrano peppers, and jalapeño pepper and cook for 5 minutes until tender. Season with salt, cumin and garlic. Stir chicken with vegetable mixture; cook for 3 to 6 minutes until no longer pink; add 2 cups water and chickpeas. Mix well.

Seal the lid and cook for 5 minutes on High Pressure. Release Pressure naturally for 5 minutes. Stir chili powder with remaining ½ cup water. Press Sauté. Boil the chili as you stir and cook until slightly thickened.

Divide chili into plates, garnish with cheese and cilantro. Over the chili, squeeze a lime wedge.

# Thyme Chicken with White Wine

Serving Size: 6 | Total Time: 45 minutes

## Ingredients

1 cup chicken stock
½ cup white wine
½ onion, chopped
2 cloves garlic, minced
3.5-pound whole chicken

Salt and black pepper to taste
½ tsp dried thyme
3 tbsp butter, melted
½ tsp paprika

## Directions

Into the pot, add onion, chicken stock, white wine, and garlic. Over the mixture, place a steamer rack. Rub pepper, salt, and thyme onto chicken; lay onto the rack breast-side up. Seal the lid, press Poultry and cook on High Pressure for 26 minutes. Release the Pressure quickly.

Preheat oven broiler. In a bowl, mix paprika and butter. Remove the rack with chicken from your pot. Get rid of onion and stock. Onto the chicken, brush butter mixture and take the rack back to the pot.

Cook under the broiler for 5 minutes until chicken skin is crispy and browned. Set chicken to a cutting board to cool for about 5 minutes, then carve and transfer to a serving platter.

# Easy Chicken with Capers & Tomatoes

Serving Size: 4 | Total Time: 45 minutes

## Ingredients

4 chicken legs
Salt and black pepper to taste
2 tbsp olive oil
1 onion, diced
2 garlic cloves, minced

1/3 cup red wine
2 cups diced tomatoes
1/3 cup capers
¼ cup fresh basil
2 pickles, chopped

## Directions

Sprinkle pepper and salt over the chicken. Warm oil on Sauté. Add in onion and Sauté for 3 minutes until fragrant. Add in garlic and cook for 30 seconds until softened. Mix the chicken with vegetables and cook for 6 to 7 minutes until lightly browned.

Add red wine to the pan to deglaze, scrape the pan's bottom to get rid of any browned bits of food; Stir in tomatoes. Seal the lid and cook on High Pressure for 12 minutes. Release the Pressure quickly.

To the chicken mixture, add basil, capers and pickles. Serve the chicken topped with the tomato sauce mixture.

# Tarragon & Garlic Chicken

Serving Size: 4 | Total Time: 30 minutes

## Ingredients

1.5 lb chicken breast, boneless and skinless
4 cups chicken broth
Salt and white pepper to taste
2 garlic cloves, crushed

A handful of fresh tarragon
2 tbsp olive oil
1 onion, finely chopped

## Directions:

Warm oil on Sauté. Stir-fry the onion for 2 minutes. Stir in garlic and cook for 2 minutes, until fragrant. Add the other ingredients except for the thyme. Adjust the seasoning, seal the lid and cook on High pressure for 15 minutes. When ready, do a quick pressure release. Serve topped with fresh thyme.

# Chicken in Sriracha Sauce with Black Beans

Serving Size: 4 | Total Time: 25 minutes

## Ingredients

½ cup soy sauce
½ cup chicken broth
3 tbsp honey
2 tbsp tomato paste
1 tbsp sriracha
1 (1 inch) piece fresh ginger, grated
3 garlic cloves, grated

4 boneless, skinless chicken drumsticks
1 tbsp cornstarch
1 tbsp water
2 tbsp toasted sesame seeds
1 tbsp sesame oil
2 cups canned black beans
2 green onions, chopped

## Directions

In the cooker, mix soy sauce, honey, ginger, tomato paste, chicken broth, sriracha, and garlic. Stir until smooth; toss in chicken to coat. Seal the lid and cook for 3 minutes on High Pressure. Release the Pressure immediately.

Open the lid and press Sauté. In a small bowl, mix water and cornstarch until no lumps remain, Stir into the sauce and cook for 5 minutes until thickened.

Stir sesame oil and 1½ tablespoons sesame seeds through the chicken mixture; garnish with extra sesame seeds and green onions. Serve with black beans.

# Pilaf with Zucchini & Chicken

Serving Size: 4 | Total Time: 40 minutes

## Ingredients

2 tsp olive oil
1 zucchini, chopped
1 cup leeks, chopped
2 garlic cloves, minced
1 tbsp chopped fresh rosemary
1 cup rice, rinsed

2 tsp chopped fresh thyme leaves
Salt and black pepper to taste
2 cups chicken stock
1 lb boneless, skinless chicken legs

## Directions

Warm oil on Sauté, add in zucchini and cook for 5 minutes until tender. Stir in thyme, leeks, rosemary, pepper, salt and garlic. Cook the mixture for 3-4 minutes. Add ½ cup chicken stock into the pot to deglaze, scrape the bottom to get rid of any browned bits of food.

When liquid stops simmering, add in the remaining stock, rice, and chicken with more pepper and salt. Seal the lid and cook on High Pressure for 5 minutes. Do a quick release.

# Hot Chicken with Coriander & Ginger

Serving Size: 6 | Total Time: 35 minutes

## Ingredients

2 pounds chicken thighs, with skin and bones
1 tbsp chili powder
1 tsp fresh basil
Salt and black pepper to taste

6 cups chicken broth
1 tbsp ginger, freshly grated
1 tbsp coriander seeds
3 garlic cloves, crushed

## Directions:

Season the meat with salt, and place it in the instant pot. Add the remaining ingredients, and cook on Meat/Stew mode for 25 minutes on High. Do a natural release, for about 10 minutes. Serve immediately.

# Best Italian Chicken Balls

Serving Size: 5 | Total Time: 35 minutes

## Ingredients

1 pound ground chicken
3 tbsp red hot sauce
1 egg
1/3 cup crumbled blue cheese
¼ cup bread crumbs
¼ cup Pecorino Romano cheese
1 tbsp ranch dressing

1 tsp dried basil
Salt and black pepper to taste
15 ounces canned tomato sauce
1 cup chicken broth
2 tbsp olive oil
A handful of parsley, chopped

## Directions

In a bowl, mix chicken, egg, Pecorino, basil, pepper, salt, ranch dressing, blue cheese, 3 tbsp hot sauce, and bread crumbs; shape the mixture into meatballs. Warm oil on Sauté mode. Add in the meatballs and cook for 2 to 3 minutes until browned on all sides.

Add in tomato sauce and broth. Seal the lid and cook on High Pressure for 7 minutes. Release the pressure quickly. Remove meatballs carefully and place to a serving plate. Top with parsley and serve.

# Tasty Indian Chicken Curry

Serving Size: 6 | Total Time: 30 minutes

## Ingredients

2 tbsp butter
1 large onion, minced
1 tbsp grated fresh ginger
1 tbsp minced fresh garlic
½ tsp ground turmeric
1 tbsp kashmiri red chili powder
1 (14.5 oz) can coconut milk, refrigerated overnight
2 pounds boneless, skinless chicken legs

3 tomatoes, pureed in a blender
½ cup chopped fresh cilantro, divided
2 tbsp Indian curry paste
2 tbsp dried fenugreek
2 tsp sugar
1 tsp garam masala
Salt to taste

## Directions

Melt butter on Sauté mode. Add in 1 teaspoon salt and onion. Cook for 2 to 3 minutes until fragrant. Stir in ginger, turmeric, garlic, and red chili powder to coat; cook for 2 more minutes.

Place water and coconut milk into separate bowls. Stir the water from the coconut milk can, pureed tomatoes, and chicken with the onion mixture. Seal the lid and cook on High Pressure for 8 minutes. Release the Pressure quickly.

Stir sugar, coconut milk, fenugreek, curry paste, half the cilantro, and garam masala through the chicken mixture; apply salt for seasoning. Simmer the mixture and cook for 10 minutes until the sauce thickens, on Sauté mode. Garnish with the rest of the cilantro before serving.

# Lemon Chicken Wings

Serving Size: 4 | Total Time: 40 minutes

## Ingredients

2 tbsp olive oil
8 chicken wings
½ tsp chili powder
½ tsp garlic powder
½ tsp onion powder

½ dried oregano
½ tsp cayenne pepper
Salt and black pepper to taste
½ cup chicken broth
2 lemons, juiced

## Directions

Coat the chicken wings with olive oil. Season with chili powder, onion powder, salt, oregano, garlic powder, cayenne, and pepper.

In the pot, add the wings and chicken broth. Seal the lid and cook on High Pressure for 4 minutes. Do a quick pressure release. Preheat an oven to high.

Onto a greased baking sheet, place the wings in a single layer and drizzle over the lemon juice. Bake for 5 minutes until skin is crispy.

# Chicken Alla Italiana

Serving Size: 4 | Total Time: 40 minutes

### Ingredients

2 tsp olive oil
1 lb chicken drumsticks, boneless, skinless
Salt and black pepper to taste
1 carrot, chopped
1 red bell pepper, chopped
1 yellow bell pepper, chopped
1 onion, chopped
4 garlic cloves, chopped
2 tsp dried oregano

1 tsp dried basil
1 tsp dried parsley
A pinch of red pepper flakes
1 (28-ounce) can diced tomatoes
½ cup dry red wine
¾ cup chicken stock
1 cup black olives, pitted and chopped
2 bay leaves

### Directions

Warm oil on Sauté mode. Season the drumsticks with pepper and salt. In batches, sear the chicken for 5-6 minutes until golden-brown. Set aside on a plate. Drain the pot and remain with 1 tablespoon of fat.

In the hot oil, Sauté onion, garlic, and bell peppers for 4 minutes until softened; add red pepper flakes, basil, parsley, and oregano, and cook for 30 more seconds. Season with salt and pepper. Stir in tomatoes, olives, chicken stock, red wine and bay leaves.

Return chicken to the pot. Seal the lid and cook on High Pressure for 15 minutes. Release the Pressure quickly. Divide chicken into four serving bowls; top with tomato mixture before serving.

# Tasty Chicken Breasts

Serving Size: 4 | Total Time: 45 minutes

### Ingredients

4 chicken breasts, boneless and skinless
Salt and black pepper to taste
2 tbsp olive oil
2 tbsp soy sauce
2 tbsp tomato paste
2 tbsp honey

2 tbsp minced garlic
½ cup chicken broth
1 tbsp cornstarch
1 tbsp water
½ cup chives, chopped

### Directions

Season the chicken with pepper and salt. Warm oil on Sauté. Add in chicken and cook for 5 minutes until lightly browned.

In a small bowl, mix garlic, soy sauce, honey, and tomato paste. Pour the mixture over the chicken. Stir in ½ cup broth. Seal the lid and cook on High Pressure for 12 minutes. Release the Pressure quickly.

Set the chicken to a bowl. Mix water and cornstarch to create a slurry. Briskly stir the mixture into the sauce left in the pan for 2 minutes until thickened. Serve the chicken with sauce and chives.

# Punjabi Chicken in Lemon-Honey Gravy

Serving Size: 4 | Total Time: 15 minutes + marinade time

## Ingredients

*Punjabi chicken:*

4 chicken thighs, skinless
½ cup Greek yogurt
1 tbsp olive oil
1 tbsp lemon juice
1 tbsp red chili powder

2 tsp salt
1 tsp garam masala
½ tsp ground turmeric
½ tbsp grated fresh ginger
½ tbsp minced garlic

*Cilantro gravy:*

A handful of fresh cilantro leaves
1 tsp cumin seeds
½ jalapeño pepper, chopped
2-3 garlic cloves
2 tsp honey

2 tsp lemon juice
¾ cup olive oil
1 tbsp of water
Salt to taste

## Directions

In a bowl, mix yogurt, lemon juice, garam masala, garlic, turmeric, red chili powder, vegetable oil, salt, and ginger. Use a paper towel to pat dry the thighs. Place into a resealable plastic bag.

Add in yogurt mixture and seal. Massage bag to ensure the marinade coats the chicken completely and place in the refrigerator for 12 hours. Take out of the fridge and set aside for 30 minutes before cooking.

Add 1 cup of water into the cooker. Apply a cooking spray to your steamer and set it in over the water. Remove chicken from marinade and arrange on the trivet.

Seal the lid and cook for 15 minutes on High Pressure. Release the Pressure quickly.

In a blender, blend cilantro, water, garlic, honey, cumin, jalapeño pepper, salt and lemon juice, until smooth. Over the chicken, drizzle sauce and serve.

# Rosemary Whole Chicken with Asparagus Sauce

Serving Size: 4 | Total Time: 40 minutes

## Ingredients

1 (3 ½ lb) young whole chicken
4 garlic cloves, minced
1 tsp olive oil
4 fresh thyme, minced
3 fresh rosemary, minced
2 lemons, zested and quartered
Salt and black pepper to taste
2 tbsp olive oil

8 oz asparagus, trimmed and chopped
1 onion, chopped
1 cup chicken stock
1 tbsp soy sauce
1 fresh thyme sprig
1 tbsp flour
Chopped parsley to garnish

## Directions

Rub all sides of the chicken with garlic, rosemary, black pepper, lemon zest, thyme, and salt. Into the chicken cavity, insert lemon wedges. Warm oil on Sauté. Add in onion and asparagus, and Sauté for 5 minutes until softened. Mix chicken stock, 1 thyme sprig, black pepper, soy sauce, and salt.

Into the inner pot, set trivet over asparagus mixture. On top of the trivet, place the chicken with breast-side up. Seal the lid, select Poultry and cook for 20 minutes on High Pressure. Do a quick release. Remove the chicken to a serving platter.

In the inner pot, sprinkle flour over asparagus mixture and blend the sauce with an immersion blender until desired consistency. Top the chicken with asparagus sauce and garnish with parsley.

# Rigatoni with Ground Turkey & Tomato Sauce

Serving Size: 4 | Total Time: 40 minutes

## Ingredients

2 tbsp canola oil
1 pound ground turkey
1 egg
¼ cup bread crumbs
2 cloves garlic, minced
1 tsp dried oregano

1 tsp cumin
1 tsp red pepper flakes
Salt and black pepper to taste
3 cups tomato sauce
8 ounces rigatoni
2 tbsp grated Grana Padano cheese

## Directions

In a bowl, combine turkey, crumbs, cumin, garlic, and egg. Season with oregano, salt, red pepper flakes, and pepper. Form the mixture into meatballs with well-oiled hands.

Warm the oil on Sauté. Cook the meatballs for 3 to 4 minutes, until browned on all sides. Remove to a plate. Add rigatoni to the cooker and cover with tomato sauce. Pour enough water to cover the pasta. Stir well. Throw in the meatballs. Seal the lid and cook for 10 minutes on High Pressure. Release the Pressure quickly. Serve topped with Grana Padano cheese.

# Sunday Turkey Lettuce Wraps

Serving Size: 4 | Total Time: 45 minutes

## Ingredients

¾ cup olive oil
4 cloves garlic, minced
3 tbsp maple syrup
2 tbsp pineapple juice
1 cup coconut milk
3 tbsp rice wine vinegar

3 tbsp soy sauce
1 tbsp Thai-style chili paste
1 lb boneless, skinless turkey breasts, cut into strips
1 romaine lettuce, leaves separated
1/3 cup chopped peanuts
¼ cup chopped fresh cilantro leaves

## Directions

In the pot, mix oil, garlic, rice wine vinegar, soy sauce, pineapple juice, maple syrup, coconut milk, and chili paste until smooth; add turkey strips and ensure they are submerged in the sauce.

Seal the lid and cook on High Pressure for 12 minutes. Release the Pressure quickly. Place the turkey at the center of each lettuce leaf; Top with cilantro and chopped peanuts.

# Ginger & Potato Chicken Thighs

Serving Size: 4 | Total Time: 30 minutes

## Ingredients

4 chicken thighs, boneless
3 large potatoes, wedged
1 tbsp lemon juice
2 garlic cloves, crushed
1 tsp ginger, ground

1 tbsp cayenne pepper
1 tsp fresh mint, finely chopped
¼ cup olive oil
½ tsp salt

## Directions

In a bowl, combine oil, lemon juice, garlic, ginger, mint, cayenne, and salt. Brush each chicken piece with this mixture. Grease the inner pot with the remaining mixture. Place the potatoes and top with chicken.

Add 1½ cups of water and seal the lid. Cook on Manual/Pressure Cook mode for 15 minutes on High. When ready, press Cancel and release the pressure naturally, for 10 minutes.

# Chicken Sausage & Navy Bean Chili

Serving Size: 6 | Total Time: 45 minutes

## Ingredients

1 tbsp olive oil
1 shallot, diced
½ cup fennel, chopped
¼ cup minced garlic
1 tbsp smoked paprika
2 tsp chili powder
2 tsp ground cumin

Salt and white pepper to taste
1 (28 oz) can crushed tomatoes
1 ½ pounds chicken sausages, chopped
1 (14-ounce) can diced tomatoes with green chilies
¾ cup buffalo wing sauce
2 (14-ounce) cans navy beans, drained and rinsed

## Directions

Warm oil on Sauté. Add the sausages and brown for 5 minutes, turning frequently. Set aside on a plate. In the same fat, Sauté shallot, roasted fennel, and garlic for 4 minutes until soft. Season with paprika, cumin, pepper, salt, and chili powder.

Stir in crushed tomatoes, diced tomatoes with green chilies, buffalo sauce, and navy beans. Return the sausages to the pot. Seal the lid and cook on High Pressure for 30 minutes. Do a quick Pressure release.

# Homemade Pesto Chicken with Green Beans

Serving Size: 4 | Total Time: 20 minutes

## Ingredients

4 chicken breasts
1 tbsp butter
1 tbsp olive oil
¼ cup dry white wine

¾ cup chicken stock
Salt and black pepper to taste
1 cup green beans, trimmed and cut pieces

### For pesto:
1 cup fresh basil
1 garlic clove, smashed
2 tbsp pine nuts

¼ cup Parmesan cheese
¼ cup extra virgin olive oil
Salt and black pepper to taste

## Directions

First make the pesto - in a bowl, mix fresh basil, pine nuts, garlic, salt, pepper and Parmesan and place in food processor. Add in oil and process until the desired consistency is attained.

Apply a thin layer of pesto to one side of each chicken breast; tightly roll into a cylinder and fasten closed with small skewers. Press Sauté. Add oil and butter. Cook chicken rolls for 1 to 2 minutes per side until browned.

Add in wine and cook until the wine has evaporated, about 3-4 minutes.

Add stock and salt, and top the chicken with green beans. Seal the lid, press Meat/Stew and cook at High Pressure for 5 minutes. Release the Pressure quickly. Serve chicken rolls with cooking liquid and green beans.

# Rice & Lentil Chicken with Parsley

Serving Size: 4 | Total Time: 35 minutes

## Ingredients

1 tsp olive oil
1 garlic clove, minced
1 small yellow onion, chopped
3 cups chicken broth
4 boneless, skinless chicken thighs

1 cup white rice
½ cup dried lentils
Salt and black pepper to taste
Chopped fresh parsley for garnish

## Directions

Warm oil on Sauté mode. Stir-fry onion and garlic for 3 minutes. Add in broth, rice, lentils, chicken, pepper and salt. Seal the lid and cook on High Pressure for 15 minutes. Do a quick release.

Remove and shred the chicken in a large bowl. Set the lentils and rice into serving plates, Top with shredded chicken and parsley to serve.

# Pea & Rice Chicken with Paprika & Herbs

Serving Size: 4 | Total Time: 30 minutes

## Ingredients

4 boneless, skinless chicken breasts, chopped
1 garlic clove, minced
½ tsp paprika
¼ tsp dried oregano
¼ tsp dried thyme
1 tsp cayenne pepper
Salt and white pepper to taste

1 tbsp oil olive
1 onion, chopped
1 tbsp tomato puree
2 cups chicken broth
1 cup rice
1 celery stalk, diced
1 cup frozen green peas

## Directions

Season chicken with garlic, oregano, white pepper, thyme, paprika, cayenne pepper, and salt. Warm the oil on Sauté. Add in onion and cook for 4 minutes until fragrant. Mix in tomato puree to coat.

Add ¼ cup chicken broth into the cooker to deglaze the pan, scrape the pan's bottom to get rid of browned bits of food. Mix in celery, rice, and seasoned chicken. Add in the remaining broth to the chicken mixture.

Seal the lid and cook on High Pressure for 8 minutes. Do a quick release. Mix in green peas, cover with the lid and let sit for 5 minutes. Serve warm.

# Awesome Chicken in Tikka Masala Sauce

Serving Size: 4 | Total Time: 40 minutes

## Ingredients

2 pounds boneless, skinless chicken thighs,
Salt and black pepper to taste
1 ½ tbsp olive oil
½ onion, chopped
2 garlic cloves, minced
3 tbsp tomato puree
1 tsp fresh ginger, minced
1 tbsp garam masala
2 tsp curry powder

1 tsp ground coriander
½ tsp ground cumin
1 jalapeño pepper, seeded and chopped
29 ounces canned tomato sauce
3 tomatoes, chopped
½ cup natural yogurt
1 lemon, juiced
¼ cup fresh chopped cilantro leaves
4 lemon wedges

## Directions

Rub black pepper and ½ teaspoon of salt onto chicken. Warm oil on Sauté. Add garlic and onion and cook for 3 minutes until soft. Stir in tomato puree, garam masala, cumin, curry powder, ginger, coriander, and jalapeño pepper; cook for 30 seconds until fragrant.

Stir in remaining ½ teaspoon salt, tomato sauce, and tomatoes. Simmer the mixture as you scrape the bottom to get rid of any browned bits; Stir in chicken to coat.

Seal the lid and cook on High Pressure for 10 minutes. Release the Pressure quickly. Press Sauté and simmer the sauce and cook for 3 to 5 minutes until thickened. Stir lemon juice and yogurt through the sauce.

Serve garnished with lemon wedges and cilantro.

# Corn & Sweet Potato Soup with Chicken

Serving Size: 8 | Total Time: 40 minutes

## Ingredients

4 boneless, skinless chicken breast, diced
3 garlic cloves, minced
1 cup chicken stock
19 ounces corn kernels, frozen
1 sweet potato, peeled and cubed
4 ounces canned diced green chiles, drained

2 tsp chili powder
1 tsp ground cumin
2 cups cheddar cheese, shredded
2 cups creme fraiche
Salt and black pepper to taste
Cilantro leaves, chopped

## Directions

Add chicken, corn, chili powder, cumin, chicken stock, sweet potato, green chiles, and garlic. Mix well. Seal the lid and cook on High Pressure for 10 minutes. Release the Pressure quickly. Set the chicken to a cutting board and use two forks to shred it. Return to the pot and stir well into the liquid.

Stir in cheese and creme fraiche; Season with pepper and salt. Cook for 2 to 3 minutes until cheese is melted. Place chowder into plates and top with cilantro.

# Chicken with Honey-Lemon Sauce

Serving Size: 4 | Total Time: 30 minutes

## Ingredients

4 boneless, skinless chicken breast, cut into chunks
1 onion, diced
4 garlic cloves, smashed
½ cup honey
3 tbsp soy sauce
2 tbsp Lime juice

2 tsp sesame oil
1 tsp rice vinegar
Salt and black pepper to taste
1 tbsp cornstarch
1 tbsp water

## Directions

Mix garlic, onion and chicken in your instant pot. In a bowl, combine honey, sesame oil, Lime juice, soy sauce, and rice vinegar; Pour over the chicken mixture. Seal the lid and cook on High Pressure for 15 minutes. Release the Pressure quickly.

Mix water and cornstarch until well dissolved; Stir into the sauce, add salt and pepper to taste. Press Sauté. Simmer the sauce and cook for 2 to 3 minutes as you stir until thickened.

# Picante Chicken with Lemon

Serving Size: 2 | Total Time: 20 minutes

## Ingredients

1 lb chicken breast, cut into ½ -inch thick slices
1 cup olive oil
1 cup chicken broth
½ cup freshly squeezed lemon juice
½ cup parsley leaves, chopped

3 garlic cloves, crushed
1 tbsp cayenne pepper
1 tsp dried oregano
½ tsp salt

## Directions

In a bowl, mix olive oil, lemon juice, parsley, garlic, cayenne, oregano, and salt. Submerge fillets in this mixture and cover. Chill for 30 minutes.

Remove from the fridge and place all inside the pot. Add in the broth. Seal the lid and cook on High Pressure for 7 minutes. Release the Pressure naturally, for about 10 minutes and serve immediately.

# Colorful Vegetable & Chicken Risotto

Serving Size: 4 | Total Time: 65 minutes

## Ingredients

10 oz chicken breasts, boneless, skinless, cut into pieces
1 cup rice
6 oz button mushrooms, stems removed
1 red bell pepper, halved, seeds removed
1 green bell pepper, halved, seeds removed
1 yellow bell pepper, halved, seeds removed
6 oz broccoli, cut into florets

½ cup sweet corn
2 carrots, peeled and chopped
2 tbsp olive oil
1 tbsp butter
Salt and black pepper to taste
1 tsp fresh basil, finely chopped
Parmesan cheese for topping

## Directions

Add rice and pour in 3 cups of water. Stir in butter, pepper and salt and seal the lid. Cook on Rice mode for 8 minutes on High. Do a quick release and remove the rice.

Heat oil on Sauté, and add carrots and broccoli. Sauté for 10 minutes. Add sweet corn and bell peppers and cook for 5 minutes, stirring constantly. Finally, stir in mushrooms, and cook for 3-4 minutes.

Remove the vegetables, mix with rice and set aside. Add the chicken to the pot and pour in 2 cups of water. Season with salt and pepper. Seal the lid and cook on High pressure for 7 minutes. Do a quick release. Open the lid, stir in rice and vegetables and serve warm sprinkled with Parmesan cheese and fresh basil.

# Fabulous Orange Chicken Stew

Serving Size: 4 | Total Time: 50 minutes

## Ingredients

2 lb chicken breast, boneless and skinless
1 cup fire-roasted tomatoes, diced
1 tbsp chili powder

Salt and white pepper to taste
1 cup orange juice
2 cups chicken broth

## Directions

Season the chicken with salt and pepper, and place in your instant pot. Add the remaining ingredients, except for the orange juice and chicken broth, and cook on Sauté mode for 10 minutes, stirring occasionally.

Press Cancel, pour in the broth and orange juice. Seal the lid and cook on Poultry for 25 minutes on High. Release the pressure naturally, for 10 minutes. Serve immediately.

# Savory Chicken Wings with Worcestershire Sauce

Serving Size: 8 | Total Time: 35 minutes

## Ingredients

8 chicken wings, bones and skin on
3 cups chicken broth
1 tsp fresh ginger, grated
1 tbsp honey
2 tbsp oil

1/3 cup Worcestershire sauce
2 spring onions, finely chopped
2 garlic cloves, crushed
1 tsp salt

## Directions

Add the chicken to the pot and pour in broth. Seal the lid and cook on Poultry for 15 minutes on High. Do a quick release. Remove chicken and broth, and wipe the pot clean.

Heat oil on Sauté, and stir-fry onions and garlic for 2-3 minutes. Add Worcestershire sauce, honey, salt, and ginger. Cook for a minute and return the wings. Stir well and cook for 2 minutes, until nice and crispy.

# Feta Cheese Turkey Balls

Serving Size: 6 | Total Time: 30 minutes

## Ingredients

1 onion, minced
½ cup plain bread crumbs
1/3 cup feta cheese, crumbled
Salt and black pepper to taste
½ tsp dried oregano
1 pound ground turkey

1 egg, lightly beaten
1 tbsp olive oil
1 carrot, minced
½ celery stalk, minced
3 cups tomato puree
2 cups water

## Directions

In a mixing bowl, combine half the onion, oregano, turkey, salt, crumbs, pepper, and egg, and stir until everything is well incorporated.

Heat oil on Sauté mode, and cook celery, remaining onion, and carrot for 5 minutes, until soft. Pour in water, and tomato puree. Adjust the seasonings. Roll the mixture into meatballs, and drop into the sauce. Seal the lid.

Press Meat/Stew and cook on High Pressure for 5 minutes. Allow the cooker to cool and release the pressure naturally for 20 minutes. Serve topped with feta cheese.

# Savory Tropical Chicken

Serving Size: 4 | Total Time: 25 minutes

## Ingredients

1 tbsp olive oil
4 boneless, skinless chicken thighs
¼ cup pineapple juice
2 tbsp ketchup
2 tbsp Worcestershire sauce

1 garlic clove, minced
1 tsp cornstarch
2 tsp water
A handful of fresh cilantro, chopped

## Directions

Warm oil on Sauté. In batches, sear chicken in oil for 3 minutes until golden brown; set aside on a plate.

Mix, pineapple juice, Worcestershire sauce, garlic, and ketchup; add to the pot to deglaze, scrape the bottom to get rid of any browned bits of food. Place the chicken into the sauce and stir well to coat.

Seal the lid cook for 5 minutes on High Pressure. Release the Pressure quickly.

In a bowl, mix water and cornstarch until well dissolved. Press Cancel and set to Sauté mode. Stir the cornstarch slurry into the sauce; cook for 2 minutes until the sauce is well thickened. Sprinkle with cilantro to serve.

# Quinoa Pilaf with Chicken

Serving Size: 4 | Total Time: 40 minutes

## Ingredients

1 lb chicken breasts, boneless, skinless
1 cup quinoa
2 cups chicken broth

Salt and black pepper to taste
Greek yogurt for topping

## Directions

Add chicken and broth to the pot and seal the lid. Cook on Poultry for 15 minutes on High. Do a quick release and remove the chicken. Add quinoa and seal the lid. Cook on Rice mode for 8 minutes on High.

Meanwhile, cut the chicken meat into bite-sized pieces and place in a large bowl. To the cooker, do a quick release. Stir in chicken, to warm, season with salt, black pepper and, top with greek yogurt.

# Spicy Ground Turkey Chili with Vegetables

Serving Size: 6 | Total Time: 55 minutes

## Ingredients

1 tbsp olive oil
1 small onion, diced
2 garlic cloves, minced
1 pound ground turkey
2 bell peppers, chopped
6 potatoes, peeled and chopped
1 cup carrots, chopped

1 cup fresh or frozen corn kernels, roasted
1 cup tomato puree
1 cup diced tomatoes
1 cup chicken broth
1 tbsp ground cumin
1 tbsp chili powder
Salt and black pepper to taste

## Directions

Warm oil on Sauté, and stir-fry onion and garlic until soft, for about 3 minutes. Stir in turkey and cook until thoroughly browned, about 5-6 minutes. Add the remaining ingredients, and stir to combine.

Seal the lid and cook for 25 minutes on High Pressure. Do a quick release. Set on Sauté and cook uncovered for 15 more minutes. Serve warm.

# Parsley & Lemon Turkey Risotto

Serving Size: 4 | Total Time: 40 minutes

## Ingredients

2 boneless turkey breasts, cut into strips
2 lemons, zested and juiced
1 tbsp dried oregano
2 garlic cloves, minced
1 ½ tbsp olive oil
1 onion, diced

2 cups chicken broth
1 cup arborio rice, rinsed
Salt and black pepper to taste
¼ cup chopped fresh parsley
8 lemon slices

## Directions

In a ziploc bag, mix turkey, oregano, salt, garlic, juice and zest of two lemons. Marinate for 10 minutes.

Warm oil on Sauté. Add onion and cook for 3 minutes; add rice and chicken broth and season with pepper and salt. Empty the ziploc having the chicken and marinade into pot. Seal the lid and cook on High Pressure for 12 minutes. Release the Pressure quickly. Garnish with lemon slices and parsley to serve.

# Chicken with Vegetables & Coconut Milk Stew

Serving Size: 4 | Total Time: 55 minutes

## Ingredients

2 cups fire-roasted tomatoes, diced
1 lb chicken breast, boneless and skinless, chopped
1 tbsp fresh basil, chopped
2 cups coconut milk
1 cup chicken broth
Salt and black pepper to taste
2 tbsp tomato paste

2 celery stalks, chopped
2 carrots, chopped
2 tbsp coconut oil
1 onion, finely chopped
3 garlic cloves, crushed
½ cup button mushrooms, sliced

## Directions:

Grease the inner pot with oil. Add celery, onion, and carrots and cook on Sauté for 7 minutes, stirring constantly. Add tomato paste, basil, garlic, and mushrooms. Continue to cook for 10 more minutes. Add the rest of the ingredients, seal the lid. and cook on Poultry for 15 minutes on High. Do a quick release.

# Grilled Chicken Drumsticks with Summer Salad

Serving Size: 4 | Total Time: 60 minutes

## Ingredients

4 chicken drumsticks
3 cups chicken broth
1 tomato, roughly chopped
2 oz lettuce, torn
1 cup kalamata olives
1 cucumber, chopped

3 tbsp olive oil
1 tbsp Dijon mustard
¼ cup white wine
1 tsp lemon juice
1 tbsp Italian seasoning mix
1 tsp salt

## Directions

In a bowl, mix mustard, 2 tbsp olive oil, Italian mix, wine, and salt. Stir and brush the meat. Wrap in aluminum foil and refrigerate for 30 minutes.

Place the tomato, lettuce, cucumber, and kalamata olive in a serving bowl. Season with salt, black pepper and add in the remaining olive oil. Stir and set aside.

Remove the drumsticks from the fridge and transfer to the pot. Pour in the broth and seal the lid. Cook on Poultry mode for 15 minutes on High Pressure.

Do a quick release and remove the drumsticks. Preheat a non-stick grill pan over high heat. Brown the drumsticks for 6-7 minutes, turning once. Serve with the salad.

# Tuscan Vegetable Chicken Stew

Serving Size: 4 | Total Time: 50 minutes

## Ingredients

1 whole chicken, 3 lb
14 oz mixed broccoli and cauliflower florets
1 onion, peeled, chopped
1 potato, peeled and chopped
3 carrots, chopped

1 tomato, peeled and chopped
A handful of yellow wax beans, whole
A handful of fresh parsley, chopped
¼ cup extra virgin olive oil
Salt and black pepper to taste

## Directions

Grease the bottom of the pot with 3 tbsp of olive oil. Stir-fry the onion, for 3-4 minutes, on Sauté mode. Add the carrots, and Sauté for 5 more minutes.

Add the remaining oil, vegetables, salt, black pepper, and top with chicken. Add 1 cup of water and seal the lid. Cook on High Pressure for 30 minutes. Release the Pressure naturally, for about 10 minutes.

# Hot Chicken with Garlic & Mushrooms

Serving Size: 3 | Total Time: 30 minutes

## Ingredients

1 lb chicken breasts, skinless, boneless, cut into pieces
1 cup button mushrooms, chopped
2 cups chicken broth
2 tbsp flour

1 tsp cayenne pepper, ground
Salt and black pepper to taste
1 tbsp olive oil
2 garlic cloves, chopped

## Directions

Grease the inner pot with oil. Add garlic and chicken, season with salt, and stir-fry for 3 minutes. Add mushrooms and Pour the chicken broth. Seal the lid. Cook on High Pressure for 8 minutes.

Release the steam naturally, for 10 minutes and stir in flour, cayenne, and black pepper. Cook for 5 minutes, on Sauté mode. Serve warm.

# Sage Chicken in Orange Gravy

Serving Size: 8 | Total Time: 45 minutes

### Ingredients

1 whole chicken (about 3.5 lb)
¼ cup oil
2 tbsp fresh sage, minced
2 tbsp lemon zest
1 tsp garlic powder
¼ tsp red pepper flakes
3 cups chicken broth

1 cup red wine
5 tbsp butter
1 cup orange juice
1 tsp sugar
½ cup flour
Salt and black pepper to taste

### Directions

Mix oil, tarragon, lemon zest, garlic, salt, black pepper, and red pepper. Rub the mixture onto chicken. Melt butter on Sauté. and brown the chicken for 3-4 minutes. Pour in broth and wine. Seal the lid and cook on Poultry for 30 minutes on High. Do a quick release and remove the chicken.

In a bowl, mix the orange juice, 1 cup of cooking liquid, flour, and sugar. Cook for 5 minutes on Sauté mode until sauce has thickened. Scatter the sauce over the chicken and serve.

# Awesome Spicy Turkey Casserole with Tomatoes

Serving Size: 5 | Total Time: 35 minutes

### Ingredients

1 tbsp olive oil
½ sweet onion, diced
3 cloves garlic, minced
1 jalapeño pepper, minced
1 pound turkey breast, cubed
2 (14-ounce) cans fire-roasted tomatoes
1 ½ cups water

1 cup salsa
2 bell peppers, cut into thick strips
2 tsp chili powder
1 tsp ground cumin
Salt to taste
5 tbsp fresh oregano, chopped

### Directions

Warm oil on Sauté. Add in garlic, onion and jalapeño and cook for 5 minutes, until fragrant. Stir turkey into the pot; cook for 5-6 minutes until browned.

Add in salsa, tomatoes, bell peppers, and water. Season with salt, cumin, and chili powder. Seal the lid, Press Soup, and cook for 10 minutes on High. Release the pressure quickly. Top with oregano and serve.

# Easy Italian Chicken Stew with Potatoes

Serving Size: 4 | Total Time: 20 minutes

### Ingredients

2 lb chicken wings
2 potatoes, peeled, cut into chunks
2 fire-roasted tomatoes, peeled, chopped
1 carrot, peeled, cut into chunks
2 garlic cloves, chopped
2 tbsp olive oil

1 tsp smoked paprika, ground
4 cups chicken broth
2 tbsp fresh parsley, chopped
Salt and black pepper to taste
1 cup spinach, chopped

### Directions

Rub the chicken with salt, pepper, and paprika, and place in the pot. Add in all remaining ingredients and seal the lid. Cook on High Pressure for 8 minutes. When ready, do a quick release. Serve hot.

# Quick Swiss Chard & Chicken Stew

Serving Size: 4 | Total Time: 30 minutes

## Ingredients

2 lb chicken breasts, boneless, skinless, cut into pieces
2 lb Swiss chard, chopped
2 cups chicken broth

2 tbsp butter, unsalted
2 tbsp olive oil
Salt and black pepper to taste

## Directions

Add the chicken, oil and broth to the pot. Season with salt and black pepper, seal the lid and cook on Manual for 13 minutes on High. Do a quick release, add Swiss chard and butter. Cook on Sauté for 5 minutes. Serve warm.

# Delicious Turkey Burgers

Serving Size: 4 | Total Time: 25 minutes

## Ingredients

1 lb ground turkey
2 eggs
1 cup flour
1 onion, finely chopped

2 tsp dried dill, chopped
Salt and black pepper to taste
1 cup sour cream

## Directions

In a bowl, add all ingredients and mix well with hands. Form the patties with the previously prepared mixture. Line parchment paper over a baking dish and arrange the patties. Pour 1 cup of water in the pot.

Lay the trivet and place the baking dish on top. Seal the lid. Cook on Pressure Cook mode for 15 minutes on High. Release the pressure naturally, for 10 minutes. Serve with lettuce and tomatoes.

# Easy Primavera Chicken Stew

Serving Size: 4 | Total Time: 55 minutes

## Ingredients

4 green onions, chopped
3 garlic cloves, peeled and crushed
3 new potatoes, peeled and chopped
8 baby carrots, chopped
4 oz can tomato sauce

1 tsp salt
8 oz chicken breast, cut into bite-sized pieces
2 cups chicken broth
2 tbsp olive oil

## Directions

Place the veggies in the instant pot and pour enough water to cover. Seal the lid and cook on Manual/Pressure Cook for 15 minutes on High. Do a quick release. Remove the vegetables along with the liquid.

Heat oil on Sauté and stir-fry the vegetables for 5 minutes. Add the remaining ingredients and seal the lid. Set on Poultry and cook for 15 minutes on High. Do a natural release, for 10 minutes and serve hot.

# Dijon Mustard Chicken Breast

Serving Size: 2 | Total Time: 35 minutes

## Ingredients

1 lb chicken breasts, boneless and skinless
¼ cup apple cider vinegar
1 tsp garlic powder
2 tbsp Dijon mustard

Salt and black pepper to taste
2 tbsp olive oil
2 cups chicken stock

## Directions

Season the chicken with garlic, salt, and black pepper. Place in the instant pot and pour in the stock. Seal the lid and cook on Poultry mode for 20 minutes on High. Do a quick release and remove the meat along with the stock.

In a bowl, mix olive oil, mustard, and apple cider vinegar. Pour into the pot and press Sauté. Place the chicken in this mixture and cook for 10 minutes, turning once. When done, remove from the pot and drizzle with the sauce.

# Bell Pepper & Chicken Stew

Serving Size: 4 | Total Time: 35 minutes

## Ingredients

1 lb chicken breasts, boneless, skinless, cut into pieces
2 potatoes, peeled, chopped
5 green bell peppers, chopped, seeds removed
2 carrots, chopped
2 ½ cups chicken broth

1 tomato, roughly chopped
A handful of freshly chopped parsley
3 tbsp extra virgin olive oil
1 tsp cayenne pepper
1 tsp salt

## Directions

Warm the oil on Sauté, and stir-fry bell peppers and carrots, for 3 minutes. Add potatoes, tomato, and parsley. Sprinkle with cayenne, and salt, and stir well.

Top with the chicken, Pour in broth and seal the lid. Cook on High Pressure for 13 minutes. When ready, do a quick Pressure release, and serve hot.

# Weekend Turkey with Vegetables

Serving Size: 4 | Total Time: 45 minutes

## Ingredients

1 lb turkey breast, chopped
1 tsp red pepper flakes
2 cups canned tomatoes, diced
3 cups chicken broth
1 tsp honey
2 cups zucchini, cubed

3 garlic cloves, chopped
1 cup onions, finely chopped
2 tbsp tomato paste
1 cup baby carrots, chopped
Salt and black pepper to taste
2 tbsp olive oil

## Directions:

Mix all ingredients in your instant pot. Seal the lid and cook on Meat/Stew mode for 25 minutes on High Pressure. When ready, do a quick release and open the lid. Serve immediately.

# Cranberry Turkey with Hazelnuts

Serving Size: 5 | Total Time: 40 minutes

## Ingredients

1 lb turkey breast, boneless, skinless, cut into thick slices
3 tbsp butter, softened
2 cups fresh cranberries
1 cup toasted hazelnuts, chopped
1 cup red wine

1 tbsp fresh rosemary, chopped
2 tbsp olive oil
2 tbsp orange zest
Salt and black pepper to taste

## Directions

Rub the turkey with oil and sprinkle with orange zest, salt, pepper, and rosemary. Melt butter in pot, and brown turkey breast for 5-6 minutes, on Sauté mode. Pour in wine, cranberries and 1 cup of water. Seal the lid. Cook on High Pressure for 25 minutes. Do a quick release. Serve with chopped hazelnuts.

# Spiced Chicken Thighs with Garlic

Serving Size: 4 | Total Time: 1 hour 30 minutes

## Ingredients

4 chicken thighs
1 cup chicken broth
1 cup olive oil
¼ cup apple cider vinegar
3 garlic cloves, crushed
½ cup freshly squeezed lemon juice

1 tbsp fresh basil, chopped
2 tbsp fresh thyme, chopped
1 tbsp fresh rosemary, chopped
1 tsp cayenne pepper
1 tsp salt

## Directions

In a bowl, add oil, vinegar, garlic, juice, basil, thyme, rosemary, salt, and cayenne. Submerge thighs into this mixture and refrigerate for one hour. Remove from the fridge and pat dry with kitchen paper.

Pour the broth in the pot. Set the trivet and place the chicken on it. Seal the lid and cook on Steam mode for 15 minutes on High. Do a quick release and remove the chicken and broth; wipe clean.

Press Sauté, warm oil and brown the chicken thighs for 5 minutes, turning once, until nice and golden.

# Rosemary Chicken Thighs with Mushrooms & Garlic

Serving Size: 2 | Total Time: 30 minutes

## Ingredients

2 chicken thighs, boneless and skinless
6 oz button mushrooms
3 tbsp olive oil
1 tsp fresh rosemary, finely chopped

2 garlic cloves, crushed
½ tsp salt
1 tbsp butter
1 tbsp Italian seasoning

## Directions

Heat a tablespoon of olive oil on Sauté. Add chicken thighs and sear for 5 minutes. Set aside. Pour in the remaining oil, and add mushrooms, rosemary, and Italian seasoning mix. Stir-fry for 5 minutes.

Add in butter, chicken, and 2 cups of water. Seal the lid and cook on Pressure Cook mode for 13 minutes on High. Do a quick release. Remove the chicken and mushrooms from the cooker and serve with garlic.

# Potato Skins with Shredded Turkey

Serving Size: 4 | Total Time: 30 minutes

## Ingredients

2 cups vegetable broth
1 tsp chili powder
1 tsp ground cumin
½ tsp onion powder
½ tsp garlic powder

1 pound turkey breasts
4 potatoes
2 tbsp fresh cilantro, chopped
1 fresno chili pepper, chopped
Salt and black pepper to taste

## Directions

In the pot, combine broth, cumin, garlic powder, onion powder, and fresno chili powder. Toss in turkey to coat. Place a steamer rack over the turkey. On top of the rack, set the steamer basket.

Use a fork to pierce the potatoes and transfer to the steamer basket. Seal the lid and cook for 20 minutes on High. Release the pressure quickly. Remove rack and steamer basket from the cooker. Shred the turkey in a bowl.

Place the potatoes on a plate. Cut in half each potato lengthwise and scoop out the insides. Season with salt and pepper. Stuff with shredded turkey. Top with cilantro, and chili pepper.

# Festive Chicken with Bacon

Serving Size: 4 | Total Time: 45 minutes

## Ingredients

1 whole chicken (3.5 lb)
3 tbsp butter
¼ cup Worcestershire sauce
2 cups chicken stock

6 oz bacon
1 tbsp flour
White pepper and salt to taste

## Directions

Rub the meat with salt and pepper. Place in the instant pot along with stock and Worcestershire sauce. Seal the lid and cook on High Pressure for 40 minutes. Do a quick release and remove to a bowl.

Melt butter on Sauté mode. Stir-fry the bacon for 2 minutes, until crispy.

Stir in flour and 1 cup of cooking juices and cook for 4 minutes, until the sauce thickens. Transfer the chicken to a platter and drizzle the gravy over.

# Turkish-Style Roasted Turkey

Serving Size: 6 | Total Time: 50 minutes

## Ingredients

2 lb boneless turkey breast, halved
2 garlic cloves, crushed
1 tsp dried basil
Salt and white pepper to taste
3 whole cloves

½ cup soy sauce
½ cup lemon juice
1 tbsp cane sugar
¼ cup oil
3 cups chicken broth

## Directions

Place the meat in a ziploc bag and add basil, cloves, soy sauce, oil, cane sugar, salt, pepper, and lemon juice. Pour in 1 cup of broth and seal. Shake and Refrigerate for 30 minutes.

Heat oil on Sauté and stir fry the garlic for 2 minutes. Add in the along with 2 tbsp of the marinade and the remaining broth. Seal the lid. Cook on Poultry for 25 minutes on High. Release the Pressure naturally.

# Homemade Turkey Pepperoni Pizza

Serving Size: 4 | Total Time: 25 minutes

## Ingredients

1 whole wheat Italian pizza crust
1 cup fire-roasted tomatoes, diced
1 tsp oregano
½ tsp dried basil

½ cup turkey pepperoni, chopped
7 oz Gouda cheese, grated
2 tbsp olive oil

## Directions

Grease a baking pan with oil. Line some parchment paper and place the pizza crust in it.

Spread the fire-roasted tomatoes over the pizza crust and sprinkle with oregano and basil. Make a layer with cheese and top with pepperoni.

Add a trivet inside the pot and pour in 1 cup of water. Seal the lid, and cook for 15 minutes on High Pressure. Do a quick release. Remove the pizza from the pot using a parchment paper.

# Roast Goose with White Wine

Serving Size: 10 | Total Time: 40 minutes

## Ingredients

2 lb goose fillets, cut into 1-inch thick slices
1 cup onions, finely chopped
4 tbsp butter, softened
2 garlic cloves, crushed

1 cup white wine
2 tbsp fresh celery, chopped
1 tsp dried thyme
Salt and white pepper to taste

## Directions

Season the meat with salt and white pepper. Place in the pot and add wine and thyme. Pour in 2 cups of water, Seal the lid and set on Meat/Stew.

Cook for 25 minutes on High Pressure. When ready, do a quick release and set aside. Melt butter on Sauté, and stir-fry onions and garlic, for 3-4 minutes. Add the fillets, one at the time, and brown on both sides for 2 minutes.

# Herby Chicken with Peach Gravy

Serving Size: 4 | Total Time: 45 minutes

## Ingredients

4 chicken breasts
¼ cup olive oil
1 cup onions, chopped
¼ cup celery stalks, chopped
2 peaches, cut into chunks

½ tsp dried thyme
½ tsp dried sage
1 cup cider
2 cups chicken stock
Salt and black pepper to taste

## Directions

Heat oil on Sauté, and stir-fry the onions for 2-3 minutes, until soft. Add celery stalks and peaches, and cook for 5 minutes, stirring occasionally.

Meanwhile, rub the meat with salt, pepper, thyme and sage. Add it in the pot along with cider and stock. Seal the lid and cook on High Pressure for 35 minutes. Do a quick release.

# Spicy Chicken Thighs

Serving Size: 4 | Total Time: 45 minutes

## Ingredients

1 lb chicken thighs
2 tbsp oil
4 cups chicken broth
1 tsp salt

2 tsp Lime zest
1 tsp chili powder
½ cup tomato puree
1 tbsp sugar

## Directions

Season the meat evenly with salt and chili powder on both sides. Warm oil on Sauté, and add the thighs. Briefly brown on both sides and then set aside. Add the tomato puree, sugar, and lime zest.

Cook for 10 minutes to obtain a thick sauce. Add the chicken thighs and pour in the broth. Seal the lid and cook on Poultry mode for 20 minutes on High pressure. When done, do a quick release and serve.

# Brussels Sprouts & Zucchini Chicken

Serving Size: 4 | Total Time: 50 minutes

## Ingredients

4 chicken thighs, boneless and skinless
1 cup chicken stock
½ cauliflower head, roughly chopped
2 tomatoes, roughly chopped
½ pound Brussels sprouts

2 zucchinis, chopped
1 small onion, peeled and chopped
3 tbsp olive oil
1 tsp salt

## Directions

Heat oil, and stir-fry onion for 2 minutes on Sauté. Add vegetables and stir-fry for 5 minutes. Add the remaining ingredients and seal the lid. Cook on Poultry for 15 minutes on High. Do a quick release.

# Duck Breasts with Honey-Mustard Glaze

Serving Size: 4 | Total Time: 45 minutes

## Ingredients

1 lb duck breast
1 tbsp oil
1 tsp onion powder
1 cup honey
¼ cup soy sauce

¼ cup dry sherry
1 tbsp Dijon mustard
3 cups chicken broth
Salt and black pepper to taste

## Directions

Rub the meat with onion powder, salt, and pepper and place it in the instant pot. Pour the broth, seal the lid and cook on Meat/Stew mode for 35 minutes on High Pressure.

Do a quick release and remove from the pot. Heat oil on Sauté, add soy sauce, honey, sherry, and Dijon. Stir well and cook for 3-4 minutes. Add the meat and coat well. Serve the meat topped with the sauce.

# Savory Chicken Wings in Yogurt-Garlic Sauce

Serving Size: 6 | Total Time: 42 minutes

## Ingredients

12 chicken wings
3 tbsp olive oil

1 tsp salt
3 cups chicken broth

*Yogurt sauce:*
½ cup sour cream
1 cup yogurt

2 garlic cloves, peeled and crushed

## Directions

Heat oil on Sauté. Brown the wings for 6 minutes, turning once. Pour in broth, salt, and seal the lid. Cook on Poultry for 15 minutes on High. Do a natural release. In a bowl, mix sour cream, yogurt and garlic. Chill the wings for a while and drizzle with yogurt sauce.

# Beef, Pork and Lamb

## Braised Beef Ribs with Mushrooms

Serving Size: 4 | Total Time: 1hour

### Ingredients

2 pounds beef short ribs
1 tsp smoked paprika
½ tsp dried oregano
½ tsp cayenne pepper
Salt and black pepper to taste
1 tbsp olive oil
1 small onion, chopped

4 garlic cloves, smashed
1 cup beer
1/3 cup beef broth
1 cup crimini mushrooms, chopped
1 tbsp soy sauce
1 bell pepper, diced

### Directions

In a bowl, combine pepper, paprika, cayenne, salt, and oregano. Rub the seasoning mixture on all sides of the short ribs. Warm oil on Sauté. Add mushrooms and cook until browned, about 6-8 minutes. Set aside.

Add short ribs to the instant pot, and cook for 3 minutes for each side until browned; set aside on a plate.

Throw in garlic and onion to the oil and stir-fry for 2 minutes until fragrant.

Add in beer to deglaze, scrape the pot's bottom to get rid of any browned bits of food; bring to a simmer and cook for 2 minutes until reduced slightly.

Stir in soy sauce, bell pepper and beef broth. Dip short ribs into the liquid in a single layer. Seal the lid, press Meat/Stew and cook on High for 40 minutes. Release pressure naturally, for about 10 minutes. Divide the ribs with the sauce into bowls and top with fried mushrooms.

## Savory Pot Roast with Pancetta

Serving Size: 5 | Total Time: 1 hour 30 minutes

### Ingredients

2 ½ pounds beef brisket, trimmed
Salt and black pepper to taste
2 tbsp olive oil
1 onion, chopped
3 garlic cloves, minced
1 cup beef broth
¾ cup dry red wine

2 fresh thyme sprigs
2 fresh rosemary sprigs
4 ounces pancetta, chopped
6 carrots, chopped
1 bay leaf
A handful of parsley, chopped

### Directions

Warm oil on Sauté. Fry the pancetta for 4-5 minutes until crispy. Set aside. Season the beef with pepper and salt, and brown for 5 to 7 minutes per each. Remove and set aside on a plate.

In the same oil, fry garlic and onion for 3 minutes until softened. Pour in red wine and beef broth to deglaze the bottom, scrape the bottom of the pot to get rid of any browned bits of food.

Return the beef and pancetta to the pot and add rosemary sprigs and thyme. Seal the lid and cook for 50 minutes on High Pressure. Release the Pressure quickly. Add carrots and bay leaf to the pot. Seal the lid and cook for an additional 4 minutes on High Pressure.

Release the Pressure quickly. Get rid of the thyme, bay leaf and rosemary sprigs. Place beef on a serving plate and sprinkle with parsley to serve.

# Beef Meatloaf with Potato & Ricotta Mash

Serving Size: 6 | Total Time: 45 minutes

## Ingredients

*Meatloaf:*

1 ½ pounds ground beef
1 onion, diced
1 egg
1 potato, grated

¼ cup tomato puree
1 tsp garlic powder
Salt and black pepper to taste

*Mashed potatoes:*

4 potatoes, chopped
2 cups water
½ cup milk

2 tbsp butter
Salt and black pepper to taste
1 cup ricotta cheese

## Directions

In a bowl, combine ground beef, egg, 1 tsp pepper, garlic powder, potato, onion, tomato puree, and 1 tsp salt to obtain a consistent texture. Shape the mixture into a meatloaf and place onto an aluminum foil. Arrange potatoes in the pot and pour water over them.

Place a trivet onto potatoes and set the foil sheet with meatloaf onto the trivet. Seal the lid and cook on High Pressure for 22 minutes. Release the Pressure quickly. Take the meatloaf from the pot and set on a cutting board to cool before slicing.

Drain the liquid out of the pot. Mash potatoes in the pot with ½ teaspoon pepper, milk, ricotta cheese, 1 teaspoon salt, and butter until smooth and all the liquid is absorbed. Divide potatoes into serving plates and lean a meatloaf slice to one side of the potato pile before serving.

# Homemade Cuban Ropa Vieja

Serving Size: 6 | Total Time: 1 hour 10 minutes

## Ingredients

2 pounds beef skirt steak
3 ½ cups beef stock
2 bay leaves
¼ cup olive oil
1 red onion, halved and chopped
1 green bell pepper, chopped
1 red bell pepper, chopped
¼ cup minced garlic

1 tsp dried oregano
1 tsp ground cumin
1 cup tomato sauce
1 cup dry red wine
1 tbsp vinegar
Salt and black pepper to taste
¼ cup cheddar cheese, shredded

## Directions

Season the skirt steak with pepper and salt. Add water to the cooker; mix in bay leaves and flank steak. Seal the lid and cook on High Pressure for 35 minutes. Release the Pressure quickly.

Remove skirt steak to a cutting board and allow to sit for about 5 minutes. When cooled, shred the beef using two forks. Drain the pressure cooker, and reserve the bay leaves and 1 cup liquid.

Warm oil on Sauté mode. Add onion, bell peppers, cumin, garlic, and oregano and continue cooking for 5 minutes until vegetables are softened.

Stir in reserved liquid, tomato sauce, bay leaves and wine. Return shredded beef to the pot with vinegar; season with pepper and salt.

Seal the lid and cook on High Pressure for 15 minutes. Release Pressure naturally for 10 minutes, then turn steam vent valve to Venting to release the remaining Pressure quickly. Serve with shredded cheese.

# Vietnamese-Style Rice Noodle Soup

Serving Size: 6 | Total Time: 1 hour 10 minutes

## Ingredients

2 tbsp coconut oil
1 yellow onion, quartered
¼ cup minced fresh ginger
2 tsp coriander seeds
2 tsp ground cinnamon
2 tsp ground cloves
9 cups water
2 pounds beef neck bones
Salt and black pepper to taste

8 ounces rice noodles
3 tbsp sugar
2 tbsp fish sauce
10 ounces sirloin steak
A handful of fresh cilantro, chopped
2 scallions, chopped
2 jalapeño peppers, chopped
2 cups Swiss chard, chopped
1 red onion, chopped

## Directions

Melt oil on Sauté mode. Add ginger and yellow onion, and cook for 4 minutes until the onion soften. Stir in cloves, cinnamon and coriander, and cook for 1 minute until soft. Add in water, salt, beef meat and bones. Seal the lid and cook on High Pressure for 30 minutes. Release the pressure naturally for 8 minutes.

Transfer the meat to a large bowl; cover with it enough water and soak for 10 minutes. Drain the water and slice the beef. In hot water, soak rice noodles for 8 minutes until softened and pliable; drain and rinse with cold water. Drain the liquid from cooker into a separate pot through a fine-mesh strainer; get rid of any solids.

Add fish sauce and sugar to the broth. Transfer into the cooker and simmer on Sauté mode.

Place the noodles in four separate soup bowls. Top with steak slices, scallions, swiss chard, jalapeño pepper, cilantro, red onion, and pepper. Spoon the broth over each bowl to serve.

# Short Ribs with Red Wine & Cheese Cream Sauce

Serving Size: 6 | Total Time: 1 hour

## Ingredients

3 pounds beef short ribs
Salt and black pepper to taste
2 tbsp olive oil
1 onion, chopped
1 large carrot, chopped
1 celery stalk, chopped
3 garlic cloves, chopped
2 cups beef broth

1 (14.5-ounce) can diced tomatoes
½ cup dry red wine
¼ cup red wine vinegar
2 bay leaves
¼ tsp red pepper flakes
2 tbsp chopped parsley
½ cup cheese cream

## Directions

Season short ribs with 1 teaspoon black pepper and 1 teaspoon salt. Warm olive oil on Sauté. Add in short ribs and sear for 3 minutes each side until browned. Set aside on a bowl.

Drain everything only to be left with 1 tablespoon of the remaining fat from the pot. Set on Sauté, and stir-fry garlic, carrot, onion, and celery in the hot fat for 4 to 6 minutes until fragrant. Stir in broth, wine, flakes, vinegar, tomatoes, bay leaves, and remaining pepper and salt.

Set on Sauté and bring the mixture to a boil. With the bone-side up, lay short ribs into the braising liquid. Seal the lid and cook on High Pressure for 40 minutes. Release the Pressure quickly. Set the short ribs on a plate. Get rid of bay leaves. Skim and get rid of the fat from the surface of braising liquid.

Using an immersion blender, blend the liquid for 1 minute; add cheese cream, pepper and salt, and blitz until smooth. Arrange the ribs onto a serving plate, pour the sauce over and top with parsley.

# Awesome Beef Chili with Bacon

Serving Size: 6 | Total Time: 1hour 15 minutes

## Ingredients

2 pounds stewing beef, trimmed
Salt and black pepper to taste
4 ounces smoked bacon, cut into strips
2 tsp olive oil
1 onion, diced
2 bell peppers, diced
3 garlic cloves, minced

1 tbsp ground cumin
1 tsp chili powder
½ tsp cayenne pepper
1 chipotle in adobo sauce, finely chopped
2 cups beef broth
29 ounces canned whole tomatoes
15 ounces canned kidney beans, drained

## Directions

Set on Sauté mode and fry the bacon until crispy, about 5 minutes. Set aside.

Rub the beef with ½ teaspoon black pepper and 1 teaspoon salt. In the bacon fat, brown beef for 5-6 minutes; Transfer to a plate. Warm the oil. Add in garlic, peppers and onion and Sauté for 3 to 4 minutes until soft. Stir in cumin, cayenne pepper, the extra pepper, salt, chipotle, chili powder and cook for 30 seconds until soft.

Return beef and bacon to the pot with vegetables and spices; add in tomatoes and broth. Seal the lid and cook on High Pressure for 45 minutes. Release the Pressure quickly. Stir in beans. Let simmer on Keep Warm for 10 minutes until flavors combine.

# Italian Beef Meatballs with Pomodoro Sauce

Serving Size: 6 | Total Time: 35 minutes

## Ingredients

1 ½ pounds ground beef
1/3 cup warm water
¾ cup grated Parmigiano-Reggiano cheese
½ cup bread crumbs
1 egg
2 tbsp fresh parsley

¼ tsp garlic powder
¼ tsp dried oregano
Salt and black pepper to taste
½ cup capers
1 tsp olive oil
3 cups marinara sauce

## Directions

In a bowl, mix ground beef, parsley, garlic powder, pepper, oregano, crumbs, egg, and salt; shape into meatballs. Warm oil on Sauté mode. Add meatballs to the oil and brown for 2-3 minutes and all sides.

Pour water and marinara sauce over the meatballs. Seal the lid and cook on High Pressure for 10 minutes. Release the Pressure quickly. Serve in large bowls topped with capers and Parmigiano-Reggiano cheese.

# Dijon & Lemon Beef Steak

Serving Size: 3 | Total Time: 50 minutes

## Ingredients

3 rib-eye steaks, boneless
2 tbsp lemon juice
3 tbsp canola oil

3 tbsp Dijon mustard
Salt and black pepper to taste
3 cups beef broth

## Directions

In a bowl, mix lemon juice, oil, mustard, salt, and pepper. Brush the steaks with this mixture and set aside. Pour the beef broth in the instant pot.

Place the steamer tray and arrange the steaks on top. Seal the lid and cook on High Pressure for 35 minutes. Do a quick release and remove the broth. Press Sauté and brown steaks on both sides for 3-4 minutes.

# Habanero Beef Brisket with Red Wine

Serving Size: 4 | Total Time: 1 hour 20 minutes

## Ingredients

2 tsp smoked paprika
½ tsp dried oregano
Salt and black pepper to taste
1 tbsp Worcestershire sauce
½ tsp ground cumin
½ tsp garlic powder
1 tsp habanero powder

¼ tsp cayenne pepper
2 pounds beef brisket
2 tbsp olive oil
1 cup beef broth
¼ cup red wine
A handful of parsley, chopped

## Directions

In a bowl, combine oregano, cumin, cayenne, garlic powder, salt, paprika, pepper, Worcestershire sauce and habanero powder. Rub the seasoning mixture on the beef to coat.

Warm olive oil on Sauté. Add in beef and cook for 3 to 4 minutes each side until browned completely. Pour in beef broth and red wine. Seal the lid and cook on High Pressure for 50 minutes. Release the pressure naturally, for about 10 minutes.

Place the beef on a cutting board and allow to cool for 10 minutes before slicing. Arrange the beef slices on a serving platter, Pour the cooking sauce over and scatter with parsley to serve.

# Homemade Southern Pot Roast with Pepperoncini

Serving Size: 6 | Total Time: 1 hour 40 minutes

## Ingredients

1 tbsp canola oil
2 pounds chuck roast
Salt and black pepper to taste
¼ cup butter
1 onion, finely chopped
1 tsp onion powder
1 tsp garlic powder

½ tsp dried thyme
½ tsp dried parsley
6 cups beef broth
½ cup pepperoncini juice
10 pepperoncini
5 potatoes, peeled and chopped
2 bay leaves

## Directions

Warm oil on Sauté mode. Season chuck roast with pepper and salt, then sear in hot oil for 2 to 4 minutes per side until browned. Set aside.

Melt butter and cook onion for 3 minutes until fragrant. Sprinkle with dried parsley, onion powder, dried thyme, and garlic powder and stir for 30 seconds.

Stir in bay leaves, broth, pepperoncini juice, potatoes, and pepperoncini. Nestle chuck roast down into the liquid. Seal the lid and cook on High for 60 minutes. Release Pressure naturally, for about 10 minutes. Set the chuck roast to a cutting board and use two forks to shred. Serve immediately.

# Thyme Beef with Mushrooms & Cherry Tomatoes

Serving Size: 4 | Total Time: 30 minutes

## Ingredients

1 lb beef steaks
1 lb button mushrooms, chopped
2 tbsp vegetable oil
Salt and black pepper to taste

1 bay leaf
1 tbsp dried thyme
6 oz cherry tomatoes

## Directions

Rub steaks with salt, pepper, and thyme. Place in the instant pot. Pour in 3 cups of water, add bay leaf and seal the lid. Cook on High pressure for 13 minutes. Do a quick release and set the steaks aside. Heat oil on Sauté, and stir-fry mushrooms and tomatoes for 5 minutes. Add steaks and brown on both sides.

# Grandma's Beef and Vegetable Stew

Serving Size: 6 | Total Time: 1 hour 5 minutes

## Ingredients

¼ cup flour
1 tsp paprika
2 pounds beef chuck, cubed
2 tbsp olive oil
2 tbsp butter
1 onion, diced
3 garlic cloves, minced
1 cup dry red wine
2 cups beef stock

1 tbsp dried Italian seasoning
2 tsp Worcestershire sauce
4 cups potatoes, diced
2 celery stalks, chopped
3 cups carrots, chopped
3 tomatoes, chopped
2 bell peppers, chopped
Salt and black pepper to taste
A handful of fresh parsley, chopped

## Directions

In a bowl, mix black pepper, beef, flour, paprika, and 1 teaspoon salt. Toss the ingredients and ensure the beef is well-coated. Warm butter and oil on Sauté mode. Add in beef and cook for 8- 10 minutes until browned. Set aside on a plate. To the same fat, add garlic, onion, and celery, bell peppers, and cook for 4-5 minutes.

Deglaze with wine, scrape the bottom to get rid of any browned beef bits. Pour in remaining salt, beef stock, Worcestershire sauce, and Italian seasoning. Return beef to the pot; add carrots, tomatoes, and potatoes.

Seal the lid, press Meat/Stew and cook on High Pressure for 35 minutes. Release Pressure naturally for 10 minutes. Taste and adjust the seasonings as necessary. Serve on plates and scatter over the parsley.

# Marvellous Swedish Meatballs with Cauliflower Mash

Serving Size: 6 | Total Time: 45 minutes

## Ingredients

¾ pound ground beef
¾ pound ground pork
1 large egg, beaten
½ onion, minced
¼ cup bread crumbs
1 tbsp water
Salt and black pepper to taste
4 tbsp butter

2 cups beef stock
3 tbsp flour
½ tsp red wine vinegar
1 ¾ cups heavy cream
4 tbsp blue cheese, crumbled
1 head cauliflower, cut into florets
¼ cup sour cream
¼ cup fresh chopped parsley

## Directions

In a bowl, mix beef, onion, salt, bread crumbs, pork, egg, water, and pepper; shape meatballs. Warm 2 tbsp of butter on Sauté mode. Add meatballs and cook until browned, about 5-6 minutes. Set aside to a plate. Pour beef stock in the pot to deglaze, scrape the pan to get rid of browned bits of food.

Stir vinegar and flour with the liquid in the pot until smooth; bring to a boil. Stir ¾ cup heavy cream into the liquid. Arrange meatballs into the gravy. Place trivet onto meatballs. Arrange cauliflower florets onto the trivet. Seal the lid and cook on High Pressure for 8 minutes. Release the Pressure quickly.

Set the cauliflower in a mixing bowl. Add in the remaining 1 cup heavy cream, pepper, sour cream, salt, and 2 tbsp butter and use a potato masher to mash the mixture. Add the blue cheese and mix well. Spoon the mashed cauliflower onto serving bowls; top with gravy and meatballs. Garnish with parsley to serve.

# Traditional French Beef Stew

Serving Size: 5 | Total Time: 40 minutes

## Ingredients

1 lb boneless chuck steak, trimmed, cut chunks
¼ cup flour
Salt and black pepper to taste
1 cup pancetta, chopped
½ cup red burgundy wine
1 ¼ cups beef broth

1 carrot, diced
2 cups portobello mushrooms, quartered
4 shallots, chopped
3 garlic cloves, crushed
A handful of parsley, chopped

## Directions

Toss beef with black pepper, salt, and flour in a large bowl to coat. Set on Sauté mode. Cook pancetta for 5 minutes until brown and crispy. Pour in approximately half the beef and cook for 5 minutes each side until browned all over. Transfer the pancetta and beef to a plate. Sear remaining beef and transfer to the plate.

Add beef broth and wine to the cooker to deglaze the pan, scrape the pan's bottom to get rid of any browned bits of food. Return beef and pancetta to cooker; stir in garlic, carrot, shallots, and mushrooms. Seal the lid and cook on High Pressure for 32 minutes. Release the pressure quickly. Garnish with parsley and serve.

# Friday Night Chili Con Carne

Serving Size: 6 | Total Time: 1 hour

## Ingredients

Salt and black pepper to taste
1 tsp sweet paprika
1 tsp cayenne pepper
1 tsp chili powder
½ tsp onion powder
14 oz canned black beans, drained and rinsed

1 (4-pound) beef brisket
1 cup beef broth
2 bay leaves
2 tbsp Worcestershire sauce

## Directions

In a bowl, combine pepper, paprika, chili powder, cayenne pepper, salt, onion powder, bay leaves and garlic salt; rub onto brisket pieces to coat. Add the brisket to your instant pot. Cover with Worcestershire sauce and broth.

Seal the lid and cook on High Pressure for 50 minutes. Release the pressure naturally. Transfer the brisket to a cutting board. Drain any liquid present in the pot using a fine-mesh strainer; get rid of any solids and fat.

Slice brisket, arrange the slices onto a platter, add the black beans on side and spoon the cooking liquid over the slices and beans to serve.

# Butternut Squash & Beef Stew

Serving Size: 6 | Total Time: 35 minutes

## Ingredients

2 tbsp canola oil
2 pounds stew beef, cut into 1-inch chunks
1 cup red wine
1 onion, chopped
1 tsp garlic powder
1 tsp salt

3 whole cloves
1 bay leaf
3 carrots, chopped
½ butternut pumpkin, chopped
2 tbsp cornstarch
3 tbsp water

## Directions

Warm oil on Sauté mode. Brown the beef for 5 minutes on each side. Deglaze the pot with wine, scrape the bottom to get rid of any browned beef bits. Add in onion, salt, bay leaf, cloves, and garlic powder. Seal the lid, press Meat/Stew and cook on High for 15 minutes.

Release the Pressure quickly. Add in pumpkin and carrots without stirring. Seal the lid and cook on High Pressure for 5 minutes. Release the Pressure quickly.

In a bowl, mix water and cornstarch until cornstarch dissolves completely; mix into the stew. Allow the stew to simmer while uncovered on Keep Warm for 5 minutes until you attain the desired thickness.

# Mushroom Beef Stroganoff

Serving Size: 6 | Total Time: 1 hour

## Ingredients

¼ cup flour
Salt and black pepper to taste
2 pounds beef stew meat
2 tbsp olive oil
1 onion, chopped
2 garlic cloves, minced

1 cup beef broth
3 cups fresh mushrooms, chopped
8 ounces sour cream
1 tbsp chopped fresh parsley
1 cup long-grain rice, cooked

## Directions

In a large bowl, combine salt, pepper and flour. Add beef and massage to coat beef in flour mixture.

Warm oil on Sauté mode. Brown the beef for 4 to 5 minutes. Add garlic and onion and cook for 3 minutes until fragrant. Add beef broth to the pot. Seal the lid and cook on High Pressure for 35 minutes. Release the Pressure quickly. Open the lid and stir mushrooms and sour cream into the beef mixture.

Seal the lid and cook on High Pressure for 2 minutes. Release the Pressure quickly. Scoop over cooked rice before serving. Season the stroganoff with pepper, parsley and salt

# Stuffed Onions with Beef & Rice

Serving Size: 4 | Total Time: 30 minutes

## Ingredients

10 sweet onions, peeled
1 lb of lean ground beef
½ tbsp rice
3 tbsp olive oil
1 tbsp dry mint, ground
1 tsp cayenne pepper, ground

½ tsp cumin, ground
1 tsp salt
½ tbsp sour cream
½ cup bread crumbs
A handful of fresh parsley, finely chopped

## Directions

Cut a ¼-inch slice from top of each onion and trim a small amount from the bottom end, this will make the onions stand upright. Place onions in a microwave-safe dish, and Pour one cup of water.

Cover with a tight lid and microwave for 10-12 minutes or until onions soften. Remove onions and cool slightly. Carefully remove inner layers of onions with a paring knife, leaving about a ¼-inch onion shell.

In a bowl, combine beef, rice, oil, mint, cayenne pepper, cumin, salt, and bread crumbs. Use one tablespoon of the mixture to fill the onions. Grease the inner pot with oil. Add onions and pour 2.5 cups of water.

Seal the lid and cook on Manual/Pressure Cook for 10 minutes on High. Do a quick release. Top with parsley and serve with sour cream and pide bread.

# Beef Short Ribs with Asparagus Sauce

Serving Size: 6 | Total Time: 1 hour 15 minutes

## Ingredients

3 ½ lb boneless beef short ribs, cut into pieces
Salt and black pepper to taste
3 tbsp olive oil
1 onion, diced
1 cup dry red wine
1 tbsp tomato puree
2 carrots, peeled and chopped
2 garlic cloves, minced

5 sprigs parsley, chopped
2 sprigs rosemary, chopped
3 sprigs oregano, chopped
4 cups beef stock
10 ounces mushrooms, quartered
1 cup asparagus, trimmed chopped
1 tbsp cornstarch
¼ cup cold water

## Directions

Season the ribs with black pepper and salt. Warm oil on Sauté. In batches, add the short ribs to the oil and cook for 3 to 5 minutes each side until browned. Set aside. Add onion and Sauté for 4 minutes until soft.

Add tomato puree and red wine into the pot to deglaze, scrape the bottom to get rid of any browned beef bits. Cook for 2 minutes until wine reduces slightly. Return the ribs to the pot and top with carrots, oregano, rosemary, and garlic. Add in stock and press Cancel.

Seal the lid, press Meat/Stew and cook on High for 35 minutes. Release Pressure naturally for 10 minutes. Transfer ribs to a plate. Strain and get rid of herbs and vegetables, and return cooking stock to inner pot. Add mushrooms and asparagus to the broth. Press Sauté and cook for 2 to 4 minutes until soft.

In a bowl, mix water and cornstarch until cornstarch dissolves completely. Add the cornstarch mixture into the broth as you stir for 1 to 3 minutes until the broth thickens slightly. Season the sauce with black pepper and salt. Pour the sauce over ribs, add chopped parsley for garnish before serving.

# Beef & Jasmine Rice Porridge

Serving Size: 6 | Total Time: 50 minutes

## Ingredients

1 cup jasmine rice
2 cloves garlic, minced
1 (1 inch) piece fresh ginger, minced
6 cups beef stock
1 cup kale, roughly chopped

1 cup water
2 pounds ground beef
Salt and black pepper to taste
Fresh cilantro, chopped

## Directions

Run cold water and rinse rice. Add garlic, rice, and ginger into the pot. Pour water and stock into the pot and Spread the beef on top of rice.

Seal the lid and cook on High Pressure for 30 minutes. Release pressure naturally, for 10 minutes.

Stir in kale to obtain the desired consistency. Season with pepper and salt. Top with cilantro to serve.

# Ground Beef & Eggplant Casserole

Serving Size: 2 | Total Time: 35 minutes

## Ingredients

2 eggplants, peeled, cut lengthwise
Salt and black pepper to taste
1 cup lean ground beef
1 onion, chopped

1 tsp olive oil
2 tomatoes
3 tbsp freshly chopped parsley

## Directions

Place eggplants in a bowl and Season with salt. Let sit for 10 minutes. Rinse well and drain.

Grease the inner pot with oil. Stir-fry onion for 2 minutes, until soft.

Add ground beef, tomatoes, and cook for 5 minutes. Remove from the pot and transfer to a deep bowl. Make a layer with eggplant slices in the pot.

Spread the ground beef mixture over and sprinkle with black pepper and parsley. Make another layer with eggplants and repeat until you've used up all ingredients.

Seal the lid and cook on High Pressure for 12 minutes. Do a quick release.

# Chili Beef & Turnip Stew

Serving Size: 6 | Total Time: 30 minutes

## Ingredients

1 tbsp olive oil
1 yellow onion, chopped
Salt to taste
4 garlic cloves, minced
2 tbsp tomato puree
1 tbsp chili powder
2 tsp ground cumin
1 tsp dried oregano

½ tsp ground turmeric
A pinch of cayenne pepper
1 pound ground beef meat
1 (28-ounce) can whole tomatoes
2 cups beef stock
1 pound turnips, peeled and cubed
2 tomatoes, chopped
1 bell pepper, chopped

## Directions

Warm oil on Sauté mode. Add in onion with a pinch of salt and cook for 3 to 5 minutes until softened.

Stir in garlic, chili powder, turmeric, cumin, tomato paste, oregano, and cayenne pepper; cook for 2 to 3 minutes as you stir until very soft and sticks to the pot's bottom.

Add beef and cook for 5 minutes until completely browned. Stir in tomatoes, turnips, bell pepper, and stock. Seal the lid and cook on High Pressure for 15 minutes. Release the pressure quickly.

# Easy Roast Beef with Bearnaise Sauce

Serving Size: 6 | Total Time: 35 minutes

## Ingredients

2 lb beef scotch fillet
6 tbsp butter
1 cup white wine
1 onion, chopped
1 tsp fresh basil, chopped

4 egg yolks
2 tbsp lemon juice
4 peppercorns
2 cups beef broth
Salt and black pepper to taste

## Directions

Melt butter on Sauté, and stir-fry the onion until translucent, for about 3 minutes. Add in wine, basil, peppercorns, salt, pepper, and lemon juice. Stir well and seal the lid. Cook on High Pressure for 3 minutes.

Do a quick Pressure release and stir in egg yolks. Add in beef fillets, pour in broth and seal the lid. Cook on Meat/Stew for 25 minutes on High Pressure.

Do a quick release.

# Sticky Baby Back BBQ Ribs

Serving Size: 6 | Total Time: 40 minutes

## Ingredients

2 tbsp olive oil
1 rack baby back ribs, cut into bones
1 tbsp mustard powder
1 tbsp smoked paprika
1 tbsp dried oregano

Salt and black pepper to taste
1/3 cup ketchup
1 cup barbecue sauce
½ cup apple cider

## Directions

In a bowl, thoroughly combine salt, mustard, paprika, oregano, and black pepper. Rub the mixture over the ribs. Warm oil on Sauté mode. Add in the ribs and sear for 1 to 2 minutes for each side until browned.

Pour apple cider and barbecue sauce into the pot. Turn the ribs to coat. Seal the lid, press Meat/Stew and cook on High Pressure for 30 minutes. Release the Pressure quickly.

Preheat a broiler. Cook the ribs with the sauce under the broiler for about 7 until the ribs become sticky and have a dark brown color. Transfer the ribs to a serving plate. Baste with the sauce to serve.

# Hearty Beef Stew with Vegetables

Serving Size: 4 | Total Time: 40 minutes

## Ingredients

1 lb beef stew meat, chopped
2 onions, peeled, chopped
3 potatoes, peeled, chopped
1 cup green peas
1 tsp salt

1 tsp cayenne pepper
1 tbsp apple cider vinegar
3 tbsp olive oil
3 cups beef broth
A handful of freshly chopped parsley

## Directions

Heat oil on Sauté mode. Stir-fry the onions until translucent. Add the meat and potatoes, and brown for about 10 minutes. Add peas, and season with salt and cayenne pepper. Pour in broth and apple cider.

Seal the lid and set on Meat/Stew for 25 minutes on High. Do a quick release and top with parsley.

# Penne with Beef & Tomato Sauce

Serving Size: 5 | Total Time: 45 minutes

## Ingredients

1 pack (16 oz.) penne
6 oz beef, braising steak cut into chunks
1 onion, chopped
1 tomato peeled, diced
1 tbsp tomato paste

3 tbsp butter, unsalted
Salt and black pepper to taste
1 tsp cayenne pepper
1 tbsp vegetable oil

## Directions

Heat oil on Sauté and stir-fry the onion, until translucent. Add tomato, tomato paste, butter, a pinch of salt, black pepper and cayenne pepper. Cook until tomato softens, stirring occasionally. Add beef chunks and 1 cup water.

Give it a good stir, seal the lid and cook for 14 minutes on High Pressure. Do a quick release and set the meat aside. Add in penne and 2 cups of water. Seal the lid and cook on High Pressure for 4 minutes.

Do a quick release and transfer the macaroni to a large bowl, Stir in the beef sauce and serve.

# Beef Fillets with Onion

Serving Size: 6 | Total Time: 50 minutes

## Ingredients

2 lb beef fillets, cut into bite-sized pieces
4 onions, chopped
3 tbsp tomato paste
2 tbsp oil

1 tbsp butter, melted
2 tbsp fresh parsley, chopped
Salt and black pepper to taste

## Directions

Grease the instant pot with 2 tbsp of oil. Make the first layer of meat. Add onions, tomato paste, parsley, salt, and pepper. Stir and Pour 2 cups of water.

Seal the lid and cook on Meat/Stew mode for 30 minutes on High. Release the steam naturally, for about 10 minutes. Stir in 1 tbsp of butter and serve warm.

# Beef Gyros with Yogurt & Dill

Serving Size: 4 | Total Time: 55 minutes

## Ingredients

1 pound beef sirloin, cut into thin strips
1 onion, chopped
1/3 cup beef broth
2 tbsp fresh lemon juice
2 tbsp olive oil
2 tsp dry oregano

1 clove garlic, minced
Salt and black pepper to taste
4 slices pita bread
1 cup Greek yogurt
2 tbsp fresh dill, chopped

## Directions

In the pot, mix beef, beef broth, oregano, garlic, lemon juice, pepper, onion, olive oil, and salt.

Seal the lid and cook on High Pressure for 30 minutes. Release Pressure naturally for 15 minutes, then turn steam vent valve to Venting to release the remaining Pressure quickly. Divide the beef mixture between the pita bread, Top with yogurt and dill, and roll up to serve.

# Moroccan Beef & Cherry Stew

Serving Size: 4 | Total Time: 1 hour 20 minutes

## Ingredients

2 tbsp olive oil
1 onion, chopped
1 ½ pounds stewing beef, trimmed
1 tsp ground cinnamon
½ tsp paprika
½ tsp turmeric
½ tsp salt

¼ tsp ground ginger
¼ tsp ground allspice
1-star anise
1 cup water
1 tbsp honey
1 cup dried cherries, halved
¼ cup toasted almonds, slivered

## Directions

Set on Sauté mode and warm olive oil. Add in onion and cook for 3 minutes. Mix in beef and cook for 2 minutes each side until browned. Stir in anise, cinnamon, turmeric, allspice, salt, paprika, and ginger; cook for 2 minutes until aromatic. Add in honey and water. Seal the lid, press Meat/Stew and cook on High Pressure for 50 minutes.

In a bowl, soak dried cherries in hot water until softened. Once ready, release pressure naturally for 15 minutes. Drain cherries and stir into the tagine. Top with toasted almonds before serving.

# Red Wine Beef & Vegetable Hotpot

Serving Size: 6 | Total Time: 35 minutes

## Ingredients

2 lb beef meat for stew
¾ cup red wine
1 tbsp ghee
6 oz tomato paste
6 oz baby carrots, chopped
2 sweet potatoes, cut into chunks

1 onion, finely chopped
½ tsp salt
4 cups beef broth
½ cup green peas
1 tsp dried thyme
3 garlic cloves, crushed

## Directions:

Heat the ghee on Sauté. Add beef and brown for 5-6 minutes. Add onion and garlic, and keep stirring for 3 more minutes. Add the remaining ingredients and seal the lid. Cook on Meat/Stew for 20 minutes on High pressure. Do a quick release and serve immediately.

# Stewed Beef with Potatoes

Serving Size: 4 | Total Time: 60 minutes

## Ingredients

1 lb beef shoulder
1 lb potatoes, cut into chunks
2 carrots, chopped
1 onion, finely chopped
4 tbsp olive oil
2 tbsp tomato paste

1 tbsp flour
4 cups beef broth
1 tbsp fresh celery, chopped
1 tbsp fresh parsley, chopped
1 cayenne pepper, chopped
Salt and black pepper to taste

## Directions

Warm oil on Sauté. Stir-fry onion, carrots, and potatoes for 7-8 minutes. Stir in flour and press Cancel. Add the remaining ingredients. Seal the lid and cook on High pressure for 40 minutes. Do a quick release.

# Easy Lamb & Spinach Soup

Serving Size: 5 | Total Time: 45 minutes

## Ingredients

1 lb lamb shoulder, cut into bite-sized pieces
10 oz fresh spinach leaves, chopped
3 eggs, beaten

5 cups vegetable broth
3 tbsp olive oil
1 tsp salt

## Directions

Place in your instant pot the lamb along with the remaining ingredients. Seal the lid, press Soup/Broth and cook for 30 minutes on High Pressure. Do a natural pressure release, for about 10 minutes.

# Tasty Beef Cutlets with Vegetables

Serving Size: 4 | Total Time: 45 minutes

## Ingredients

2 large beef cutlets
3 potatoes, whole
1 onion, whole
3 carrots, whole
6 oz cauliflower, into florets

3 tbsp olive oil
1 tbsp butter
Salt and black pepper to taste
½ tbsp chili pepper, ground
3 cups beef broth

Sprinkle the meat with salt and pepper, and place it in your instant pot. Peel onion, carrots, potatoes. Add the cauliflower. Pour broth, seal the lid and cook on High Pressure for 25 minutes. Release the Pressure naturally, for about 10 minutes. Remove the meat and vegetables. Melt butter and oil on Sauté, and add chili pepper. Stir and add the meat. Brown on both sides and serve immediately.

# Easy Wax Beans with Ground Beef

Serving Size: 4 | Total Time: 20 minutes

**Ingredients**

1 lb ground beef
1 lb wax beans
1 small onion, chopped
1 tbsp tomato paste
2 cups beef broth
2 garlic cloves, crushed

2 tbsp olive oil
2 tbsp fresh parsley, finely chopped
1 tsp salt
½ tsp paprika
1 tbsp Parmesan cheese, grated

**Directions**

Grease the pot with olive oil. Stir-fry the onion and garlic, for a few minutes until translucent on Sauté. Add beef, tomato paste, parsley, salt, and paprika.

Cook for 5 more minutes, stirring constantly. Add wax beans and beef broth. Press Cancel and seal the lid. Cook on High Pressure for 4 minutes. Do a natural release. Top with Parmesan and serve hot.

# Beef Arancini with Potatoes

Serving Size: 4 | Total Time: 40 minutes

**Ingredients**

1 lb lean ground beef
6 oz rice
2 onions, peeled, chopped
2 garlic cloves, crushed

1 egg, beaten
1 large potato peeled, chopped
3 tbsp olive oil
1 tsp salt

**Directions**

In a bowl, combine beef, rice, onions, garlic, egg, and salt. Shape the mixture into 15-16 meatballs. Grease the inner pot with 1 tbsp of olive oil.

Press Sauté and cook the meatballs for 3-4 minutes, or until slightly brown. Remove the meatballs. Add the remaining oil and make a layer of potato.

Top with meatballs, cover with water, and seal the lid. Adjust the release steam handle. Cook on Meat/Stew mode for 15 minutes on High. Do a quick release.

# Carrot Casserole with Beef & Potato

Serving Size: 3 | Total Time: 20 minutes

**Ingredients**

1 lb lean beef, with bones
2 carrots
1 potato, sliced

3 tbsp olive oil
½ tsp salt

**Directions**

Mix all ingredients in the instant pot. Pour enough water to cover and seal the lid. Cook on High Pressure for 15 minutes. Do a quick release and serve hot.

# Homemade Beef Goulash with Cabbage & Potatoes

Serving Size: 6 | Total Time: 45 minutes

## Ingredients

2 lb beef stew meat
3 potatoes, cut into chunks
1 large onion, roughly chopped
1 large carrot, chopped
1 cabbage head, shredded
1 cup sun-dried tomatoes, diced

4 cups beef broth
3 tbsp tomato paste
1 tsp tabasco sauce
Salt and white pepper to taste
3 tbsp butter

## Directions

Heat oil on Sauté and cook the onion until translucent, for 2 minutes. Add the tomato paste and stir. Add the remaining ingredients and seal the lid. Cook on High pressure for 35 minutes. Do a quick release.

# Creamy Beef & Cauliflower Chili

Serving Size: 6 | Total Time: 20 minutes

## Ingredients

1 lb beef stew meat
1 tbsp cauliflower, chopped
1 medium onion, chopped
2 cups beef broth
2 cups heavy cream

1 cup water
1 tsp Italian seasoning
1 tsp salt
½ tsp ground chili pepper

## Directions

Add all ingredients in your instant pot. Seal the lid and cook on High Pressure for 15 minutes. When ready, do a quick release and serve immediately.

# Beef Bones with Beans & Chili Pepper

Serving Size: 4 | Total Time: 30 minutes

## Ingredients

14.5 oz canned beans
12 oz beef bones
1 onion, peeled, chopped
3 garlic cloves
1 carrot, chopped

1 tbsp fresh parsley, chopped
1 bay leaf
Salt and black pepper to taste
1 chili pepper, minced
3 tbsp vegetable oil

## Directions

Place all other ingredients in the instant pot. Pour water enough to cover. Seal the lid. Cook on High Pressure for 15 minutes. Release the steam naturally, for 10 minutes. Let it chill for a while before serving.

# Beef Lasagna with Eggplant & Almonds

Serving Size: 4 | Total Time: 30 minutes

## Ingredients

3 eggplants, halved
2 lb stewed beef, boneless, sliced
2 tomatoes, chopped
2 red bell peppers, sliced, seeds removed
¼ tbsp tomato paste

1 bunch of fresh parsley, chopped
3 oz toasted almonds, chopped
2 tbsp capers, rinsed, drained
¼ cup extra virgin olive oil
1 tsp salt

## Directions

Grease the instant pot with 2 tbsp of olive oil. Make the first layer with halved eggplants tucking the ends gently to fit in.

Make the second layer with beef slices, tomatoes and red bell peppers. Spread the tomato paste evenly over, sprinkle with almonds and salted capers.

Add the remaining olive oil, salt and pepper. Pour 1 ½ cups of water and seal the lid. Cook on High Pressure for 13 minutes. Do a quick release. Serve with fresh parsley.

# Traditional Turkish Dolma (Stuffed Peppers)

Serving Size: 4 | Total Time: 35 minutes

## Ingredients

2 lb red bell peppers, stems and seed removed
1 onion, finely chopped
1 lb lean ground beef
¼ cup rice
½ cup tomatoes, chopped

1 tomato, sliced
½ tsp salt
1 tsp cayenne pepper
3 tbsp olive oil

## Directions

In a bowl, combine meat, onion, rice, tomatoes, salt, and cayenne. Stir well to combine. Use 2 tbsp of this mixture and fill each pepper.

Make sure to leave at least ½ inch of headspace. Grease the bottom of your instant pot with cooking spray. Make the first layer with tomato slices.

Arrange the peppers and add 2 cups of water. Seal the lid, and cook on High Pressure for 15 minutes. Do a natural Pressure release, for 10 minutes.

# Sirloin Steaks with Red Wine

Serving Size: 4 | Total Time: 1 hour 25 minutes

## Ingredients

2 lb beef sirloin
1 cup red wine
2 cups beef consomme
2 bay leaves
2 tbsp olive oil
Salt and black pepper to taste

1 large onion, chopped
1 stalk celery, diced
1 tbsp tomato puree
2 cloves garlic, minced
2 sprigs fresh parsley

## Directions

Rub the meat with salt and pepper on all sides. Heat oil on Sauté and sear the beef for 4-5 minutes. Set aside.

In the same oil, add onion, celery, garlic, and tomato puree. Cook for 4-5 minutes, until soft. Pour in wine to deglaze the bottom of the pot, scrape to remove browned bits.

Bring the meat back to the pot, add consomme, parsley and bay leaf. Seal the lid, and cook on High Pressure for 50 minutes. Do a natural pressure release, for 10 minutes.

Slice the sirloin and spoon over the cooking sauce to serve.

# Pesto Beef Sandwiches with Peperoncini Peppers

Serving Size: 4 | Total Time: 40 minutes

## Ingredients

1 ½ pounds beef steak, cut into strips
Salt and black pepper to taste
1 tbsp olive oil
¼ cup dry red wine
1 cup beef broth
1 tbsp oregano

1 tsp onion powder
1 tsp garlic powder
4 hoagie rolls, halved
8 slices mozzarella cheese
½ cup pepperoncini peppers, chopped
4 tbsp pesto

## Directions

Season the beef strips with salt and pepper. Warm oil on Sauté and sear the beef for 2 to 3 minutes for each side until browned. Add wine into the pot to deglaze, scrape the bottom to get rid of any browned beef bits. Stir garlic powder, beef broth, onion powder, and oregano into the pot.

Seal the lid, press Meat/Stew and cook for 25 minutes on High. Release Pressure naturally for 10 minutes. Spread each bread half with pesto, put beef on top, place pepperoncini over, add mozzarella cheese slices and cover with the second half of bread to serve.

# Eggplant & Beef Stew with Parmesan

Serving Size: 6 | Total Time: 60 minutes

## Ingredients

9 oz beef neck, cut into bite-sized pieces
1 eggplant, chopped
2 cups fire-roasted tomatoes
½ tbsp fresh green peas
1 tbsp cayenne pepper
1 tbsp beef broth

4 tbsp olive oil
2 tbsp tomato paste
1 tbsp ground chili pepper
½ tsp salt
Parmesan cheese, for garnish

## Directions

Rub the meat with salt, cayenne, and chili pepper. Grease the instant pot with oil and brown the meat for 5-7 minutes, or until golden, on Sauté mode.

Add all the remaining ingredients and seal the lid. Cook on Meat/Stew mode for 40 minutes on High. Do a natural release, for 10 minutes. Serve warm, sprinkled with freshly grated Parmesan Cheese.

# T-Bone Steaks with Basil & Mustard

Serving Size: 4 | Total Time: 1 hour 35 minutes

## Ingredients

1 lb T-bone steak (2 pieces)
Salt and black pepper to taste
2 tbsp Dijon mustard

¼ cup oil
½ tsp dried basil, crushed

## Directions

Whisk together oil, mustard, salt, pepper, and basil. Brush each steak and Refrigerate for 1 hour. Meanwhile, insert the steamer tray in the instant pot.

Pour 3 cups of water and arrange the steaks on the tray. Seal the lid and cook on Steam mode for 25 minutes on High. Do a quick release and open the pot. Discard the liquid, remove the tray, and hit Sauté. Brown the steaks, one at the time, for 5 minutes, turning once.

# Bulgarian-Style Moussaka with Beef & Potatoes

Serving Size: 4 | Total Time: 30 minutes

## Ingredients

2 lb potatoes, peeled, chopped
1 lb lean ground beef
1 onion, peeled, chopped
Salt and black pepper to taste

½ cup milk
2 eggs, beaten
1 tbsp vegetable oil
Sour cream for serving

## Directions

Grease the bottom of the pot with oil. Make one layer of potatoes and brush with milk. Spread the ground beef on top and make another layer of potatoes.

Brush well with the remaining milk. Seal the lid, and cook for 15 minutes on High Pressure. When ready, do a quick release. Open the lid, add salt, pepper, and make the final layer with the beaten eggs. Seal the lid and let it stand for about 10 minutes. Top with sour cream to serve.

# Thyme Ground Beef Roll

Serving Size: 6 | Total Time: 60 minutes

## Ingredients

2 lb ground beef
2 large eggs
½ tsp minced garlic
1 cup all-purpose flour

1 tsp dried thyme, ground
3 tbsp olive oil
½ tsp salt

## Directions

In a bowl, combine the meat, garlic, flour, and eggs. Sprinkle with thyme, rosemary and salt. Mix with hands until well incorporated, and set aside.

Grease a baking dish with olive oil. Form the meatloaf at the bottom. Add 1 ½ cups of water and place a trivet in your cooker. Lay the baking dish on the trivet. Seal the lid, Press Meat/Stew and cook for 40 minutes on High. Do a quick release. Carefully transfer the meatloaf to a serving dish. Garnish with vegetable salad or mashed potatoes, to serve.

# Veal Chops with Greek Yogurt

Serving Size: 4 | Total Time: 60 minutes

## Ingredients

2 lb boneless veal shoulder, cubed
3 large tomatoes, roughly chopped
2 tbsp flour
3 tbsp butter
1 tbsp cayenne pepper

1 tsp salt
1 tbsp parsley, finely chopped
1 cup Greek yogurt for serving
1 pide bread

## Directions

Grease the bottom of the inner pot with 1 tbsp of butter. Make a layer with veal pieces and Pour water to cover. Season with salt and seal the lid. Cook on High pressure for 45 minutes. Do a quick release.

Meanwhile, melt the remaining butter in a skillet. Add the cayenne pepper, and flour, and briefly stir-fry - for about 2 minutes. Slice pide bread and arrange on a serving plate. Place the meat and tomatoes on top.

Drizzle with cayenne pepper, Top with yogurt and sprinkle with parsley.

# Vegetables with Veal & Pork

Serving Size: 4 | Total Time: 45 minutes

## Ingredients

1 lb lean veal cuts, cut into bite-sized pieces
1 lb pork tenderloin, cubed
12 oz button mushrooms, sliced
3 carrots, chopped
2 tbsp butter, softened

1 tbsp olive oil
1 tbsp cayenne pepper
Salt and black pepper to taste
A bunch fresh of parsley leaves, chopped
3 oz celery root, finely chopped

## Directions

Heat the olive oil and butter in the Instant Pot on Sauté. Add in veal, pork, mushrooms, carrots, salt, pepper, cayenne pepper, and celery, and cook for 5 minutes. Stir in 2 cups of water. Seal the lid, and cook on High pressure for 13 minutes.

Do a quick release Open the lid and adjust the seasoning. Serve warm sprinkled with parsley.

# Simple Beef with Rice & Cheese

Serving Size: 4 | Total Time: 55 minutes

## Ingredients

2 lb beef shoulder
1 cup rice
2 cups beef broth

3 tbsp butter
¼ cup Parmesan cheese, grated
Salt and black pepper to taste

## Directions

Rinse the meat and rub with salt. Place it in the pot and pour in broth. Seal the lid and cook on Meat/Stew for 25 minutes on High Pressure. Do a quick release, remove the meat but keep the broth.

Add rice and stir in 1 tbsp of butter. Season with black pepper and salt. Seal the lid, and cook on Rice mode for 8 minutes on High. Do a quick release.

Remove the rice and wipe the pot clean. Melt 2 tbsp of butter on Sauté. Add meat and lightly brown for 10 minutes.

Serve with rice topped with Parmesan cheese.

# Classic Mushroom Beef Stroganoff

Serving Size: 6 | Total Time: 45 minutes

## Ingredients

1 lb beef steak, cut into bite-sized pieces
1 cup button mushrooms, chopped
1 cup sour cream
2 cups beef broth
3 tbsp Worcestershire sauce

3 tbsp olive oil
1 tbsp flour
1 onion, chopped
2 garlic cloves, minced
Salt and black pepper to taste

## Directions

In a bowl, mix flour, a pinch of salt and pepper. Coat steaks with this mixture.

Place the meat and broth in the inner pot. Seal the lid and cook for 10 minutes on High Pressure. Do a quick release. Add mushrooms, onion, and garlic, and Worcestershire sauce. Seal the lid and cook on High Pressure for 15 minutes. Do a quick release. Stir in sour cream. Let simmer for 10 minutes, and serve.

# Tasty Spicy Beef

Serving Size: 6 | Total Time: 45 minutes

## Ingredients

2 lb lean beef, cut into bite-sized pieces
5 onions, peeled, chopped
5 garlic cloves, peeled, crushed
1 jalapeño pepper, chopped
1 bell pepper, chopped

Salt and black pepper, to taste
1 tsp cayenne pepper
2 tbsp tomato sauce
2 tbsp vegetable oil

## Directions

Heat oil on Sauté. Stir-fry onions, garlic, for 2-3 minutes. Add the meat, salt, pepper, cayenne pepper, jalapeño pepper, and tomato sauce. Mix well and pour enough water to cover.

Seal the lid and cook for 20 minutes on High Pressure. Do a quick pressure release.

# Green Pea & Beef Ragout

Serving Size: 4 | Total Time: 15 minutes

## Ingredients

2 lb beef, tender cuts, boneless, cut into bits
2 cups green peas
1 onion, diced
1 tomato, diced
3 cups beef broth
½ cup tomato paste

1 tsp cayenne pepper, ground
1 tbsp flour
1 tsp salt
½ tsp dried thyme, ground
½ tsp red pepper flakes

## Directions

Add all ingredients in the instant pot. Seal the lid, press Manual/Pressure Cook and cook for 10 minutes on High Pressure.

When done, release the steam naturally, for 10 minutes and serve.

# Calf's Liver Venetian-Style

Serving Size: 2 | Total Time: 40 minutes

## Ingredients

1 lb calf's liver, rinsed
3 tbsp olive oil
2 garlic cloves, crushed
1 tbsp fresh mint, finely chopped

½ tsp cayenne pepper
1 tsp salt
½ tsp Italian seasoning

## Directions

In a bowl, mix oil, garlic, mint, cayenne, salt and Italian seasoning. Brush the liver and chill for 30 minutes. Remove from the fridge and pat dry with paper.

Place the liver into the inner pot. Seal the lid and cook on High Pressure for 5 minutes.

When ready, release the steam naturally, for about 10 minutes.

# Garlic Pork Chops with Creamy Gravy & Broccoli

Serving Size: 6 | Total Time: 45 minutes

## Ingredients

*Pork Chops:*

Salt and black pepper to taste
1 tsp garlic powder
1 tsp onion powder
1 tsp red pepper flakes
6 boneless pork chops

*Gravy:*

3 tbsp flour
½ cup heavy cream

1 broccoli head, broken into florets
1 cup vegetable stock
¼ cup butter, melted
¼ cup milk

Salt and black pepper to taste

## Directions

Combine salt, garlic powder, pepper flakes, onion, and black pepper. Rub the mixture onto pork chops. Place stock, milk, and broccoli in the instant pot. Lay the pork chops on top. Seal the lid and cook for 15 minutes on High Pressure. Release the Pressure quickly.

Transfer the pork chops and broccoli to a plate. Press Sauté and simmer the liquid remaining in the pot. Mix cream and flour. Pour into the simmering liquid and cook for 4 to 6 minutes until thickened and bubbly. Season with pepper and salt. Top the chops with gravy, drizzle butter over broccoli and serve.

# Apricot Jam-Glazed Ham

Serving Size: 12 | Total Time: 40 minutes

## Ingredients

¼ cup water
5 pounds smoked ham
¾ cup apricot jam
½ cup brown sugar
Juice from 1 lime

2 tsp mustard
½ tsp ground cardamom
¼ tsp ground nutmeg
Black pepper to taste

## Directions

Into the pot, add water and ham. In a bowl, mix jam, lime juice, cardamom, pepper, nutmeg, mustard, and sugar. Pour the mixture over the ham. Seal the lid and cook on High Pressure for 10 minutes. Release the pressure quickly. Transfer the ham to a cutting board; allow to sit for 10 minutes. Press Sauté.

Simmer the liquid and cook for 4 to 6 minutes until thickened into a sauce. Slice ham and place onto a serving bowl. Drizzle with sauce before serving.

# Paprika Pork Fajitas with Cotija Cheese

Serving Size: 5 | Total Time: 1 hour 30 minutes

## Ingredients

1 tbsp ground cumin
2 tsp dried oregano
1 tsp paprika
1 tsp onion powder
Salt and black pepper to taste
½ tsp ground cinnamon
3 pounds boneless pork shoulder
¾ cup vegetable broth

¼ cup pineapple juice
1 lime, juiced
4 cloves garlic, crushed
2 bay leaves
5 corn tortillas, warmed
½ cup queso Cotija, crumbled

## Directions

In a bowl, combine cumin, paprika, pepper, onion powder, oregano, salt, and cinnamon; toss in pork to coat. Place the pork in the Pressure cooker and allow settling for 15 to 30 minutes.

Add in broth, garlic, lime juice, bay leaves, and pineapple juice. Seal the lid and cook on High Pressure for 50 minutes. Release Pressure naturally for 15 minutes, then release the remaining pressure quickly.

Preheat oven to 450°F. Transfer the pork to a rimmed baking sheet and use two forks to shred the meat.

Reserve juices in the instant pot. Bake in the oven for 10 minutes until crispy. Skim and get rid of fat from the liquid remaining in the pot. Dispose of the bay leaves. Over the pork, pour the liquid and serve alongside warm corn tortillas and queso Cotija.

# Cannellini Bean & Italian Sausage Stew with Spinach

Serving Size: 6 | Total Time: 45 minutes

## Ingredients

1 tbsp olive oil
1 lb Italian sausages, halved
1 celery stalk, chopped
1 carrot, chopped
1 onion, chopped
1 sprig fresh sage

1 sprig fresh rosemary
1 bay leaf
1 cup cannellini beans, soaked and rinsed
2 cups vegetable stock
3 cups fresh spinach
1 tsp salt

## Directions

Warm oil on Sauté. Add in sausage pieces and sear for 5 minutes until browned; set aside on a plate.

To the pot, add celery, onion, bay leaf, sage, carrot, salt, and rosemary; cook for 3 minutes to soften slightly. Stir in vegetable stock and beans. Arrange seared sausage pieces on top of the beans.

Seal the lid, press Bean/Chili and cook on High for 10 minutes. Release Pressure naturally for 20 minutes, do a quick release. Get rid of bay leaf, rosemary and sage. Mix spinach into the mixture to serve.

# Saucy Baby Back Ribs

Serving Size: 4 | Total Time: 45 minutes

## Ingredients

2 pounds baby back pork ribs
4 cups orange juice

Juice from 1 lemon

*For BBQ sauce:*
2 tbsp honey
½ cup ketchup
Juice from ½ lemon
1 tbsp Worcestershire sauce

1tsp mustard
2 tsp paprika
½ tsp cayenne pepper
Salt to taste

## Directions

Mix all BBQ ingredients in a bowl, until well incorporated. Set aside. Place ribs in your instant pot, and add in lemon juice and orange juice.

Seal the lid, press Meat/Stew and cook on High Pressure for 20 minutes. Release Pressure naturally for 15 minutes. Meanwhile, preheat oven to 400°F. Line the sheet pan with aluminum foil.

Transfer the ribs to the prepared sheet. Do away with the cooking liquid. Onto both sides of ribs, brush barbecue sauce. Bake ribs in the oven for 10 minutes until sauce is browned and caramelized; set the ribs aside and cut into individual bones to serve.

# Pork Sausage Hot Dogs with Bell Peppers & Beer

Serving Size: 6 | Total Time: 15 minutes

## Ingredients

1 tbsp olive oil
6 pork sausage links
1 green bell pepper, chopped into strips
1 red bell pepper, chopped into strips
1 yellow bell pepper, chopped into strips

2 spring onions, chopped
1 ½ cups beer
6 hot dog rolls
Salt and black pepper to taste

## Directions

Warm oil on Sauté. Add in sausage links and sear for 5 minutes until browned; set aside on a plate. Into the instant pot, add chopped peppers. Lay the sausages on top. Add beer into the pot and season with salt and pepper.

Seal the lid and cook for on High Pressure 5 minutes. Release the Pressure quickly. Serve sausages in hot dog rolls topped with onions and bell peppers.

# Pork Sausages with Potato & Celeriac Mash

Serving Size: 4 | Total Time: 45 minutes

## Ingredients

1 tbsp olive oil
4 pork sausages
1 onion
2 cups vegetable broth
½ cup water
4 potatoes, peeled and diced
1 cup celeriac, chopped

2 tbsp butter
¼ cup milk
Salt and black pepper to taste
1 tbsp heavy cream
1 tsp Dijon mustard
½ tsp dry mustard powder
Fresh flat-leaf parsley, chopped

## Directions

Warm oil on Sauté mode. Add in sausages and cook for 1 to 2 minutes for each side until browned. Set the sausages to a plate. To the same pot, add onion and Sauté for 3 minutes until fragrant. Press Cancel.

Add sausages on top of onion and pour water and broth over them. Place a trivet over onion and sausages. Put potatoes and celeriac in the steamer basket and transfer it to the trivet.

Seal the lid and cook for 11 minutes on High Pressure. Release the pressure quickly. Transfer potatoes and celeriac to a bowl and set sausages on a plate and cover them with aluminum foil.

Using a potato masher, mash potatoes and celeriac together with black pepper, milk, salt and butter until mash becomes creamy and fluffy. Adjust the seasonings.

Set on Sauté mode. Add the onion mixture and bring to a boil. Cook for 5 to 10 minutes until the mixture is reduced and thickened. Into the gravy, stir in dry mustard, salt, pepper, mustard and heavy cream. Place the mash in 4 bowls in equal parts, top with a sausage or two, and gravy. Garnish with parsley.

# Christmas Ham with Honey-Mustard Glaze

Serving Size: 10 | Total Time: 30 minutes

## Ingredients

½ cup apple cider
¼ cup honey
1 tbsp Dijon mustard
¼ cup brown sugar
2 tbsp orange juice

2 tbsp pineapple juice
½ tsp ground cinnamon
¼ tsp grated nutmeg
A pinch of ground cloves
1 (5-pound) ham, bone-in

## Directions

Set on Sauté. Mix in apple cider, mustard, pineapple juice, cloves, cinnamon, sugar, honey, orange juice, and nutmeg; cook until sauce becomes warm and the sugar and spices are completely dissolved.

Lay ham into the sauce. Seal the lid and cook on High Pressure for 10 minutes. Release the Pressure quickly. As the ham cooks, preheat the oven's broiler. Line aluminum foil to a baking sheet.

Transfer the ham to the prepared baking sheet. On Sauté, cook the remaining liquid for 4 to 6 minutes until you have a thick and syrupy glaze. Brush the glaze onto ham.

Set the glazed ham in the preheated broiler and bake for 3 to 5 minutes until the glaze is caramelized. Place the ham on a cutting board and slice. Transfer to a serving bowl and drizzle glaze over the ham.

# Beer Pulled Pork Tacos

Serving Size: 5 | Total Time: 2 hours

## Ingredients

3 tbsp sugar
3 tsp taco seasoning
Salt and black pepper to taste
2 lb pork shoulder, trimmed, cut into chunks
1 cup beer
1 cup vegetable broth, ¼ cup plus

2 tbsp lemon juice
¼ cup mayonnaise
2 tbsp honey
2 tsp mustard
3 cups shredded cabbage
5 taco tortillas

## Directions

In a bowl, combine sugar, taco seasoning, and black pepper. Rub onto pork pieces to coat well. Allow settling for 30 minutes. Into the pot, add broth, pork, and beer. Seal the lid and cook on High Pressure for 50 minutes.

Meanwhile in a bowl, mix mayonnaise, mustard, lemon juice, cabbage and honey until well coated.

Release the pressure naturally for 15 minutes. Transfer the pork to a cutting board and allow cooling for a few minutes, then shred with two forks. Skim and get rid of fat from liquid in the Pressure cooker. Return pork to the pot and mix with the liquid.

Toast the tortillas in a skillet over medium heat for about 30 seconds per side. Fill each tortilla with pork and slaw to serve.

# Authentic Cuban Pork Shoulder

Serving Size: 8 | Total Time: 2 hours 30 minutes

## Ingredients

½ cup orange juice
¼ cup lime juice
¼ cup canola oil
¼ cup chopped fresh cilantro
1 tsp red pepper flakes

8 cloves garlic, minced
1 tbsp ground cumin
1 tbsp fresh oregano
Salt and black pepper to taste
3 pounds pork shoulder

## Directions

In a bowl, mix orange juice, canola oil, cumin, salt, pepper, oregano, pepper flakes, lime juice, and garlic. Add into a large plastic bag alongside the pork. Seal and massage the bag to ensure the marinade covers the pork completely.

Place in the refrigerator for two hours. In the instant pot, set your removed pork from bag.

Add the marinade on top. Seal the lid and cook on High Pressure for 50 minutes. Release Pressure naturally for 15 minutes. Transfer the pork to a cutting board and use a fork to break into smaller pieces. Skim and get rid of the fat from liquid in the cooker. Serve the liquid with pork and sprinkle with cilantro.

# Mushroom & Carrot Pork Stew

Serving Size: 2 | Total Time: 45 minutes

## Ingredients

2 pork chops, bones removed and cubed
1 cup crimini mushrooms, sliced
2 large carrots, chopped
½ tsp garlic powder
Salt and black pepper to taste

2 tbsp butter
1 cup beef broth
1 tbsp apple cider vinegar
2 tbsp cornstarch

## Directions

Season the meat with salt and pepper. Add butter and pork chops to the pot and brown for 10 minutes, stirring occasionally, on Sauté mode. Add mushrooms and cook for 5 minutes. Add the remaining ingredients and seal the lid. Cook on High Pressure for 25 minutes. Do a quick release and serve hot.

# Caribbean-Flavoured Pulled Pork with Mango Sauce

Serving Size: 6 | Total Time: 1 hour 15 minutes

## Ingredients

1 ½ tsp onion powder
1 tsp dried thyme
Salt and black pepper to taste
1 tsp cayenne pepper
1 tsp ground allspice
½ tsp ground nutmeg

½ tsp ground cinnamon
3 pounds pork shoulder
1 mango, cut into chunks
1 tbsp olive oil
½ cup water
2 tbsp fresh cilantro, minced

## Directions

In a bowl, combine onion, thyme, allspice, cinnamon, black pepper, sea salt, cayenne, and nutmeg. Coat the pork shoulder with olive oil. Season with seasoning mixture. Warm oil on Sauté. Add in the pork and cook for 5 minutes until browned completely. To the pot, add water and mango chunks.

Seal the lid, press Meat/Stew and cook on High Pressure for 45 minutes. Release the pressure naturally for 15 minutes, then quick release the remaining pressure. Transfer the pork to a cutting board to cool.

To make the sauce, pour the cooking liquid in a food processor and pulse until smooth. Use two forks to shred the pork and arrange on a serving platter. Serve the pork topped with mango salsa and cilantro.

# Cumin Pork Chops with Peach Sauce

Serving Size: 4 | Total Time: 20 minutes

## Ingredients

4 pork chops
1 tsp cumin seeds
Salt and black pepper to taste

2 cups peaches, sliced
1 tbsp vegetable oil
¾ cup vegetable stock

## Directions

Sprinkle salt, cumin, and black pepper on the pork chops. Set on Sauté and warm oil. Add the chops and cook for 3 to 5 minutes until browned and set aside on a bowl.

Arrange peach slices at the bottom of the cooker. Place the pork chops on top of the plumes. Add any juice from the plate over the pork and apply stock around the edges.

Seal lid and cook on High Pressure for 8 minutes. Do a quick Pressure release. Transfer the pork chops to a serving plate and spoon over the peach sauce before serving.

# Pork Chops in Honey-Mustard Sauce

Serving Size: 4 | Total Time: 50 minutes

## Ingredients

2 lb pork chops
1 cup beef broth
2 tbsp oil
¼ cup honey

1 tbsp Dijon mustard
½ tsp cinnamon
1 tsp ginger, grated
Salt and black pepper to taste

## Directions

Season the chops with salt and pepper. Heat oil on Sauté and brown the chops for 2-3 minutes, on each side. In a bowl, mix honey, mustard, cinnamon, and ginger. Whisk together and drizzle over chops.

Pour in broth and seal the lid. Cook on High Pressure for 30 minutes. Do a quick release and serve hot.

# Chickpea & Pork Stew with Bell Peppers

Serving Size: 6 | Total Time: 40 minutes

## Ingredients

1 tbsp olive oil
3 pounds boneless pork shoulder, trimmed and cubed
1 white onion, chopped
15 ounces canned chickpeas, drained and rinsed
½ cup sweet paprika
2 tsp salt

1 tbsp chili powder
1 bay leaf
2 red bell peppers, chopped
6 cloves garlic, minced
1 tbsp cornstarch

## Directions

Set on Sauté, add pork and oil, and allow cooking for 5 minutes until browned. Add in the onion, paprika, bay leaf, salt, 1 ½ cups of water, chickpeas, and chili powder. Seal the lid and cook on High Pressure for 8 minutes.

Do a quick release and discard bay leaf. Remove 1 cup of cooking liquid from the pot; add to a blender alongside garlic, water, cornstarch, and red bell peppers, and blend well until smooth. Add the blended mixture into the stew and mix well.

# Honey & White Wine Pork

Serving Size: 4 | Total Time: 30 minutes

## Ingredients

1 pound pork loin, cut into chunks
2 tbsp white wine
15 ounces canned peaches, chopped
¼ cup beef stock
2 tbsp sweet chili sauce

2 tbsp honey
2 tbsp soy sauce
2 tbsp cornstarch
¼ cup water

## Directions

Into the pot, mix soy sauce, beef stock, wine, honey, juice from the canned peaches, and sweet chili sauce. Stir in pork to coat. Seal the lid and cook on High Pressure for 5 minutes.

Release pressure naturally for 10 minutes, then release the remaining pressure quickly. Remove the pork to a serving plate. Chop the peaches into small pieces.

In a bowl, mix water with cornstarch until well dissolved; stir the mixture into the pot. Press Sauté and cook for 5 more minutes until you obtain the desired thick consistency. Add in the chopped peaches and stir well. Serve the pork topped with peach sauce and enjoy.

# Pulled Pork Carnitas Wraps with Lime & Cilantro

Serving Size: 12 | Total Time: 1 hour

## Ingredients

2 tsp grapeseed oil
1 (5-pound) boneless pork shoulder
1 onion, chopped
2 garlic cloves, minced
2 oranges, juiced
2 limes, juiced
2 tbsp sweet smoked paprika

1 tbsp dried oregano
1 ½ cups water
2 jalapeño peppers, chopped
1 avocado, sliced
Fresh cilantro leaves, chopped
12 corn tortillas, warmed

## Directions

Warm oil on Sauté. Add in pork and cook for 5 minutes until golden brown. Transfer the pork to a plate.

Add garlic and onion to the pot and cook for 2 to 3 minutes until soft. Add lime and orange juices into the pan to deglaze, scrape the bottom to get rid of any browned bits of food. Stir in black pepper, paprika, salt and oregano. Return the pork to pot; stir to coat in seasoning and liquid.

Seal the lid and cook for 35 minutes on High Pressure. Release the pressure quickly.

Press Sauté. When the liquid starts to simmer, use two forks to shred the pork. Cook for 10 more minutes until liquid is reduced by half. Serve in warmed tortillas topped with jalapeños, avocado and cilantro.

# Spiced Pork with Orange & Cinnamon

Total Time: 60 minutes | Serving Size: 8

## Ingredients

2 tbsp olive oil
5 pounds pork shoulder
1 cinnamon stick
2 cups orange juice
1 tbsp cumin
½ tsp garlic powder

¼ tsp onion powder
1 onion, chopped
1 jalapeño pepper, diced
2 tsp thyme
½ tsp oregano
Salt and black pepper to taste

## Directions

Place half of the oil in a small bowl. Add all of the spices and stir well to combine the mixture. Rub it all over the meat, making sure that the pork is well-coated.

Heat the remaining oil on Sauté. Add the pork and sear it on all sides until browned. Transfer to a plate. Pour the orange juice into the pan and deglaze the bottom with a spatula.

Add the rest of the ingredients and stir to combine well. Return the pork to the pot. Seal the lid, select the Pressure Cook cooking mode for 40 minutes, on High Pressure.

When ready, allow for a natural pressure release, for about 10 minutes. Grab two forks and shred the pork inside the pot. Stir to combine with the juices, and serve.

# Red Wine Pork Stew with Basil & Tomatoes

Serving Size: 4 | Total Time: 45 minutes

## Ingredients

16 oz pork tenderloin, cut into bite-sized pieces
1 onion, peeled, chopped
2 tbsp vegetable oil
4 tomatoes, peeled, diced

½ tbsp red wine
½ tbsp beef broth
A handful of fresh basil
Salt and black pepper to taste

Heat oil and stir-fry the onion, until translucent. Add the meat, salt, pepper, wine, tomatoes, and basil. Cook for 10 minutes.Pour in broth, seal the lid and cook on High Pressure for 25 minutes. Do a quick release.

# Pork Chops with Brussels Sprouts

Total Time: 40 minutes | Serving Size: 4

**Ingredients**

1 pound pork chops
1 cup onions, sliced
1 cup carrots, sliced
1 tbsp butter
2 cups brussels sprouts

1 tbsp arrowroot
1 tsp garlic, minced
1 cup vegetable stock
½ tsp dried thyme
Salt and black pepper to taste

**Directions**

Melt butter on Sauté mode. Add the pork chops, and cook on all sides until golden in color. Transfer to a plate. Add the onions, and cook for 3 minutes, then add the garlic.

Saute for one more minute. Return the pork chops to the pot and pour the stock over. Season with salt and pepper. Seal the lid and cook on High Pressure for 15 minutes.

When the timer goes off, do a quick pressure release. Stir in thyme, carrots and brussel sprouts. Seal the lid again, and cook for 3 minutes on High Pressure. Do a quick pressure release.

Transfer the chops and veggies to a serving platter. Whisk the arrowroot into the pot and cook on Sauté until it thickens. Adjust the seasoning. Pour the sauce over the chops and veggies. Serve immediately.

# Garlic Pork Chops on Puréed Butternut Squash

Serving Size: 4 | Total Time: 45 minutes

**Ingredients**

3 tbsp olive oil
2 sprigs thyme, chopped
2 sprigs rosemary, chopped
4 pork chops
1 cup mushrooms, chopped
4 cloves garlic, minced

1 cup vegetable broth
1 tbsp soy sauce
1 pound butternut squash, cubed
1 tbsp olive oil
1 tsp cornstarch

**Directions**

Set on Sauté and heat rosemary, thyme and 2 tbsp of oil. Add the pork chops and sear for 1 minute for each side until lightly browned.

Sauté garlic and mushrooms in the instant pot for 5-6 minutes until mushrooms are tender. Add soy sauce and broth. Transfer pork chops to a wire trivet and place inside the pot. Over the chops, place a cake pan. Add butternut squash in the pan and drizzle with 1 tbsp olive oil.

Seal the lid and cook on High Pressure for 10 minutes. Release the pressure quickly. Remove the pan and trivet from the pot. Stir cornstarch into the mushroom mixture for 2 to 3 minutes until the sauce thickens.

Transfer the mushroom sauce to an immersion blender and blend until you attain the desired consistency. Scoop sauce into a cup with a pour spout. Smash the squash into a purée and spoon into a serving platter. Top with the pork chops and drizzle with gravy.

# Pork Shoulder with Honey, Garlic and Ginger

Serving Size: 6 | Total Time: 1 hour 20 minutes

## Ingredients

2 lb pork shoulder, boneless
1 garlic head, divided into cloves
Salt and black pepper to taste
½ tsp red pepper flakes
1 tbsp butter, unsalted

2 tsp fresh ginger, grated
3 tbsp apple cider vinegar
2 tbsp honey
3 tbsp soy sauce
1 tsp garlic powder

## Directions

In a bowl, combine apple cider, honey, soy sauce, garlic powder, and ginger. Brush the meat with this mixture and set aside. Brown the pork, evenly on all sides, on Sauté. Then, add 1 cup of water and garlic. Seal the lid and cook on High Pressure for 35 minutes on High.

Do a quick release. Season with salt, pepper, and red pepper flakes. Add butter and cook until the liquid evaporates – for 10 minutes, on Sauté mode.

# Classic Pork Goulash

Serving Size: 4 | Total Time: 40 minutes

## Ingredients

12 oz pork neck, cut into bite-sized pieces
2 tbsp flour
4 tbsp vegetable oil
2 onions, peeled, chopped
1 carrot, chopped
A handful of chopped celery

10 oz button mushrooms
4 cups beef broth
1 chili pepper, chopped
1 tbsp cayenne pepper
Salt and black pepper to taste

## Directions

Heat oil on Sauté. Add onions and cook for 2 minutes, until translucent. Add flour, chili pepper, carrot, celery, cayenne pepper, and continue to cook for 2 more minutes, stirring constantly.

Press Cancel, and add meat, mushrooms, beef broth, and water. Season with salt and pepper. Seal the lid and cook on Manual/Pressure Cook mode for 30 minutes on High Pressure. Do a quick release and serve immediately.

# Spicy Garlic Pork

Serving Size: 4 | Total Time: 50 minutes

## Ingredients

1 lb pork shoulder
2 tbsp olive oil
3 Jalapeño peppers, seeded and chopped
2 Japones chiles, chopped
1 tsp ground cumin

3 cups water
1 large onion, chopped
2 garlic cloves, crushed
3 cups beef broth
Salt and black pepper to taste

## Directions:

Heat oil on Sauté and cook the jalapeño peppers for 3 minutes. Add in all the spices, garlic and onion and stir-fry for another 2 minutes, until soft. Add in the pork shoulder, water, beef broth and the pureed mixture.

Seal the lid, and cook on Meat/Stew for 30 minutes on High. Release the pressure quickly and serve hot.

# Spring Onion & Ground Pork Egg Casserole

Total Time: 30 minutes | Serving Size: 5

## Ingredients

1 tbsp butter, melted
1 cup spring onions, chopped
1 pound ground pork, chopped

6 eggs
Salt and black pepper, to taste
1 cup water

## Directions

In a bowl, break the eggs and whisk until frothy. Mix in the onions and ground meat, and season with the salt and pepper. Grease a casserole dish with 1 tablespoon of melted butter. Pour the egg mixture into the dish.

Place a metal trivet in the pressure cooker and add 1 cup of water. Select RICE mode and cook for 25 minutes on High. Do a quick pressure release and serve immediately.

# Delicious Pork in Button Mushroom Gravy

Serving Size: 6 | Total Time: 60 minutes

## Ingredients

2 lb pork shoulder
1 cup button mushrooms, chopped
2 tbsp butter, unsalted
1 tbsp balsamic vinegar
½ tsp garlic powder

1 tsp salt
¼ cup soy sauce
2 bay leaves
1 cup beef broth
2 tbsp cornstarch

## Directions

Rinse the meat and rub with salt and garlic powder. Melt butter on Sauté. Brown the meat for 5 minutes on each side. Stir in soy sauce and bay leaves. Cook for 2 minutes before, add in beef broth and balsamic vinegar. Seal the lid and set on Meat/Stew mode. Cook for 30 minutes on High Pressure.

When done, do a quick release and Stir in mushrooms. Cook until tender, for about 5 minutes, on Sauté mode. Stir in cornstarch and cook for 2 minutes.

# Pork Loin with Apples & Rutabaga

Serving Size: 4 | Total Time: 40 minutes

## Ingredients

1 tbsp olive oil
1 pound pork loin, cut into cubes
2 apples, peeled and chopped
1 large rutabaga, chopped
1 onion, diced
1 celery stalk, diced

1 tbsp parsley, chopped
½ cup leeks, sliced
1 ½ cups beef broth
½ tsp cumin
½ tsp thyme
Salt and black pepper to taste

## Directions

Heat half of the olive oil on Sauté. Add the pork and cook until it browned on all sides. Remove to a plate. Add leeks, onion, celery, and drizzle with the remaining oil.

Stir to combine and cook for 3 minutes. Add the pork back to the cooker, pour the broth over, and stir in all of the herbs and spices. Seal the lid, and cook on High Pressure for 10 minutes.

After the beep, do a quick pressure release. Stir in the rutabaga and apples. Seal the lid again and cook for 5 minutes on High. Do a quick pressure release, and serve right away.

# Pulled Pork with Homemade Barbecue Sauce

Serving Size: 8 | Total Time: 70 minutes

## Ingredients

4 pounds pork shoulder
1 tbsp onion powder
1 tbsp garlic powder

Salt and black pepper to taste
1 tbsp chili powder
2 cups vegetable stock

*For BBQ Sauce:*
6 dates, soaked
¼ cup tomato paste

½ cup coconut aminos

## Directions

In a small bowl combine onion powder, garlic powder, salt, black pepper, and chili powder. Rub the mixture onto the pork. Place the pork inside your pressure cooker.

Pour the stock around the meat, not over it, and then seal the lid. Select Pressure Cook mode and set the timer to 60 minutes, on High Pressure.

Meanwhile, place all sauce ingredients in a food processor and pulse until smooth. Release the pressure quickly. Grab two forks and shred the meat inside the pot. Pour the sauce over and stir to combine.

# Maple Pulled Pork with Tomatoes

Serving Size: 6 | Total Time: 45 minutes

## Ingredients

2 lb pork shoulder
½ cup maple syrup
½ cup sun-dried tomatoes, diced
3 cups beef stock

2 tbsp mustard powder
½ cup brown sugar
2 tbsp salt
1 cup fresh cilantro, chopped

## Directions

Rub the meat with salt and sugar, and place it in the pot. Add the remaining ingredients except for the cilantro. Seal the lid and cook on High Pressure for 30 minutes. Allow the Pressure to release naturally, for 10 minutes. Shred the pork with two forks, transfer to a plate and top with cilantro to serve.

# Garlic Pork Meatloaf with Ketchup Glaze

Serving Size: 6 | Total Time: 70 minutes

## Ingredients

1 pound ground sausage
1 pound ground pork
1 cup cooked rice
1 cup milk
½ tsp cayenne powder

½ tsp marjoram
2 eggs, beaten
2 garlic cloves, minced
1 onion, diced
Salt and black pepper to taste

*Topping:*
2 tbsp brown sugar

1 cup ketchup

## Directions

In a bowl, crack the eggs and whisk them with milk. Stir in the meat, cayenne, marjoram, rice, onion, salt, black pepper, and garlic. With hands, mix in the ingredients to combine and form meatloaf mixture.

Grease a baking dish with cooking spray. Add and shape the meatloaf mixture inside. Whisk together the ketchup and sugar and pour over the meatloaf. Place the trivet inside the pressure cooker, and pour 1 cup of water. Lay the dish on top, seal the lid and cook on Soup/Broth for 50 minutes on High. Do a quick release.

# Pork Loin with Pineapple Sauce

Serving Size: 6 | Total Time: 30 minutes

## Ingredients

2 lb pork loin, cut into 6 equal pieces
16 ounces canned pineapples
1 cup vegetable broth
1 tbsp brown sugar
3 tbsp olive oil
½ cup tomato paste
1 cup sliced onions

½ tsp ginger, grated
Salt and black pepper to taste
¼ cup tamari
¼ cup rice wine vinegar
½ tbsp cornstarch
1 tbsp water

## Directions

Heat the 2 tbsp oil on Sauté. Cook the onions a few minutes, until translucent. Add the pork and stir in the rest of the ingredients, except for water and cornstarch. Seal the lid and cook for 20 minutes on Soup/Broth on High. Release the pressure quickly.

In a bowl, mix cornstarch and water, with a fork, until slurry. Stir in the cornstarch slurry in the pressure cooker, and cook for 2 more minutes, or until thickened, on Sauté. Serve hot to enjoy!

# Tasty Pork Butt with Fennel & Mushrooms

Serving Size: 8 | Total Time: 30 minutes

## Ingredients

1 pound pork butt, sliced
2 cups mushrooms, sliced
1 fennel bulb, chopped
½ cup white wine

1 tsp garlic, minced
½ cup vegetable broth
Salt and black pepper, to taste

## Directions

Grease with cooking spray and heat on Sauté mode. Brown the pork slices and for a few minutes. Stir in the remaining ingredients. Season with salt and pepper.

Seal the lid and cook for 20 minutes on Meat/Stew on High. When done, do a quick release.

# Cabbage & Pork Soup

Serving Size: 6 | Total Time: 20 minutes

## Ingredients

1 pound ground pork
1 onion, diced
2 pounds napa cabbage, chopped
1 potato, diced
6 button mushrooms, sliced

3 scallions, sliced
2 carrots, chopped
1 tbsp butter
4 cups vegetable broth
Salt and black pepper to taste

## Directions

Melt butter on Sauté, and add the pork. Cook until it browned, breaking it with a spatula. Once browned, add onion and mushrooms, and cook for another 4-5 minutes.

Season with salt and pepper. Pour in vegetable broth and stir in the remaining ingredients. Seal the lid, cook on Pressure Cook for 6 minutes on High.

Do a quick release. Ladle into serving bowls and serve.

# Steamed Red Cabbage with Crispy Bacon

Serving Size: 8 | Total Time: 25 minutes

## Ingredients

1 pound red cabbage, chopped
8 bacon slices, chopped
1 ½ cups beef broth

2 tbsp butter
Salt and black pepper to taste

## Directions

Add the bacon slices in your pressure cooker, and cook for 5 minutes, until crispy, on Sauté. Stir in the cabbage, broth, salt, pepper, and butter. Seal the lid, select Steam mode for 10 minutes on High pressure. When ready, release the pressure naturally, for 10 minutes.

# Tasty Buckwheat & Pork Stew

Serving Size: 4 | Total Time: 50 minutes

## Ingredients

8 oz buckwheat porridge, cooked
1 lb pork tenderloin
1 carrot, chopped
1 onion, finely chopped
3 tbsp vegetable oil

1 tsp dry marjoram
Salt and black pepper to taste
1 garlic clove
½ cup white wine
2 cups vegetable broth

## Directions

Heat oil on Sauté. Add onion, garlic and stir-fry for 2 minutes, until fragrant and translucent. Add carrot and meat. Cook for 5 minutes, until lightly browned. Add the remaining ingredients. Seal the lid and cook on High pressure for 35 minutes. Do a quick release and stir in the porridge. Serve hot.

# Sweet & Spicy Pulled Pork

Serving Size: 8 | Total Time: 65 minutes

## Ingredients

3 lb pork shoulder
1 cup onions, finely chopped
2 tbsp butter, unsalted
1 tbsp cayenne pepper
1 tsp salt

1 cup beef broth
3 tbsp maple syrup
2 tbsp soy sauce
1/3 cup Worcestershire sauce
2 bay leaves

## Directions

On Sauté, stir-fry butter, onions, cayenne, and salt, for 4 minutes. Add maple syrup, soy sauce, Worcestershire sauce, and bay leaves. Cook for 5 minutes. Add meat and pour in the broth. Seal the lid and cook on High pressure for 40 minutes. When done, do a quick release and serve hot.

# Rice Chowder with Bacon & Green Peas

Serving Size: 4 | Total Time: 20 minutes

## Ingredients

2 cups basmati rice
1 cup bacon, chopped
1 medium onion, chopped
½ cup green peas
3 tbsp olive oil

2 garlic cloves, chopped
1 tsp dried thyme
1 tsp salt
4 cups beef broth

Heat oil on Sauté, and stir-fry onion and garlic for 2-3 minutes, or until translucent. Add all the remaining ingredients and seal the lid. Cook on High Pressure for 5 minutes. When ready, release the Pressure naturally for 10 minutes. Stir well, and plate in a serving bowl.

# Pork Chops in Cinnamon Apple Sauce

Serving Size: 4 | Total Time: 1 hour

### Ingredients

4 pork loin chops, 1-inch thick
2 tbsp oil
1 tbsp butter
3 apples, peeled, cored, chopped
¼ cup soy sauce

1 cup beef broth
2 tbsp honey
¼ tsp cinnamon
Salt and black pepper to taste

### Directions

Heat oil on Sauté and briefly brown the chops for 3 minutes on each side. Remove and melt the butter.

Add apples, soy sauce, broth, honey, and cinnamon. Cook until apples are slightly tender. Add the chops back, seal the lid and cook on Meat/Stew for 40 minutes on High. Do a quick release. Adjust the seasoning and serve.

# Pork Tenderloin with Balsamic & Butter

Serving Size: 4 | Total Time: 50 minutes

### Ingredients

2 lb pork tenderloin
2 tbsp butter, unsalted
2 tbsp brown sugar
2 tbsp balsamic vinegar

2 garlic cloves, crushed
1 cup beef broth
Salt and black pepper to taste
1 tbsp cornstarch

### Directions

Melt butter on Sauté and stir-fry garlic for 1 minute. Add sugar and vinegar, and cook for 1 more minute. Rub the meat with salt and pepper. Place in your instant pot and Pour in the broth. Seal the lid.

Cook on High Pressure for 35 minutes. Do a quick release and set the meat aside. Stir in cornstarch in the remaining liquid and cook for 1 minute on Sauté to thicken the sauce. Drizzle over meat and serve.

# White Peas with Jalapeño & Bacon

Serving Size: 4 | Total Time: 30 minutes

### Ingredients

1 lb white peas
4 slices bacon
1 onion, chopped
1 jalapeño pepper, chopped
2 tbsp flour

2 tbsp butter
1 tbsp cayenne pepper
3 bay leaves, dried
Salt and black pepper to taste

### Directions

Melt butter on Sauté, and stir-fry the onion for 2-3 minutes, until translucent. Add bacon, peas, jalapeño pepper, bay leaves, salt, cayenne, and pepper. Stir in 2 tbsp of flour and add 3 cups of water. Seal the lid and cook on High Pressure for 15 minutes. Release the steam naturally, for 10 minutes.

# Homemade Braised Pork Belly

Serving Size: 10 | Total Time: 30 minutes

## Ingredients

2 lb pork belly slices
2 tbsp oil
½ tsp cinnamon, ground
¼ tsp nutmeg, ground

¼ cup honey
¼ cup red wine
2 cups orange juice
1 cup water

## Directions

Heat oil on Sauté, and brown the pork for 3 minutes. Add the remaining ingredients, Seal the lid and cook on High Pressure for 20 minutes. Do a quick release. Press Sauté and bring to a boil. Let simmer until the excess liquid evaporates. Serve warm.

# Vegetable & Ground Pork Stew

Serving Size: 6 | Total Time: 25 minutes

## Ingredients

1 ¼ pounds ground pork
1 cup cabbage, shredded
½ cup chopped celery
2 red onions, chopped
2 large tomatoes, chopped
1 carrot, shredded
2 cups water

1 red bell pepper, chopped
1 green bell pepper, chopped
1 yellow bell pepper, chopped
¼ tsp cumin
1 tsp red pepper flakes
Salt and black pepper, to taste
Freshly chopped coriander leaves, for garnish

## Directions

Coat with cooking spray. Add the pork and cook them until browned on Sauté. Stir in the remaining ingredients, and pour the water. Seal the lid and set to Pressure Cook for 15 minutes on High. Do a quick pressure release. Sprinkle with freshly chopped coriander, to serve.

# Thyme Pork Loin with Apples & Daikon

Serving Size: 4 | Total Time: 30 minutes

## Ingredients

1 pound pork loin, cut into cubes
1 onion, diced
1 daikon, chopped
1 cup vegetable broth
½ cup white wine
2 granny smith apples, peeled and diced
½ cup sliced leeks

1 tbsp vegetable oil
1 celery stalk, diced
2 tbsp dried parsley
¼ tsp thyme
½ tsp cumin
¼ tsp lemon zest
Salt and black pepper, to taste

## Directions

Season the pork with thyme, salt and pepper. Heat oil on Sauté mode. Add pork and cook for a few minutes, until browned. Add the onion and cook for 2 more minutes, until soft.

Stir in the remaining ingredients, except for the apples. Seal the lid and cook for 15 minutes on Pressure Cook mode on High. When ready, release the pressure quickly. Stir in apples, seal the lid again, and cook on High for another 5 minutes. Do a quick release.

# Pancetta Kale with Beans & Chickpeas

Serving Size: 8 | Total Time: 30 minutes

## Ingredients

5 cups water
1 pack (2 oz) onion soup mix
¼ cup olive oil
1 tbsp garlic, minced
1 ½ pounds canned chickpeas, soaked overnight

2 tsp mustard
½ pound pancetta slices, chopped
1 onion, chopped
1 cup kale, chopped
Salt and black pepper to taste

## Directions

Heat the oil and cook the onion, garlic, and pancetta for 5 minutes on Sauté mode. Add 1 cup of water, soup mix, salt, and pepper, and cook for 5 more minutes. Then, add the chickpeas and 4 cups of water.

Add in the kale and mustard. Seal the lid and cook for 15 minutes on Pressure Cook on High Pressure. Once cooking is completed, perform a quick pressure release and serve immediately.

# Pork with Onions & Cream Sauce

Serving Size: 6 | Total Time: 45 minutes

## Ingredients

1 ½ lb pork shoulder, cut into pieces
2 onions, chopped
1 ½ cups sour cream
1 cup tomato puree
½ tbsp cilantro

¼ tsp cumin
¼ tsp cayenne pepper
1 garlic clove, minced
Salt and black pepper, to taste

## Directions

Coat with cooking spray the inner pot and add the pork. Cook for 3-4 minutes on Sauté mode until lightly browned. Add onions and garlic and cook for 3 minutes, until fragrant. Press Cancel.

Stir in the remaining ingredients and seal the lid. Select Soup/Broth and cook for 30 minutes on High. When it beeps, let sit for 5 minutes before quick release the pressure.

# Easy Pork Balls with Apple Sauce

Serving Size: 8 | Total Time: 50 minutes

## Ingredients

2 ½ pounds ground pork
¼ cup tamari sauce
3 garlic cloves, minced
½ tbsp dried thyme
½ cup diced onions

2 tsp honey
¼ cup apple juice
1 ½ cups water
1 cup breadcrumbs
Salt and black pepper to taste

## Directions

Whisk together honey, tamari, apple juice, water, and thyme in the pressure cooker. Season with salt and pepper. Set on Sauté mode and cook for 15 minutes, lid off.

Meanwhile, combine all the remaining ingredients in a bowl. Shape meatballs out of the mixture. Drop the meatballs into the sauce, and press Cancel.

Seal the lid, and set on Pressure Cook mode for 15 minutes on High. When done, release the pressure naturally, for 10 minutes. Serve immediately.

# Boneless Short Ribs with Wine Mushroom Sauce

Serving Size: 4 | Total Time: 70 minutes

## Ingredients

2 lb boneless pork short ribs, cut into 3-inch pieces
Salt and black pepper to taste
½ onion, chopped
½ cup red wine
3 tbsp oil
Minced parsley to garnish

½ tbsp tomato paste
2 carrots, sliced
2 cups mushrooms, sliced
1 tbsp cornstarch

## Directions

Rub the ribs on all sides with salt and black pepper. Heat the oil on Sauté and brown short ribs on all sides, about 6-7 minutes Remove ribs to a plate. Add onion and cook for 3-5 minutes. Pour in wine and tomato paste to deglaze by scraping any browned bits from the bottom of the cooker. Cook for 2 minutes until wine has reduced slightly. Return ribs to the pot and cover with carrots. Pour 1 cup of water over ribs and carrots.

Hit Cancel to stop Sauté mode. Seal the lid, and select Meat/Stew on High Pressure for 35 minutes. When ready, let pressure release naturally for 10 minutes. Transfer ribs and carrots to a plate.

To the pot, add mushrooms. Press Sauté and cook the mushrooms for 2-4 minutes. In a bowl, add 2 tbsp of water and cornstarch and mix until smooth. Pour this slurry into the pot, stirring constantly, until it thickens slightly, 2 minutes. Season gravy with salt and pepper to taste. Pour over the ribs and garnish with minced parsley.

# Fennel Pork Butt with Mushrooms

Serving Size: 8 | Total Time: 30 minutes

## Ingredients

1 pound pork butt, sliced
2 cups mushrooms, sliced
1 fennel bulb, chopped
½ cup white wine

1 tsp garlic, minced
½ cup vegetable broth
Salt and black pepper, to taste

## Directions

Grease with cooking spray and heat on Sauté mode. Brown the pork slices and for a few minutes. Stir in the remaining ingredients. Season with salt and pepper. Seal the lid and cook for 20 minutes on Meat/Stew on High. When done, do a quick release.

# Savory Pork Chops with Brussel Sprouts

Serving Size: 4 | Total Time: 30 minutes

## Ingredients

4 pork chops
½ pound Brussel sprouts
¼ cup sparkling wine
1 ½ cups beef stock
2 shallots, chopped

1 tbsp olive oil
1 cup celery stalk, chopped
1 tbsp coriander
Salt and black pepper to taste

## Directions

Heat olive oil on Sauté. Add the pork chops and cook until browned on all sides. Stir in the remaining ingredients. Seal the lid and cook for 20 minutes on Meat/Stew on High. Release the pressure quickly.

# Turmeric Pork Meatloaf with Ketchup Topping

Serving Size: 4 | Total Time: 30 minutes

## Ingredients

### For the Meatloaf:

2 pounds ground pork
2 garlic cloves, minced
1 cup bread crumbs
1 large-sized egg
1 cup milk

2 small onions, finely chopped
Salt and black pepper, to taste
½ tsp turmeric powder
½ tsp dried oregano

### For the Topping:

1 cup ketchup
2 tbsp brown sugar
¼ cup tomato paste

1 tsp garlic powder
½ tsp onion powder
½ tsp cayenne pepper

## Directions

Place the trivet at the bottom of your pressure cooker and pour 1 cup of water. Lightly grease a round sheet pan, that fits in your pressure cooker.

Combine ground pork, bread crumbs, milk, onions, egg, garlic, salt, pepper, oregano, and turmeric powder together in a mixing bowl. Shape into a loaf and place onto the prepared sheet pan.

In another bowl, mix the ingredients for the topping. Spread the topping over the meatloaf and lower the sheet pan onto the trivet. Seal the lid, select Pressure Cook and cook for 24 minutes on High. Do a quick pressure release. Remove to a cutting board and slice before serving.

# German-Style Sauerkraut & Pork Stew

Serving Size: 4 | Total Time: 25 minutes

## Ingredients

1 pound ground pork
4 cups sauerkraut, shredded
1 cup tomato puree
1 cup vegetable stock

1 red onion, chopped
2 garlic cloves, minced
2 bay leaves
Salt and black pepper to taste

## Directions

Add onion, garlic, and cook until soft and fragrant, on Sauté. Add the pork and cook it until lightly browned. Stir in the remaining ingredients, and season with salt, and black pepper.

Seal the lid and cook for 20 minutes on Meat/Stew on High. When done, press Cancel and release the pressure quickly. Discard the bay leaves, serve and enjoy.

# Party Apple-Glazed Pork Ribs

Serving Size: 4 | Total Time: 45 minutes

## Ingredients

½ cup apple cider vinegar
2 pounds pork ribs

3 ½ cups apple juice
Salt and black pepper to taste

## Directions

Pour apple juice and apple cider vinegar into the pressure cooker and lower the trivet. Season the pork ribs with salt and pepper, and place on top of the trivet and seal the lid. Cook on High pressure for 30 minutes. Once it goes off, let the valve drop on its own for a natural release, for about 10 minutes.

# Garlic-Spicy Ground Pork with Peas

Serving Size: 6 | Total Time: 55 minutes

## Ingredients

2 pounds ground pork
1 onion, diced
1 can diced tomatoes
1 can peas
5 garlic cloves, crushed
3 tbsp butter
1 serrano pepper, chopped

1 cup beef broth
1 tsp ground ginger
2 tsp ground coriander
Salt and black pepper to taste
¾ tsp cumin
¼ tsp cayenne pepper
½ tsp turmeric

## Directions

Melt butter on Sauté mode. Add onion and cook for 3 minutes, until soft. Stir in the spices and garlic and cook for 2 more minutes. Add pork and cook until browned.

Pour broth and add serrano pepper, peas, and tomatoes. Seal the lid and cook for 30 minutes on Meat/Stew on High. When ready, release the pressure naturally for 10 minutes.

# Baby Carrot & Onion Pork Chops

Serving Size: 4 | Total Time: 30 minutes

## Ingredients

1 pound pork chops
1 pound baby carrots
1 onion, sliced
1 tbsp butter

1 cup vegetable broth
1 tsp garlic powder
Salt and black pepper, to taste

## Directions

Season the pork with salt and pepper. Melt butter on Sauté, and brown the pork on all sides. Stir in carrots and onion and cook for 2 more minutes, until soft. Pour in the broth, and add garlic powder. Season with salt and pepper. Seal the lid and cook for 20 minutes on Meat/Stew on High. When ready, release the pressure quickly.

# Pork Tenderloin with Cherries & Apples

Serving Size: 4 | Total Time: 55 minutes

## Ingredients

1 ¼ pounds pork tenderloin
1 chopped celery stalk
2 cups apples, peeled and chopped
1 cup cherries, pitted
½ cup apple juice

½ cup water
¼ cup onions, chopped
Salt and black pepper to taste
2 tbsp olive oil

## Directions

Heat oil on Sauté mode, and cook the onions and celery for 5 minutes until softened. Season the pork with salt and pepper, and add to the cooker. Brown for 2-3 minutes per side.

Then, top with apples and cherries, and pour the water and apple juice. Seal the lid and cook on Meat/Stew mode for 40 minutes, on High pressure.

Once ready, do a quick pressure release. Slice the pork tenderloin and arrange on a serving platter. Spoon the apple-cheery sauce over the pork slices, to serve.

# Merlot Pork Chops

Serving Size: 4 | Total Time: 40 minutes

## Ingredients

4 pork chops
3 carrots, chopped
1 tomato, chopped
1 onion, chopped
2 garlic cloves, minced
¼ cup merlot red wine
½ cup beef broth

1 tsp dried oregano
2 tbsp olive oil
2 tbsp flour
2 tbsp water
2 tbsp tomato paste
1 beef bouillon cube
Salt and black pepper to taste

## Directions

Heat the oil on Sauté mode. In a bowl, mix in flour, pepper, and salt. Coat the pork chops. Place them in the pressure cooker and cook for a few minutes, until browned on all sides.

Add the carrots, onion, garlic, and oregano. Cook for 2 more minutes. Stir in the remaining ingredients and seal the lid. Cook on Soup/Broth and cook for 25 minutes on High. When ready, do a natural pressure release, for 10 minutes, and serve immediately.

# Vegetable Casserole with Smoked Bacon

Serving Size: 4 | Total Time: 30 minutes

## Ingredients

½ pound smoked bacon, chopped
½ cup carrots, sliced
2 cups water
1 cup vegetable stock

¾ cup half and half
4 golden potatoes, peeled and chopped
4 endives, halved lengthwise
Salt and black pepper to taste

## Directions

Set on Sauté mode and add the bacon. Cook for 2 minutes until slightly crispy. Add the potatoes, carrots, water, and vegetable stock. Seal the lid and cook for 10 minutes on High Pressure. Press Cancel and release the pressure quickly. Add the endives and cook for 5 more minutes on High Pressure. Press Cancel again and quick-release the pressure.

Strain the bacon and veggies and return them to the pressure cooker. Add the half and half and season with salt and pepper. Cook on Sauté mode, for 3 more minutes, lid off.

# Friday Night BBQ Pork Butt

Serving Size: 6 | Total Time: 55 minutes

## Ingredients

2 pounds pork butt
¼ tsp garlic powder
Salt and black pepper to taste
1 cup barbecue sauce

¼ tsp cumin powder
½ tsp onion powder
1 ½ cups beef broth

## Directions

In a bowl, combine the barbecue sauce and all of the spices. Brush the pork with the mixture. On Sauté, coat with cooking oil. Add the pork, and sear on all sides, for a few minutes.

Pour the beef broth around the meat. Seal the lid and cook for 40 minutes on Meat/Stew on High. When ready, press Cancel and wait 5 minutes before releasing the pressure quickly.

# Tasty Cajun Pork Chops

Serving Size: 4 | Total Time: 80 minutes

## Ingredients

2 pounds pork chops
1 cup beef broth
1 onion, diced

*Marinade:*
2 tbsp fish sauce
½ tsp Cajun seasoning
2 tsp garlic, minced

2 tbsp potato starch
1 carrot, chopped
Salt and black pepper to taste

½ cup soy sauce
1 tbsp sesame oil

## Directions

Combine marinade ingredients in a bowl. Add in the pork chops and let marinate for 30 minutes.

Coat the pressure cooker with cooking spray. Add onion and carrot and cook until soft on Sauté. Add the pork chops along with the marinade. Whisk in the broth and starch.

Seal the lid and cook for 40 minutes on Meat/Stew on High. Do a quick release and serve.

# Broccoli & Cauliflower Pork Sausages

Serving Size: 6 | Total Time: 20 minutes

## Ingredients

1 pound pork sausage, sliced
½ pound broccoli florets
½ pound cauliflower florets
10 ounces canned mushroom soup

10 ounces canned cauliflower soup
10 ounces evaporated milk
Salt and black pepper to taste

## Directions

Place roughly ¼ of the sausage slices in your pressure cooker. In a bowl, whisk together the soups, salt, pepper, and milk. Pour some of the mixtures over the sausages.

Top the sausage slices with ¼ of the cauliflower and broccoli florets. Pour some of the soup mixtures again. Repeat the layers until you use up all ingredients. Seal the lid, and cook on Pressure Cook for 10 minutes, on High. When ready, do a quick release.

# One-Pot Pork Sausages with Peppers & Onions

Serving Size: 8 | Total Time: 20 minutes

## Ingredients

8 pork sausages
2 large sweet onions, sliced
4 red bell peppers, cut into strips
1 tbsp olive oil

½ cup beef broth
¼ cup white wine
1 tsp garlic, minced
Salt and black pepper to taste

## Directions

On Sauté, add the sausages, and brown them for a few minutes. Remove to a plate and discard the liquid. Press Cancel. Wipe clean the cooker and heat the oil on Sauté mode.

Stir in onions and bell peppers. Stir-fry them for 5 minutes, until soft. Add garlic and cook for a minute. Add the sausages and pour in broth and wine. Season with salt and pepper. Seal the lid and cook for 5 minutes on High pressure. Once done, do a quick pressure release.

# Oregano Pork with Apples & Dijon Mustard

Serving Size: 6 | Total Time: 60 minutes

## Ingredients

3 pounds pork roast
2 apples, peeled and sliced
3 tbsp Dijon mustard
1 tbsp dried oregano
½ cup white wine

1 cup water
1 tbsp garlic, minced
1 tbsp olive oil
Salt and black pepper to taste

## Directions

Brush the pork with mustard. Heat oil on Sauté, and sear the pork on all sides, for a few minutes. Add apples and stir in the remaining ingredients.

Seal the lid and cook for 40 minutes on Meat/Stew on High Pressure. When ready, release the pressure naturally for 10 minutes. The internal temperature should be at least 160 F.

# Beef Steaks with Onion Gravy

Serving Size: 4 | Total Time: 30 minutes

## Ingredients

4 round beef steaks
2 onions, sliced
1 ½ cups beef broth
1 tsp garlic, minced
1 tbsp dried parsley
½ tsp rosemary

1 tbsp oil
½ tsp red pepper flakes
¼ cup half and half
2 tbsp flour
Salt and black pepper to taste

## Directions

Heat the oil on Sauté mode. Add the beef and brown the steaks on all sides. Remove to a plate. Sauté the onions and garlic for 2 minutes, until translucent and fragrant.

Return the steaks to the pressure cooker. Stir in the salt, pepper, pepper flakes, rosemary, parsley, and pour in broth. Seal the lid and cook for 20 minutes on Meat/Stew on High.

When ready, do a quick pressure release, and stir in the flour and half and half. Cook for 3 more minutes, until thickened, with the lid off, on Sauté mode. Serve immediately.

# Easy Pork Fillets with Peachy Sauce

Serving Size: 6 | Total Time: 30 minutes

## Ingredients

1 lb pork loin fillets
16 ounces canned peach
½ tsp cilantro, ground
½ tsp ginger, finely chopped
½ cup Worcestershire sauce
¼ cup apple cider vinegar
½ tsp garlic, minced

Salt and black pepper to taste
1 cup onions, sliced
1 tbsp brown sugar
2 tbsp olive oil
1 cup tomato sauce
1 tbsp arrowroot slurry

## Directions

On Sauté mode, heat oil. Cook onions until tender, for about 4 minutes. Stir in the remaining ingredients, except for the arrowroot. Seal the lid, Select Meat/Stew and cook for 20 minutes on High. Do a quick pressure release. Stir in the arrowroot slurry and cook on Sauté, until the sauce thickens.

# Cinnamon BBQ Pork Ribs

Serving Size: 6 | Total Time: 60 minutes

## Ingredients

3 pounds pork ribs
½ cup apple jelly
1 cup barbecue sauce
1 onion, diced
2 tbsp ground cloves

½ cup water
1 tbsp brown sugar
1 tsp Worcestershire sauce
1 tsp ground cinnamon
Salt and black pepper to taste

## Directions

Whisk together all ingredients in your pressure cooker, except the ribs. Place the ribs inside and seal the lid. Set the cooker to Meat/Stew mode and cook for 50 minutes on High. Release the pressure naturally.

# Fruity Pork Steaks

Serving Size: 4 | Total Time: 358 minutes

## Ingredients

4 pork steaks
¼ cup milk
8 prunes, pitted
½ cup white wine
2 apples, peeled and sliced

¼ cup heavy cream
1 tbsp fruit jelly
½ tsp ground ginger
Salt and black pepper to taste

## Directions

Place all ingredients, except the jelly, in your pressure cooker. Stir to combine well, and season with salt and pepper. Seal the lid and cook on High Pressure for 15 minutes. Once done, wait 5 minutes and do a quick pressure release. Stir in the jelly, serve, and enjoy.

# Pork Sirloin Chili

Serving Size: 6 | Total Time: 45 minutes

## Ingredients

3 pounds sirloin pork roast
1 tbsp honey
1 tsp chili powder
1 tbsp rosemary

1 tbsp olive oil
1 ¼ cups water
Salt and black pepper to taste
2 tbsp lemon juice

## Directions

Combine the spices, in a bowl, and rub them onto the pork. Heat oil on Sauté mode and sear the pork on all sides. Stir in the remaining ingredients and seal the lid. Cook for 30 minutes, on Meat/Stew on High. Do a natural pressure release, for 15 minutes.

# Apple Cider Pork Chops

Serving Size: 4 | Total Time: 35 minutes

## Ingredients

1 lb pork fillets
½ lb granny smith apples, cut into wedges
2 leeks, white part only, cut into rings
2 tbsp olive oil
1 ¼ cups apple cider

1 tsp chili pepper
Salt and black pepper, to taste
1 tsp dry rosemary
1 tsp dry thyme

## Directions

On Sauté mode, heat 1 tbsp of olive oil. Season the pork with salt, black and chili pepper. Brown the fillets for about 4 minutes per side. Set aside. Heat the remaining oil in the pressure cooker.

Add in leeks and Sauté until soft, for about 4 minutes. Add in apples, rosemary, thyme and pour in cider. Place the pork loin among the apples and leeks. Seal the lid and cook for 20 minutes on Meat/Stew on High.

Once cooking is complete, perform a quick pressure release and remove the lid. To serve, arrange the pork on a plate and pour the apple leeks mixture over the pork tenderloins.

# Chili-Braised Pork Chops with Tomatoes

Serving Size: 4 | Total Time: 30 minutes

## Ingredients

| | |
|---|---|
| 4 pork chops | ½ cup beer |
| 1 onion, chopped | ½ cup vegetable stock |
| 2 tbsp chili powder | 1 tsp olive oil |
| 14 oz canned tomatoes with green chilies | Salt and black pepper to taste |
| 1 garlic clove, minced | |

## Directions

Heat oil on Sauté mode. Add onion, garlic, and chili powder and cook for 2 minutes. Add the pork chops and cook until browned on all sides.

Stir in the tomatoes, stock, and beer. Season with salt and pepper. Seal the lid and cook for 20 minutes on Meat/Stew on High. When ready, quick release the pressure and serve hot.

# White Mushrooms & Pork Chops with Tomato Sauce

Serving Size: 4 | Total Time: 35 minutes

## Ingredients

| | |
|---|---|
| 4 large bone-in pork chops | 1 tsp garlic, minced |
| 1 cup tomato sauce | ½ cup water |
| 1 ½ cups white button mushrooms, sliced | 1 tbsp oil |
| 1 onion, chopped | Salt and black pepper, to taste |

## Directions

Heat oil on Sauté. Add garlic, onion and cook for 2 minutes, until soft and fragrant. Add pork and cook until browned on all sides. Stir in the remaining ingredients and seal the lid. Cook for 20 minutes on Meat/Stew on High. When ready, do a quick pressure release.

# Awesome Herby Pork Butt with Yams

Serving Size: 4 | Total Time: 25 minutes

## Ingredients

| | |
|---|---|
| 1 pound pork butt, cut into 4 equal pieces | ¼ tsp oregano |
| 1 pound yams, diced | 1 ½ tsp sage |
| 2 tsp butter | 1 ½ cups beef broth |
| ¼ tsp thyme | Salt and black pepper, to taste |

## Directions

Season the pork with thyme, sage, oregano, salt, and pepper. Melt butter on Sauté mode. Add pork and cook until brown, for a 5 minutes. Add the yams and pour the broth. Seal the lid and cook for 20 minutes on Meat/Stew on High. Do a quick release and serve hot.

# Garlic Mashed Potatoes with Italian Sausages

Serving Size: 6 | Total Time: 30 minutes

## Ingredients

1 ½ cups water
6 Italian sausages
1 tbsp olive oil
2 garlic cloves, smashed
4 large potatoes, peeled and cut into chunks

1/3 cup butter, melted
¼ cup milk
Salt and black pepper to taste
1 tbsp chopped chives

## Directions

Select Sauté and heat olive oil. Cook for 8-10 minutes, turning periodically until browned. Set aside. Wipe the pot with paper towels. Add in water and set steamer rack over water and steamer basket onto the rack. Place potatoes to the steamer basket. Seal the lid and cook on High Pressure for 12 minutes.

Release the pressure quickly. Remove basket and rack from the pot. Drain water from the pot. Return potatoes to pot. Add in salt, butter, pepper, garlic, and milk and use a hand masher to mash until no large lumps remain. Using an immersion blender, blend potatoes on Low for 1 minute until fluffy and light.

Avoid over-blending to ensure the potatoes do not become gluey! Transfer the mash to a serving plate, Top with sausages and scatter chopped chives over to serve.

# Pork Belly with Maple Syrup, Garlic & Tamari Sauce

Serving Size: 6 | Total Time: 40 minutes

## Ingredients

4 garlic cloves, sliced
½ tsp ground cloves
1 tsp grated fresh ginger
1 ½ pounds pork belly, sliced
2 ¼ cups water
¼ cup white wine

½ cup Yellow onions, peeled and chopped
¼ cup tamari sauce
1 tsp sugar maple syrup
4 cups white rice, cooked, warm
Salt and black pepper to taste

## Directions

Brown pork belly, for about 6 minutes per side, on Sauté mode. Add the remaining ingredients. Seal the lid and cook for 25 minutes on Pressure Cook on High Pressure. Cook until the meat is tender. Switch the pressure release valve to open, and do a quick pressure release. Serve with rice.

# Macaroni & Cheddar Cheese with Chorizo

Serving Size: 6 | Total Time: 25 minutes

## Ingredients

1 pound macaroni
3 ounces chorizo, chopped
3 cups water
1 tbsp garlic powder

2 tbsp minced garlic
2 cups milk
2 cups cheddar cheese, shredded
Salt to taste

## Directions

On Sauté and stir-fry chorizo until crispy, for about 6 minutes. Set aside. Wipe the pot with kitchen paper. Add in water, macaroni, garlic, and salt to taste. Seal lid and cook on for 5 minutes High Pressure.

Release the pressure quickly. Stir in cheese, garlic powder, and milk until the cheese melts. Divide the mac and cheese between serving bowls. Top with chorizo and serve.

# Delicious Pork & Garbanzo Bean Chili

Serving Size: 10 | Total Time: 55 minutes

## Ingredients

1 lb garbanzo beans, soaked overnight
1 tbsp olive oil
2 onions, finely chopped
2 ½ pounds ground pork
1 small jalapeño with seeds, minced
6 garlic cloves, minced
¼ cup chili powder
2 tbsp ground cumin

2 tsp salt
1 tsp smoked paprika
1 tsp dried oregano
1 tsp garlic powder
¼ tsp cayenne pepper
2 ½ cups beef broth
1 (6-ounce) can tomato puree

## Directions

Add the beans and pour in cold water to cover 1 inch. Seal the lid and cook for 20 minutes on High Pressure. Release the pressure quickly.

Drain beans and rinse with cold water. Set aside. Wipe clean the pot and set to Sauté mode. Warm olive oil, add in onions, and sauté for 3 minutes until soft.

Add jalapeño, pork, and garlic, and stir-fry for 5 minutes until is cooked through. Stir in chili powder, salt, garlic powder, paprika, cumin, oregano, and cayenne, and cook until soft, about 30 seconds. Pour in broth, beans, and tomato puree.

Seal the lid and cook for 20 minutes on High Pressure. Release the pressure naturally. Open the lid, press Sauté, and cook as you stir until desired consistency is attained. Spoon chili into bowls and serve.

# Best Pork Chops with BBQ Sauce & Veggies

Serving Size: 4 | Total Time: 25 minutes

## Ingredients

4 pork rib chops
1 cup carrots, thinly sliced
1 cup turnips, thinly sliced

1 cup onions, slice into rings
1 ½ cups BBQ sauce
2 cups water

## Directions

Add the pork chops in your cooker. Pour in half cup of BBQ sauce and 2 cups of water. Select Meat/Stew mode. Stir in the onions, turnips, and carrots. Lock the lid and cook for 20 minutes on High. Once ready, release the pressure quickly. Open the lid, drizzle with the remaining BBQ sauce and serve.

# Pork Ribs with Onions

Serving Size: 4 | Total Time: 35 minutes

## Ingredients

1 ½ cups tomato puree
1 tbsp garlic, minced
1 ½ cups water
Salt and black pepper to taste

½ tsp dried sage
1 ¼ cups sweet onions
½ cup carrots, thinly sliced
1 lb cut pork spare ribs

## Directions

Brown the ribs on Sauté. Pour in water and tomato puree. Add the remaining ingredients. Seal the lid and cook for 30 minutes on Pressure Cook on High. Once ready, do a quick pressure release and serve.

# Modern Minestrone with Pancetta

Serving Size: 6 | Total Time: 35 minutes

### Ingredients

2 tbsp olive oil
2 ounces pancetta, chopped
1 onion, diced
1 parsnip, peeled and chopped
2 carrots, peeled and cut into rounds
2 celery stalks,
2 garlic cloves, minced
1 tbsp dried basil
1 tbsp dried thyme

1 tbsp dried oregano
6 cups vegetable broth
2 cups green beans, trimmed and chopped
1 (15-ounce) can diced tomatoes
1 (15-ounce) can chickpeas, rinsed and drained
1 ½ cups small shaped pasta
Salt and black pepper to taste
½ cup grated Parmesan cheese

### Directions

Heat oil on Sauté. Add onion, carrots, garlic, pancetta, celery, and parsnip, and cook for 5 minutes until they become soft. Stir in basil, oregano, beans, broth, tomatoes, pepper, salt, thyme, chickpeas, and pasta.

Seal the lid and cook for 6 minutes on High Pressure. Release pressure naturally for 10 minutes, then release the remaining pressure quickly.

Ladle the soup into bowls and serve garnished with Parmesan.

# Beer Pork Roast with Mushrooms

Serving Size: 8 | Total Time: 50 minutes

### Ingredients

3 pounds pork roast
8 ounces mushrooms, sliced
12 ounces root beer

10 ounces cream mushroom soup
1 package dry onion soup

### Directions

In the pressure cooker, whisk together mushroom soup, dry onion soup mix, and root beer. Add the mushrooms and pork.

Seal the lid, and set to Meat/Stew mode for 40 minutes on High. When ready, let sit for 5 minutes before doing a quick pressure release.

# Roast Lamb Leg with Potatoes

Serving Size: 6 | Total Time: 35 minutes

### Ingredients

2 lb lamb leg
2 garlic cloves
1 tbsp fresh thyme, chopped
1 lb potatoes
1 lemon, chopped

3 tbsp oil
¼ cup red wine vinegar
1 tsp brown sugar
1 tsp salt

### Directions

Place the potatoes in the pot, and pour enough water to cover. Season with salt, add garlic, and seal the lid. Set on Meat/Stew mode. Cook for 20 minutes on High Pressure. Do a quick release and remove potatoes; reserve the liquid. Rub the meat with oil and thyme. Place in the pot.

Pour in red wine vinegar, sugar, and add lemon. Add 1 cup of the reserved liquid and seal the lid. Cook on High Pressure for 7 minutes. Do a quick release.

# Rosemary Lamb Chops with Mashed Potatoes

Serving Size: 8 | Total Time: 40 minutes

## Ingredients

8 lamb chops
Salt to taste
3 sprigs rosemary leaves, chopped
3 tbsp butter, softened
1 tbsp olive oil
1 tbsp tomato puree

1 green onion, chopped
1 cup beef stock
5 potatoes, peeled and chopped
1/3 cup milk
4 cilantro leaves, for garnish

## Directions

Rub rosemary leaves and salt to the lamb chops. Warm oil and 2 tbsp of butter on Sauté mode. Brown lamb chops for 1 minute per each side; set aside on a plate.

In the pot, mix tomato puree and green onion; cook for 2-3 minutes. Add beef stock into the pot to deglaze, scrape the bottom to get rid of any browned bits of food. Return lamb chops alongside any accumulated juices to the pot. Set a steamer rack on lamb chops. Place steamer basket on the rack. Arrange potatoes in the steamer basket. Seal the lid and cook on High Pressure for 4 minutes. Release the Pressure quickly.

Remove trivet and steamer basket from the pot. In a high speed blender, add potatoes, milk, salt, and remaining butter. Blend well until you obtain a smooth consistency. Divide the potato mash onto serving dishes. Lay lamb chops on the mash. Drizzle with cooking liquid obtained from the cooker, and sprinkle with cilantro.

# Simple Roast Lamb

Serving Size: 4 | Total Time: 40 minutes

## Ingredients

2 lb lamb leg
1 tbsp garlic powder
3 tbsp extra virgin olive oil

Salt and black pepper to taste
4 rosemary sprigs, chopped

## Directions

Grease the inner pot with oil. Rub the meat with salt, pepper, and garlic powder, and place in the instant pot. Pour enough water to cover and seal the lid. Cook on Meat/Stew for 30 minutes on High. Do a quick release. Make sure the meat is tender and falls off the bones. Top with cooking juices and rosemary.

# Leg of Lamb with Garlic and Pancetta

Serving Size: 6 | Total Time: 50 minutes

## Ingredients

2 lb lamb leg
6 garlic cloves
1 large onion, chopped
6 pancetta slices

1 tsp rosemary
Salt and black pepper to taste
2 tbsp oil
3 cups beef broth

## Directions:

Heat oil on Sauté. Add pancetta and onion, making two layers. Season with salt and cook for 3 minutes, until lightly browned.

Meanwhile, place the meat in a separate dish. Using a sharp knife, make 6 incisions into the meat and place a garlic clove in each. Rub the meat with spices and transfer to the pot. Press Cancel and pour in beef broth.

Seal the lid and cook on High pressure for 25 minutes. When done, do a natural pressure release, for about 10 minutes.

# Savory Irish Lamb Stew

Serving Size: 4 | Total Time: 30 minutes

## Ingredients

1 pound lamb, cut into pieces
1 ½ tbsp canola oil
1 onion, sliced
2 tbsp cornstarch
2 potatoes, cubed

2 carrots, chopped
2 ½ cups beef broth
½ tsp dried oregano
Salt and black pepper to taste

## Directions

Season lamb with salt and pepper. Heat canola oil on Sauté and sear the lamb until browned on all sides, about 4-5 minute. Add all the remaining ingredients, except for the cornstarch, and stir to combine.

Seal the lid and cook on High Pressure for 18 minutes. When ready, do a quick pressure release. Whisk the cornstarch with a little bit of water and stir it into the stew. Cook on Sauté for 3 more minutes, lid off. Serve hot.

# Lamb with Tomato & Green Peas

Serving Size: 3 | Total Time: 65 minutes

## Ingredients

1 cup green peas
1 lb lamb, cubed
1 tomato, roughly chopped
1 onion, peeled, chopped
2 carrots, peeled, chopped
1 celery stalk, chopped

A handful of parsley, chopped
2 garlic cloves, crushed
4 tbsp tomato sauce, canned
2 tbsp olive oil
4 cups vegetable stock
Salt and black pepper to taste

## Directions

Warm oil on Sauté and cook onion, carrots, celery, and garlic for 8 minutes until tender. Add in the lamb and sauté for another 5-6 minutes. Season with salt and black pepper.

Add in all the remaining ingredients except for the parsley and seal the lid. Cook on High Pressure for 30 minutes. Do a natural Pressure release for about 10 minutes. Top with parsley to serve.

# Lamb Stew with Lemon & Parsley

Serving Size: 4 | Total Time: 60 minutes

## Ingredients

1 lb lamb neck, boneless
2 potatoes, peeled, cut into bite-sized pieces
2 large carrots, chopped
1 tomato, diced
1 small red bell pepper, chopped

1 garlic head, whole
A handful of fresh parsley, chopped
¼ cup lemon juice
Salt and black pepper to taste
2 cups water

## Directions

Add the meat and season with salt. Add in the remaining ingredients, tuck in one garlic head in the middle of the pot and add water.

Add parsley and seal the lid. Cook on High Pressure for 45 minutes. When ready, do a quick release.

# Quick French-Style Lamb with Sesame

Serving Size: 4 | Total Time: 35 minutes

## Ingredients

1 cup rice
1 cup green peas
12 oz lamb, tender cuts, ½-inch thick
3 tbsp sesame seeds

4 cups beef broth
1 tsp salt
½ tsp dried thyme
3 tbsp butter

## Directions

Mix the meat in the pot with broth. Seal the lid and cook on High Pressure for 13 minutes. Do a quick release. Remove the meat but keep the liquid. Add rice and green peas. Season with salt and thyme. Stir well and top with the meat. Seal the lid and cook on Rice for 8 minutes on High. Do a quick release and stir in butter and sesame seeds.

# Garlic Lamb with Thyme

Serving Size: 4 | Total Time: 60 minutes

## Ingredients

2 lb lamb, cubed
2 garlic cloves, minced
1 cup onions, chopped
1 cup red wine
2 cups beef stock

2 tbsp butter, softened
2 celery stalks, chopped
1 tbsp fresh thyme
2 tbsp flour
Salt and black pepper to taste

## Directions

Rub the lamb with salt and pepper. Melt butter on Sauté and cook onions, celery, and garlic for 5 minutes. Add lamb and fry until browned, for about 5-6 minutes. Dust the flour and stir. Pour in the stock and red wine, seal the lid, and cook on High Pressure for 30 minutes. Do a natural release, for 10 minutes. Serve garnished with thyme.

# Traditional Lamb with Vegetables

Serving Size: 6 | Total Time: 25 minutes

## Ingredients

1 lb lamb chops, 1-inch thick
1 cup water
1 cup green peas, rinsed
3 carrots, chopped
3 onions, chopped

1 potato, chopped
1 tomato, roughly chopped
3 tbsp olive oil
1 tbsp paprika
Salt and black pepper to taste

## Directions

Grease the instant pot with olive oil. Rub salt onto meat and make a bottom layer. Add peas, carrots, onions, potato, and tomato. Season with paprika. Add olive oil, water, salt, and pepper. Give it a good stir and seal the lid. Cook on Meat/Stew mode for 20 minutes on High Pressure. When ready, do a natural Pressure release.

# *Fish and Seafood*

## Awesome Shrimp with Okra & Brussels Sprouts

Serving Size: 8 | Total Time: 60 minutes

### Ingredients

1 lb large shrimp, cleaned, rinsed
6 oz Brussels sprouts, outer leaves removed
4 oz of okra, whole
2 carrots, chopped
2 cups vegetable broth
2 tomatoes, diced
2 tbsp tomato paste

½ tsp cayenne pepper, ground
Salt and black pepper to taste
1 cup olive oil, plus 2 tbsp
¼ cup balsamic vinegar
1 tbsp fresh rosemary, chopped
1 small celery stalk, for decoration
2 tbsp sour cream, optionally

### Directions

Mix oil, vinegar, rosemary, salt, and pepper in a large bowl. Stir and submerge the shrimp into the mixture. Toss well to coat and refrigerate for 20 minutes. Add tomatoes, tomato paste, 2 tbsp olive oil, and cayenne pepper.

Cook on Sauté for 5 minutes, stirring constantly. Remove to a bowl, cover and set aside. Pour in broth, and add Brussels sprouts, carrots, and okra. Sprinkle with salt, black pepper and seal the lid.

Cook on High pressure for 15 minutes. Then, do a quick release. Remove the vegetables and add shrimp in the remaining broth. Seal the lid again and cook on Steam for 3 minutes on High.

Do a quick release and set aside. Add the remaining oil, and cooked vegetables. Cook for 2-3 minutes, stirring constantly, on Sauté. Remove to a bowl. Top with sour cream and drizzle with shrimp marinade.

## Seafood Chowder with Mussels & Oyster Crackers

Serving Size: 4 | Total Time: 20 minutes

### Ingredients

2 cups oyster crackers
2 tbsp olive oil
¼ cup grated pecorino romano cheese
½ tsp garlic powder
Salt and black pepper to taste
2 pancetta slices
2 celery stalks, chopped
1 medium onion, chopped
1 tbsp flour

¼ cup white wine
1 cup water
20 oz canned mussels, drained, liquid reserved
1 pound potatoes, peeled and cut chunks
1 tsp dried rosemary
1 bay leaf
1 ½ cups heavy cream
2 tbsp chopped fresh chervil

### Directions

Fry pancetta on Sauté for 5 minutes, until crispy. Remove to a paper towel–lined plate and set aside. Sauté the celery and onion in the same fat for 1 minute, stirring, until the vegetables soften.

Mix in the flour to coat the vegetables. Pour in the wine simmer. Cook for about 1 minute or until reduced by about one-third. Pour in the water, the reserved mussel liquid, potatoes, salt, rosemary, and bay leaf.

Seal the lid and cook on High Pressure for 4 minutes. Do a natural pressure release for 5 minutes. Stir in the mussels and heavy cream. Press Sauté and bring the soup to a simmer to heat the mussels through. Discard the bay leaf. Spoon the soup into bowls and crumble the pancetta over the top. Garnish with the chervil, cheese, and crackers, on side.

# Mediterranean Cod with Cherry Tomatoes

Serving Size: 4 | Total Time: 20 minutes

## Ingredients

1 lb cherry tomatoes, halved
1 bunch fresh thyme sprigs
4 fillets cod
1 tsp olive oil
1 clove garlic, pressed
Salt and black pepper to taste

2 cups water
1 cup white rice
1 cup kalamata olives
2 tbsp pickled capers
1 tbsp olive oil

## Directions

Line a parchment paper on the basket of the pot. Place about half the tomatoes in a single layer on the paper. Sprinkle with thyme, reserving some for garnish. Arrange cod fillets on top. Sprinkle with olive oil.

Spread the garlic, pepper, salt, and remaining tomatoes over the fish. In the pot, mix rice and water.

Lay a trivet over the rice and water. Lower steamer basket onto the trivet. Seal the lid, and cook for 7 minutes on Low Pressure. Release the Pressure quickly. Remove the steamer basket and trivet from the pot. Use a fork to fluff rice. Plate the fish fillets and apply a garnish of olives, reserved thyme, remaining olive oil, and capers. Serve with rice.

# Thyme Sea Bass with Turnips

Serving Size: 4 | Total Time: 15 minutes

## Ingredients

1 ½ cups water
1 lemon, chopped
4 sea bass fillets
4 sprigs thyme

1 white onion, chopped into thin rings
2 turnips, chopped
Salt and black pepper to taste
2 tsp olive oil

## Directions

Add water and set a rack into the pot. Line a parchment paper to the bottom of the steamer basket. Place lemon slices in a single layer on the rack.

Arrange fillets on the top of the lemons, cover with onion and thyme sprigs. Top with turnips. Drizzle pepper, salt, and olive oil over the mixture. Put steamer basket onto the rack. Seal lid and cook on Low pressure for 8 minutes. Release the pressure quickly. Serve over the delicate onion rings and thinly turnips.

# Mussels With Lemon & White Wine

Serving Size: 5 | Total Time: 15 minutes

## Ingredients

1 cup white wine
½ cup water
1 tsp garlic powder

2 pounds mussels, cleaned and debearded
Juice from 1 lemon

## Directions

In the pot, mix garlic powder, water and wine. Put the mussels into the steamer basket, rounded-side should be placed facing upwards to fit as many as possible.

Insert rack into the cooker and lower steamer basket onto the rack. Seal the lid and cook on Low Pressure for 1 minute. Release the pressure quickly. Remove unopened mussels. Coat the mussels with the wine mixture and lemon juice to serve.

# Paprika Salmon with Dill Sauce

Serving Size: 2 | Total Time: 15 minutes

## Ingredients

2 salmon fillets
Juice from ½ lemon
¼ tsp paprika

*For sauce:*
¼ cup fresh dill
Juice from ½ lemon

Salt and black pepper to taste
2 cups water

Sea salt to taste
¼ cup olive oil

## Directions

In a food processor, blend all the chutney ingredients until creamy. Set aside.

To your cooker, add the water and place a steamer basket. Arrange salmon fillets skin-side down on the steamer basket. Drizzle lemon juice over salmon and sprinkle with paprika. Seal the lid and cook for 3 minutes on High Pressure. Release the pressure quickly. Season the fillets with pepper and salt and top with the dill sauce to serve.

# Hot Shrimp & Potato Chowder

Serving Size: 4 | Total Time: 25 minutes

## Ingredients

4 slices pancetta, chopped
4 tbsp minced garlic
1 onion, chopped
2 potatoes, chopped
16 ounces canned corn kernels
4 cups vegetable stock

1 tsp dried rosemary
Salt and black pepper to taste
1 lb jumbo shrimp, peeled, deveined
1 tbsp olive oil
½ tsp red chili flakes
¾ cup heavy cream

## Directions

Fry the pancetta for 5 minutes until crispy, on Sauté mode, and set aside. Add in 2 tbsp of garlic and onion, and stir-fry for 3 minutes. Add in potatoes, corn, stock, rosemary, half of the salt, and pepper.

Seal the lid and cook on High Pressure for 10 minutes. Do a quick Pressure release. Remove to a serving bowl. In a bowl, toss the shrimp in the remaining garlic, salt, olive oil, and flakes.

Wipe the pot clean and fry shrimp for 3-4 minutes per side, until pink. Mix in the heavy cream and cook for 2 minutes. Add shrimp to chowder, garnish with the reserved pancetta and serve immediately.

# Shrimp Boil with Chorizo Sausages

Serving Size: 4 | Total Time: 30 minutes

## Ingredients

3 red potatoes
3 ears corn, cut into rounds
2 cups water
1 cup white wine
4 chorizo sausages, chopped

1 lb shrimp, peeled and deveined
2 tbsp of seafood seasoning
Salt to taste
1 lemon, cut into wedges
¼ cup butter, melted

## Directions

Add all ingredients, except butter and lemon wedges. Do not stir. Seal the lid and cook for 2 minutes on High Pressure. Release the pressure quickly. Drain the mixture through a colander. Transfer to a serving platter. Serve with melted butter and lemon wedges.

# Herby Trout with Farro & Green Beans

Serving Size: 4 | Total Time: 20 minutes

## Ingredients

1 cup farro
2 cups water
4 skinless trout fillets
8 ounces green beans
1 tbsp olive oil
Salt and black pepper to taste

4 tbsp melted butter
½ tbsp sugar
½ tbsp lemon juice
½ tsp dried rosemary
2 garlic cloves, minced
½ tsp dried thyme

## Directions

Pour the farro and water in the pot and mix with green beans and olive oil. Season with salt and black pepper,

In another bowl, mix together the remaining black pepper and salt, butter, sugar, lemon juice, rosemary, garlic, and thyme. Coat the trout with the buttery herb sauce. Insert a trivet in the pot and lay the trout fillets on the trivet. Seal the lid and cook on High Pressure for 12 minutes. Do a quick release and serve immediately.

# Clean-Hands Party Rice, Veggies & Shrimp

Serving Size: 5 | Total Time: 25 minutes

## Ingredients

¼ cup olive oil
1 onion, chopped
1 red bell pepper, diced
2 garlic cloves, minced
1 tsp paprika
1 tsp turmeric
Salt and white pepper to taste

1 cup rice
¼ cup frozen green peas
2 cups fish broth
1 lb frozen shrimp, peeled and deveined
Chopped fresh parsley
1 lemon, cut into wedges

## Directions

Warm oil on Sauté mode. Add in bell pepper and onion, and cook for 5 minutes until fragrant. Mix in garlic and cook for one more minute until soft.

Add paprika, pepper, salt and turmeric to the vegetables with paprika and cook for 1 minute. Stir in fish broth and rice. Add shrimp to the rice mixture. Seal the lid and cook on High Pressure for 5 minutes.

Release the pressure quickly. Stir in green peas and let sit for 5 minutes until green peas are heated through. Serve warm garnished with parsley and lemon wedges.

# Savory Cod Fillets in Maple-Lemon Sauce

Serving Size: 3 | Total Time: 20 minutes

## Ingredients

1 lb cod fillets, skinless and boneless
1 cup maple syrup
½ cup soy sauce
3 garlic cloves, chopped

1 lemon, juiced
Salt and black pepper to taste
1 tbsp butter

## Directions

In a bowl, mix maple syrup, soy sauce, garlic, lemon juice, black pepper, and salt. Stir until combined and set aside. Grease the pot with butter. Place the fillets at the bottom and pour over the maple mixture.

Seal the lid and cook on Steam for 8 minutes on High. Release the pressure naturally, for about 5 minutes.

# Salmon with Green Peas & Rice

Serving Size: 4 | Total Time: 20 minutes

## Ingredients

1 cup rice
2 cups vegetable stock
4 skinless salmon fillets
1 cup green peas
3 tbsp olive oil
Salt and black pepper to taste
2 limes, juiced

2 tbsp honey
1 tsp sweet paprika
2 jalapeño peppers, seeded and diced
4 garlic cloves, minced
½ cup canned corn kernels, drained
2 tbsp chopped fresh dill

## Directions

Add in rice, stock, and salt. Place a trivet over the rice. In a bowl, mix oil, lime juice, honey, paprika, jalapeño, garlic, and dill. Coat the fish with the honey sauce while reserving a little for garnishing.

Lay the salmon fillets on the trivet. Seal the lid and cook on High Pressure for 8 minutes. Do a quick release. Fluff the rice with a fork and mix in the green peas and corn kernels. Transfer to a serving plate and top with the salmon. Drizzle with the remaining honey sauce and enjoy.

# Seafood Traditional Spanish Paella

Serving Size: 4 | Total Time: 30 minutes

## Ingredients

2 tbsp olive oil
1 onion, chopped
4 garlic cloves, minced
½ cup dry white wine
2 cups rice
4 cups chicken stock
1 ½ tsp sweet paprika

1 tsp turmeric powder
Salt and black pepper to taste
1 pound small clams, scrubbed
1 lb fresh prawns, peeled and deveined
1 red bell pepper, diced
1 lemon, cut in wedges

## Directions

Stir-fry onion and garlic in a tbsp of oil on Sauté mode for 3 minutes. Pour in wine to deglaze, scraping the bottom of the pot of any brown. Cook for 2 minutes, until the wine is reduced by half.

Add in rice and broth. Season with the paprika, turmeric, salt, bell pepper, and pepper. Seal the lid and cook on High Pressure for 10 minutes. Do a quick release. Remove to a plate and wipe the pot clean.

Heat the remaining oil on Sauté. Cook clams and prawns for 6 minutes, until the clams have opened and the shrimp are pink. Discard unopened clams. Arrange seafood and lemon wedges over paella, to serve.

# Salmon Fillets With Orange Sauce

Serving Size: 3 | Total Time: 30 minutes

## Ingredients

1 lb salmon fillets
1 cup orange juice, freshly squeezed
2 tbsp cornstarch

Salt and black pepper to taste
1 garlic clove, minced
1 tsp orange zest, freshly grated

## Directions

Combine together all ingredients in a large bowl. Cover and let to marinate for 10-15 minutes.

Then, add to the pot and seal the lid. Cook on High pressure for 10 minutes. Do a quick pressure release.

# Pizza with Tuna & Goat Cheese

Serving Size: 4 | Total Time: 25 minutes

## Ingredients

1 cup canned tuna, oil-free
½ cup mozzarella cheese, shredded
¼ cup goat's cheese
3 tbsp olive oil

1 tbsp tomato paste
½ tsp dried rosemary
14 oz pizza crust
1 cup olives, optional

## Directions

Grease the bottom of a baking dish with one tablespoon of olive oil. Line some parchment paper. Flour the working surface and roll out the pizza dough to the approximate size of your instant pot gently fit the dough in the previously prepared baking dish.

In a bowl, combine olive oil, tomato paste and rosemary. Whisk together and Spread the mixture over the crust. Sprinkle with goat cheese, mozzarella, olives, and tuna. Place a trivet inside the pot and pour in 1 cup of water. Seal the lid, and cook for 15 minutes on High Pressure. Do a quick release. Cut and serve.

# Spicy Haddock with Beer & Crushed Potatoes

Serving Size: 4 | Total Time: 25 minutes

## Ingredients

8 ounces beer
2 eggs
1 cup flour
½ tbsp cayenne powder
1 tbsp cumin powder

Salt and black pepper to taste
4 haddock fillets
4 potatoes, cut into ¼- to ½-inch matchsticks
2 tbsp olive oil

## Directions

In a bowl, whisk beer and eggs. In another bowl, combine flour, cayenne, cumin, black pepper, and salt. Coat each fish piece in the egg mixture, then dredge in the flour mixture, coating all sides well.

Spray a baking dish with nonstick cooking spray. Place in the fish fillets, pour ¼ cup of water and grease with cooking spray. Place the potatoes in the pot and cover with water and place a trivet over the potatoes.

Lay the baking dish on top and seal the lid. Cook on High Pressure for 15 minutes. Do a quick release. Drain and crush the potatoes with olive oil and serve with the fish.

# Cilantro Cod on Millet with Peppers

Serving Size: 4 | Total Time: 20 minutes

## Ingredients

1 tbsp olive oil
1 cup millet
1 yellow bell pepper, diced
1 red bell pepper, diced
2 cups chicken broth
1 lemon, zested and juiced

1 cup bread crumbs
4 tbsp melted butter
¼ cup minced fresh cilantro
1 tsp salt
4 cod fillets

## Directions

Combine oil, millet, yellow and red bell peppers in the pot, and cook for 1 minute on Sauté. Mix in the chicken broth. Place a trivet atop. In a bowl, mix crumbs, butter, cilantro, lemon zest, juice, and salt.

Spoon the bread crumb mixture evenly on the cod fillet. Lay the fish on the trivet. Seal the lid and cook on High for 6 minutes. Do a quick release and serve immediately.

# Quick Shrimp Gumbo with Andouille Sausage

Serving Size: 4 | Total Time: 30 minutes

## Ingredients

1 pound jumbo shrimp
2 tbsp olive oil
1/3 cup flour
1 ½ tsp cajun seasoning
1 onion, chopped
1 cup red bell pepper, chopped
2 celery stalks, chopped

2 garlic cloves, minced
1 small serrano pepper, seeded and minced
2 ½ cups chicken broth
6 oz andouille sausage, sliced
¾ cup water
2 green onions, finely sliced
Salt and black pepper to taste

## Directions

Heat olive oil on Sauté. Whisk in the flour with a wooden spoon and cook 3 minutes, stirring constantly. Stir in cajun seasoning, onion, bell pepper, celery, garlic, and serrano pepper for about 5 minutes.

Pour in the chicken broth, water, and andouille sausage. Seal and cook for 6 minutes on High Pressure.

Do a natural pressure for 5 minutes. Stir the shrimp into the gumbo to eat it up for 3 minutes. Adjust the seasoning. Ladle the gumbo into bowls and garnish with the green onions.

# Spicy Pasta with Seafood

Serving Size: 4 | Total Time: 20 minutes

## Ingredients

1 tbsp olive oil
1 onion, diced
1 garlic clove
16 ounces penne
24 ounces arrabbiata sauce

3 cups chicken broth
Salt and black pepper to taste
16 ounces scallops
¼ cup Parmesan cheese, grated
Basil leaves for garnish

## Directions

Heat oil on Sauté and stir-fry onion for 5 minutes. Add the garlic and cook until fragrant, for about 1 minute. Stir in penne, arrabbiata sauce, and 2 cups of broth. Season with the black pepper and.

Seal the lid and cook for 6 minutes on High Pressure. Do a quick release. Remove to a plate. Pour the remaining broth and add scallops. Stir to coat, seal the lid and cook on High Pressure for 4 minutes. Do a quick release. Mix in the pasta and serve topped with parmesan cheese and basil leaves.

# Spinach & Shrimp Fusilli

Serving Size: 4 | Total Time: 20 minutes

## Ingredients

1 ¼ lb shrimp, peeled and deveined
1 ½ tsp salt
1 tbsp melted butter
2 garlic cloves, minced
¼ cup white wine
10 ounces fusilli pasta

2 ½ cups water
1/3 cup tomato puree
½ tsp red chili flakes or to taste
1 tsp grated lemon zest
1 tbsp lemon juice
6 cups spinach

## Directions

On Sauté, pour white wine, bring to simmer for 2 minutes to reduce the liquid by half. Stir in the fusilli pasta, water, salt, garlic, puréed tomato, shrimp, melted butter, and chili flakes. Seal the lid. Cook for 5 minutes on High pressure. Do a quick release. Stir in lemon zest, juice, and spinach until wilted and soft.

# Crab Pilaf with Broccoli & Asparagus

Serving Size: 4 | Total Time: 20 minutes

## Ingredients

½ pound asparagus, trimmed and cut into 1-inch pieces
½ pound broccoli florets
Salt to taste
2 tbsp olive oil
1 small onion, chopped

1 cup rice
1/3 cup white wine
3 cups vegetable stock
8 ounces lump crabmeat

## Directions

Heat oil on Sauté and cook onion for 3 minutes, until soft. Stir in rice and cook for 1 minute. Pour in the wine. Cook for 2 to 3 minutes, stirring, until the liquid has almost evaporated.

Add vegetable stock and salt; stir to combine. Place a trivet atop. Arrange the broccoli and asparagus on the trivet. Seal the lid and cook on High Pressure for 8 minutes. Do a quick release.

Remove the vegetables to a bowl. Fluff the rice with a fork and add in the crabmeat, heat for a minute. Taste and adjust the seasoning. Serve immediately topped with broccoli and asparagus.

# Marinated Salmon Steaks with Garlic & Lemon

Serving Size: 3 | Total Time: 65 minutes

## Ingredients

1 lb salmon steaks
1 tsp garlic powder
½ tsp rosemary powder
1 cup olive oil

½ cup apple cider vinegar
Salt and white pepper to taste
¼ cup lemon juice

## Directions

In a bowl, mix garlic, rosemary, olive oil, apple cider vinegar, salt, lemon juice, and black pepper. Pour the mixture into a Ziploc bag along with the salmon.

Seal the bag and shake to coat well. Refrigerate for 30 minutes. Pour in 3 cups of water in the instant pot and insert the trivet. Remove the fish from the Ziploc bag and place on top. Reserve the marinade.

Seal lid and cook on Steam mode for 15 minutes on High Pressure. When ready, do a quick release and remove the steaks.

Discard the liquid and wipe clean the pot. Grease with some of the marinade and hit Sauté. Add salmon steaks and brown on both sides for 3-4 minutes.

# Black Squid Ink Tagliatelle with Seafood Mix

Serving Size: 4 | Total Time: 30 minutes

## Ingredients

1 lb fresh seafood mix
¼ cup olive oil
4 garlic cloves, crushed
1 tbsp fresh parsley, chopped

1 tsp fresh rosemary, chopped
½ tbsp white wine
1 tsp salt
17.6 oz squid ink tagliatelle, cooked

## Directions

Heat 3 tbsp olive oil on Sauté and stir-fry the garlic, for 1-2 minutes, until fragrant. Add seafood, parsley, rosemary, and salt. Give it a stir. Add the remaining oil, wine, and ½ cup of water. Seal the lid and cook on High Pressure for 4 minutes. Do a quick release and set aside. Open the instant pot, add the pasta, stir, and serve hot.

# Steamed Salmon over Creamy Polenta

Serving Size: 4 | Total Time: 20 minutes

## Ingredients

1 cup corn grits polenta
½ cup coconut milk
3 cups chicken stock
3 tbsp butter

Salt to taste
3 tbsp cajun seasoning
1 tbsp sugar
4 salmon fillets, skin removed

## Directions

Combine polenta, milk, chicken stock, butter, and salt in the pot.

In a bowl mix cajun seasoning, sugar, and salt. Oil the fillets with cooking spray and brush with the spice mixture. Insert a trivet in the pot and arrange the fillets on top. Seal the lid and cook on High Pressure for 9 minutes. Do a natural pressure release for 10 minutes.

# Mackerel with Potatoes & Spinach

Serving Size: 4 | Total Time: 30 minutes

## Ingredients

4 mackerels, skin on
1 lb of fresh spinach, torn
5 potatoes, peeled and chopped
¼ cup olive oil,
2 garlic cloves, crushed

1 tsp dried rosemary, chopped
2 sprigs of fresh mint leaves, chopped
1 lemon, juiced
Sea salt to taste

## Directions

Grease the pot with 4 tbsp olive oil. Stir-fry garlic and rosemary on Sauté, for 1 minute. Stir in spinach, a pinch of salt and cook for 4-5 minutes, until soft. Remove the spinach from the cooker and set aside.

Add the remaining oil to and make a layer of potatoes. Top with fish and drizzle with lemon juice, olive oil, and sea salt. Pour in 1 cup of water, seal the lid and cook on Steam mode for 7 minutes on High.

When ready, do a quick release. Plate the fish and potatoes with spinach, and serve immediately with mint leaves.

# Citrus Marinated Smelt with Okra & Cherry Tomatoes

Serving Size: 4 | Total Time: 35 minutes

## Ingredients

1 lb fresh smelt, cleaned, heads removed
1 cup extra virgin olive oil
½ cup freshly squeezed lemon juice
¼ cup freshly squeezed orange juice
1 tbsp Dijon mustard
1 tsp fresh rosemary, finely chopped
2 garlic cloves, crushed

1 tsp sea salt
5 oz okra
1 carrot, chopped
¼ cup green peas, soaked overnight
5 oz cherry tomatoes, halved
4 tbsp vegetable oil
2 cups fish stock

## Directions

In a bowl, mix oil, juices, dijon, garlic, salt, and rosemary. Stir well and submerge fish in this mixture.

Refrigerate for 1 hour. Meanwhile, heat vegetable oil on Sauté and stir-fry carrot, peas, cherry tomatoes, and okra, for 10 minutes. Add in the fish stock. Seal the lid and cook on Rice for 8 minutes on High.

Do a quick release and add in the fish along with half of the marinade. Seal the lid again and cook on Steam for 4 minutes on High. Release the pressure naturally, for 10 minutes. Serve immediately.

# Stuffed Tench with Garlic, Herbs & Lemon

Serving Size: 2 | Total Time: 20 minutes

## Ingredients

1 tench, cleaned and gutted
1 lemon, chopped, quartered
2 tbsp olive oil
1 tsp fresh rosemary, chopped

¼ tsp dried thyme, ground
2 garlic cloves, crushed
½ tsp sea salt

## Directions

In a bowl, mix olive oil, rosemary, thyme, garlic, and salt. Stir to combine. Brush the fish with the previously prepared mixture and stuff with lemon.

Pour 4 cups of water into the instant pot, set the steamer tray and place the fish on top. If the fish is too big and can't fit in, cut in half.

Seal the lid and cook on Steam mode for 15 minutes on High Pressure. Do a quick release. For a crispier taste, briefly brown the fish in a grill pan.

# White Wine & Rosemary Marinated Squid Rings

Serving Size: 3 | Total Time: 1 hour 10 minutes

## Ingredients

1 lb fresh squid rings
1 cup dry white wine
1 cup olive oil
2 garlic cloves, crushed
1 lemon, juiced

2 cups fish stock
¼ tsp red pepper flakes
¼ tsp dried oregano
1 tbsp fresh rosemary, chopped
1 tsp sea salt

## Directions

In a bowl, mix wine, olive oil, lemon juice, garlic, flakes, oregano, rosemary, and salt. Submerge squid rings in this mixture and cover with a lid.

Refrigerate for 1 hour. Remove the squid from the fridge and place them in the pot along with stock and half of the marinade. Seal the lid. Cook on High Pressure for 6 minutes. Release the Pressure naturally, for 10 minutes. Transfer the rings to a plate and drizzle with some marinade to serve.

# Garlic Trout Fillets with Tri-Color Pasta & Capers

Serving Size: 5 | Total Time: 50 minutes

## Ingredients

16 oz tri-color rotini pasta
6 oz trout fillets
1 cup olive oil
½ cup lemon juice
1 tsp fresh rosemary, chopped

3 garlic cloves, crushed, halved
Salt and black pepper to taste
2 tbsp fresh parsley, finely chopped
Olives and capers for serving

## Directions

In a bowl, mix oil, lemon juice, rosemary, 2 garlic cloves, black pepper, and salt. Stir well and submerge fillets in this mixture. Refrigerate for 30 minutes. Remove from the fridge and drain, reserving the liquid.

Grease the pot with some of the marinade. Add fillets, 1 cup of water, and 3 tbsp of the marinade. Seal the lid and cook on High pressure for 4 minutes. Do a quick release, add the pasta and 1 cup of water. Seal the lid and cook for 3 minutes on High. Do a quick release. Serve with capers and fresh parsley.

# Mint Salmon on Spinach Bed

Serving Size: 4 | Total Time: 30 minutes

## Ingredients

1 lb salmon fillets, boneless
1 lb fresh spinach, torn
4 tbsp olive oil
2 garlic cloves, chopped

2 tbsp lemon juice
1 tbsp fresh mint, chopped
Salt and black pepper to taste

## Directions

Place spinach in the pot, cover with water and lay the trivet on top. Rub the salmon fillets with half of the olive oil, mint, salt, pepper and garlic. Lay on the trivet. Seal the lid and cook on Steam for 5 minutes on High.

Do a quick release. Remove salmon to a serving plate. Drain the spinach in a colander. Serve the fish on a bed of spinach. Season with salt and drizzle with lemon juice.

# Seafood & Fish Stew

Serving Size: 6 | Total Time: 25 minutes

## Ingredients

2 lb different fish and seafood
3 tbsp olive oil
2 onions, peeled, chopped
2 carrots, grated

A handful of fresh parsley, chopped
2 garlic cloves, crushed
3 cups water
1 tsp sea salt

## Directions

Heat olive oil on Sauté. Stir-fry onions and garlic, for 3-4 minutes, or until translucent. Add the remaining ingredients. Seal the lid, and cook on High Pressure for 10 minutes. Do a quick release.

# Mixed Seafood with Chickpeas & Olives

Serving Size: 6 | Total Time: 25 minutes

## Ingredients

1 cup scallions, cleaned and chopped
1 medium carrot, chopped
1 lb shrimp, cleaned and deveined
1 cup chickpeas, soaked

3 cups fish broth
½ cup olives, pitted
Salt and black pepper to taste
½ tsp Italian seasoning mix

## Directions

Add all ingredients in your instant pot. Seal the lid and cook on High Pressure for 12 minutes. Release the pressure naturally, for 10 minutes. Serve warm.

# Herby Trout Fillets with Olives

Serving Size: 6 | Total Time: 1 hour 20 minutes

## Ingredients

2 lb trout fillets, skin on
½ cup olive oil
¼ cup apple cider vinegar
1 red onion, chopped
1 lemon, chopped
2 garlic cloves, crushed

1 tbsp fresh rosemary, chopped
1 tbsp dill sprigs, chopped
Sea salt and black pepper to taste
3 cups fish stock
12 black olives

## Directions

In a bowl, mix oil, apple cider, onion, garlic, rosemary, dill, sea salt, and pepper. Submerge the fillets into this mixture and refrigerate for 1 hour. Grease the bottom of the pot with 4 tbsp of the marinade and pour in the stock. Add the fish, seal the lid and cook on High pressure for 4 minutes. Do a quick release. Serve with lemon and olives.

# Spicy Mussels & Anchovies with Rice

Serving Size: 4 | Total Time: 40 minutes

## Ingredients

1 cup rice
6 oz mussels
1 onion, finely chopped
1 garlic clove, crushed
1 tbsp dried rosemary

¼ cup salted capers
1 tsp chili ground pepper
½ tsp salt
3 tbsp olive oil
4 salted anchovies

## Directions

Add rice to the pot, and pour 2 cups of water. Seal the lid and cook on Rice mode for 8 minutes on High.

Do a quick release. Remove the rice and set aside. Grease the pot with oil, and stir-fry garlic and onion, for 2 minutes, on Sauté. Add mussels and rosemary. Cook for 10 more minutes. Stir in rice and season with salt and chili pepper. Serve with anchovies and capers.

# Steamed Trout with Garlic & Fresh Herbs

Serving Size: 2 | Total Time: 30 minutes

## Ingredients

1 lb fresh trout, (2 pieces)
2 cups fish stock
1 tbsp fresh mint, chopped
¼ tsp fresh thyme, chopped
1 tbsp fresh parsley, chopped

3 garlic cloves, chopped
3 tbsp olive oil
2 tbsp fresh lemon juice
1 tsp sea salt
1 tbsp chili

## Directions

In a bowl, mix mint, thyme, parsley, garlic, olive oil, lemon juice, chili, and salt. Stir to combine. Spread the abdominal cavity of the fish and brush with the marinade. Then, brush the fish from the outside and set aside.

Insert the trivet in instant pot. Pour in the stock and place the trout on top. Seal the lid and cook on Steam mode for 15 minutes on High Pressure. Do a quick release and serve immediately.

# Seafood Medley with Rosemary Rice

Serving Size: 4 | Total Time: 30 minutes

## Ingredients

1 lb frozen seafood mix
1 cup brown rice
1 tbsp calamari ink
2 tbsp extra virgin olive oil
2 garlic cloves, crushed

1 tbsp chopped rosemary
½ tsp salt
3 cups fish stock
Freshly squeezed lemon juice

## Directions

Add in all ingredients, Seal the lid and cook on Rice mode for 10 minutes on High. Release the pressure naturally, for 10 minutes. Squeeze lemon juice and serve.

# Dilled Salmon Fillets

Serving Size: 4 | Total Time: 25 minutes

## Ingredients

4 salmon fillets
1 cup lemon juice
2 tbsp butter, softened

2 tbsp dill
Salt and black pepper to taste

## Directions

Sprinkle the fillets with salt and pepper. Insert the steamer tray and place the salmon on top. Pour in the lemon juice and 2 cups of water. Seal the lid.

Cook on Steam mode for 5 minutes on High. When done, release the Pressure naturally, for 10 minutes. Set aside the salmon and discard the liquid.

Wipe the pot clean and press Sauté. Add butter and briefly brown the fillets on both sides – for 3-4 minutes. Sprinkle with dill, to serve.

# Lime Trout with Spinach & Tomatoes

Serving Size: 3 | Total Time: 50 minutes

## Ingredients

1 lb trout fillets
6 oz fresh spinach, torn
2 tomatoes, peeled, diced
3 cups fish stock
1 tsp dried thyme

½ tsp fresh rosemary
¼ cup olive oil
¼ cup freshly squeezed lime juice
1 tsp sea salt
2 garlic cloves, crushed

## Directions

Rinse the fillets and sprinkle them with sea salt. In a bowl, mix olive oil, thyme, rosemary, and lime juice. Stir well and submerge fillets in this mixture. Refrigerate for 30 minutes; then drain the fillets.

Reserve the marinade, grease the pot with 3 tbsp of the marinade and add the fillets and stock.

Seal the lid and cook on Steam for 8 minutes on High Pressure. Do a quick release, remove the fish and set aside. Add the remaining marinade to the pot. Hit Sauté and add the tomatoes and spinach. Cook until soft. Give it a good stir and remove to a plate. Add fish, drizzle with tomato sauce and serve warm.

# Shrimp & Octopus with Tomato & Collard Greens

Serving Size: 4 | Total Time: 35 minutes

## Ingredients

1 lb collard greens, chopped
1 lb shrimp, whole
6 oz octopus, cut into bite-sized pieces
1 large tomato, peeled and chopped
3 cups fish stock

4 tbsp olive oil
3 garlic cloves
2 tbsp fresh parsley, chopped
1 tsp sea salt

## Directions

Place shrimp and octopus in the pot. Add tomato and fish stock. Seal the lid and cook on High Pressure for 15 minutes. Do a quick release. Remove shrimp and octopus, drain the liquid.

Heat olive oil on Sauté and add garlic, parsley, and stir-fry until translucent. Add collard greens and simmer for 10 minutes. Season with salt, stir and remove from the cooker. Serve with shrimp and octopus.

# Spicy Salmon Fillets with Oregano & Sea Salt

Serving Size: 4 | Total Time: 50minutes

### Ingredients

1 lb fresh salmon fillets, skin on
¼ cup olive oil
½ cup freshly squeezed lemon juice
2 garlic cloves, crushed

1 tbsp fresh oregano leaves, chopped
1 tsp sea salt
¼ tsp chili flakes
2 cups fish stock

### Directions

In a bowl, mix oil, lemon juice, garlic, oregano leaves, salt, and flakes. Brush the fillets with the mixture and refrigerate for 30 minutes. Pour the stock in, and insert the trivet.

Pat dry the salmon and place on the steamer rack. Seal the lid, and cook on Steam for 10 minutes on High. Do a quick release and serve.

# Dijon Catfish Fillets with White Wine

Serving Size: 3 | Total Time: 1 hour 5 minutes

### Ingredients

1 lb catfish fillets
1 lemon, juiced
½ cup parsley leaves, chopped
2 garlic cloves, crushed
1 onion, finely chopped
1 tbsp fresh dill, chopped

1 tbsp fresh rosemary
2 cups white wine
2 tbsp Dijon mustard
1 cup extra virgin olive oil
3 cups fish stock

### Directions

In a bowl, mix lemon juice, parsley, garlic, onion, fresh dill, rosemary, wine, mustard, and oil. Stir well to combine. Submerge fillets in this mixture and cover with a tight lid. Refrigerate for 1 hour.

Insert the trivet, remove the fish from the fridge and place it on the rack. Pour in stock along with the marinade and seal the lid. Cook on Steam for 8 minutes on High. Release the pressure quickly and serve.

# Favorite Seafood Chowder

Serving Size: 4 | Total Time: 45 minutes

### Ingredients

6 oz mackerel fillets
½ cup wheat groats, soaked
½ cup kidney beans, soaked
¼ cup sweet corn
1 lb tomatoes, peeled, roughly chopped

4 cups fish stock
4 tbsp olive oil
1 tsp sea salt
1 tsp fresh rosemary, finely chopped
2 garlic cloves, crushed

### Directions

Heat olive oil on Sauté, and stir-fry tomatoes and garlic for 5 minutes. Add rosemary, stock, salt, corn, kidney beans, and wheat groats. Seal the lid and cook on High Pressure for 25 minutes.

Do a quick release and add mackerel fillets. Seal the lid and cook on Steam for 8 minutes on High. Do a quick release, open the lid and serve immediately drizzled with freshly squeezed lemon juice.

# Chili Steamed Catfish

Serving Size: 4 | Total Time: 60 minutes

## Ingredients

1 lb flathead catfish
1 cup orange juice
¼ cup lemon juice
½ cup olive oil
1 tbsp dried thyme

1 tbsp dried rosemary
1 tsp chili flakes
1 tsp sea salt
3 cups fish stock

## Directions

In a bowl, mix orange juice, lemon juice, olive oil, thyme, rosemary, chili flakes, and salt. Brush the fish with this mixture and refrigerate for 30 minutes. Remove from the fridge, drain; reserve the marinade.

Insert the trivet in the pot. Pour in stock and marinade, and place the fish onto the top. Seal the lid and cook on High Pressure for 10 minutes. Do a quick release and serve immediately.

# Italian Steamed Sea Bream with Lemon

Serving Size: 4 | Total Time: 40 minutes

## Ingredients

2 pieces sea bream (2 lb), cleaned
¼ cup olive oil
¼ cup freshly squeezed lemon juice
1 tbsp fresh thyme sprigs

1 tbsp Italian seasoning
½ tsp sea salt
1 tsp garlic powder
4 cups fish stock

## Directions

In a bowl, mix oil, lemon juice, thyme, Italian seasoning, sea salt, and garlic powder. Brush onto fish and wrap tightly with a plastic foil. Refrigerate for 30 minutes before cooking. Pour fish stock in the pot.

Set the steamer rack and place the fish on top. Seal the lid. Cook on Steam mode for 8 minutes on High. Do a quick release, open the lid, and unwrap the fish. Serve immediately with steam vegetables.

# Pollock & Tomato Stew

Serving Size: 4 | Total Time: 35 minutes

## Ingredients

1 lb pollock fillets
4 cloves, crushed
1 lb tomatoes, peeled and chopped
2 bay leaves, whole

2 cups fish stock
Salt and black pepper to taste
1 onion, peeled and finely chopped
½ cup olive oil

## Directions

Heat 2 tbsp olive oil on Sauté. Add onion and sauté until translucent, stirring constantly, for about 3-4 minutes.

Add tomatoes and cook until soft. Press Cancel. Add the remaining ingredients and seal the lid. Cook on High pressure for 15 minutes. When ready, do a quick release and serve warm.

# Chili Deviled Eggs

Serving Size: 6 | Total Time: 15 minutes

### Ingredients

1 cup water
10 large eggs
¼ cup cream cheese

¼ cup mayonnaise
Salt and black pepper to taste
¼ tsp chili powder

### Directions

Add water, insert the steamer basket and lay the eggs inside. Seal the lid and cook on high pressure for 5 minutes. Release the pressure quickly. Drop eggs into an ice bath to cool for 5 minutes. Peel eggs and halve them.

Transfer yolks to a bowl and use a fork to mash; Stir in cream cheese, chili powder, and mayonnaise. Add pepper and salt for seasoning. Ladle yolk mixture into egg white halves.

# Traditional Italian Rice & Cheese Balls

Serving Size: 6 | Total Time: 50 minutes

### Ingredients

½ cup olive oil, plus 1 tbsp
1 white onion, diced
2 garlic cloves, minced
5 cups chicken stock
½ cup apple cider vinegar
2 cups short grain rice

1 ½ cups grated cheddar cheese,
¼ cup grated Parmesan cheese for garnish
1 cup canned Kernel sweet corn, drained
Salt and black pepper to taste
2 cups fresh bread crumbs
2 eggs

### Directions

On Sauté, heat 1 tbsp of oil and cook onion for 2 minutes until translucent. Add the garlic and sauté for a minute. Stir in the stock, vinegar and rice. Seal the lid and cook on High Pressure for 7 minutes.

Do a natural pressure release for 10 minutes. Stir in cheddar cheese, corn, salt, and pepper. Spoon into a bowl and let cool completely. Wipe clean the pot.

In a bowl, pour the bread crumbs. In a separate bowl, beat the eggs. Form balls out of the rice mixture, dip each into the beaten eggs, and coat in the breadcrumb mixture.

Heat the remaining oil on Sauté and fry arancini until crispy. Sprinkle with Parmesan cheese and serve.

# Juicy Hot Chicken Wings

Serving Size: 4 | Total Time: 15 minutes

### Ingredients

½ cup sriracha sauce
1 cup water
¼ cup ranch salad dressing mix
2 tbsp butter, melted

Juice from ½ lemon
2 pounds chicken vignettes
½ tsp paprika

### Directions

Mix chicken, water, sriracha, butter and lemon in the inner pot. Seal the lid and cook on High Pressure for 5 min minutes. Do a quick pressure release. Serve with the paprika and ranch dressing.

# Kale & Artichoke Cheese Bites

Serving Size: 8 | Total Time: 45 minutes

## Ingredients

¼ cup frozen chopped kale
¼ cup chopped artichoke hearts
¼ cup ricotta cheese
2 tbsp grated parmesan cheese
¼ cup goat cheese
1 large egg white

1 tsp dried basil
1 lemon, zested
Salt and black pepper to taste
4 frozen filo dough, thawed
1 tbsp extra-virgin olive oil

## Directions

In a bowl, combine kale, artichoke, ricotta, parmesan, goat cheese, egg white, basil, lemon zest, salt, and pepper. Place a filo dough on a clean flat surface. Brush with olive oil.

Place a second filo sheet on the first and brush with more oil. Continue layering to form a pile of four oiled sheets. Working from the short side, cut the phyllo sheets into 8 strips and half them.

Spoon 1 tablespoon of filling onto one short end of every strip. Fold a corner to cover the filling and a triangle; continue folding over and over to the end of the strip, creating a triangle-shaped filo packet.

Repeat the process with the other filo bites. Place a trivet into the pot. Pour in 1 cup of water. Place the bites on top of the trivet. Seal the lid and cook on High Pressure for 15 minutes. Do a quick release.

# Vegetarian Green Dip

Serving Size: 4 | Total Time: 15 minutes

## Ingredients

2 cups broccoli florets
1 cup water
¾ cup green bell pepper, chopped
¼ cup raw cashews
10 oz canned green chiles, drained, liquid reserved

¼ cup soy sauce
½ tsp sea salt
¼ tsp chili powder
¼ tsp garlic powder
¼ tsp cumin

## Directions

In the pot, add cashews, broccoli, green bell pepper, and water. Seal the lid and cook for 5 minutes on High Pressure. Release the pressure quickly. Drain water from the pot.

Add reserved liquid from canned green chiles, salt, garlic powder, chili powder, soy sauce, and cumin. Use an immersion blender to blend the mixture until smooth. Set aside in a mixing bowl. Stir chiles through the dip.

# Mom's Beef Fillet with Prosciutto

Serving Size: 6 | Total Time: 40 minutes

## Ingredients

2 lb beef fillets, center cut
1 onion, finely chopped
¼ cup horseradish sauce
3 tbsp butter

1 cup red wine
3 cups beef stock
6 oz prosciutto

## Directions

Melt butter on Sauté, and stir-fry the onion for 2 minutes. Add fillets, one at the time and briefly brown them on both sides, for a few minutes. Pour the wine and beef stock. Seal the lid and cook on High Pressure for 30 minutes. Do a quick release and remove the fillets on a serving platter. In a saucepan, mix horseradish sauce with prosciutto. Warm up and drizzle over the meat.

# Lemon Hummus with Spinach

Serving Size: 12 | Total Time: 50 minutes

## Ingredients

8 cups water
2 cups dried chickpeas
5 tbsp grapeseed oil
Salt to taste

½ cup tahini
5 tbsp lemon juice
2 cups spinach, chopped
5 garlic cloves, crushed

## Directions

In the instant pot, mix 2 tbsp oil, water, salt, and chickpeas. Seal the lid and cook on High Pressure for 35 minutes. Release the pressure quickly. In a small bowl, reserve ½ cup of the cooking liquid and drain chickpeas.

Mix half the reserved cooking liquid and chickpeas in a food processor and puree until no large chickpeas remain. Add remaining cooking liquid, spinach, lemon juice, salt, garlic, and tahini. Process hummus for 8 minutes until smooth. Stir in the remaining 3 tablespoons of olive oil before serving.

# Beef Dumplings with Cabbage

Serving Size: 8 | Total Time: 30 minutes

## Ingredients

8 ounces ground beef
½ cup savoy cabbage, shredded
1 carrot, grated
1 large egg, beaten
1 garlic clove, minced
2 tbsp coconut aminos

½ tbsp melted ghee
½ tbsp ginger powder
Salt and black pepper to taste
20 dumpling wrappers
2 tbsp olive oil
1 cup water

## Directions

In a bowl, mix beef, cabbage, carrot, egg, garlic, coconut aminos, ghee, ginger, salt, and pepper. Put the dumpling wrappers on a flat surface and spoon 1 tbsp of the beef filling into the middle of each wrapper.

Run the edges of the wrapper with a little water. Fold the dough to cover filling and create a semi-circle shape, pinching the edges to Seal. Then, brush the dumplings with the olive oil.

Arrange the dumplings in the pot. Pour in water, Seal the lid and cook on High Pressure for 15 minutes. Do a quick release. Drain the dumplings and place under the broiler for about 4-5 minutes.

# Chicken Wings with Teriyaki Sauce

Serving Size: 6 | Total Time: 25 minutes

## Ingredients

1 tbsp honey
1 cup teriyaki sauce
1 tsp black pepper
2 lb chicken wings

2 tbsp cornstarch
2 tbsp cold water
1 tsp sesame seeds

## Directions

In the pot, combine honey, teriyaki sauce and black pepper until the honey dissolves completely. Toss in chicken wings to coat. Seal the lid, press Poultry and cook for 10 minutes on High. Release the pressure quickly.

Transfer chicken wings to a platter. Mix cold water with the cornstarch. Press Sauté and stir in cornstarch slurry into the sauce and cook for 4 to 6 minutes until thickened. Top the chicken wings with thickened sauce. Add a garnish of sesame seeds, and serve.

# Delicious Mushroom & Garlic Pizza

Serving Size: 2 | Total Time: 25 minutes

## Ingredients

¾ cup all-purpose flour
1 cup whole wheat flour
½ tsp brown sugar
1 tsp garlic powder
2 tsp dried yeast
¼ tsp salt
1 tbsp olive oil

1 cup lukewarm water
1 cup button mushrooms, sliced
¼ cup gouda cheese, grated
2 tbsp tomato paste, sugar-free
½ tsp dried oregano
¼ cup water

## Directions

In a bowl fitted with a dough hook attachment, combine all-purpose flour with whole wheat flour, brown sugar, garlic powder, dried yeast, and salt. Mix well and gradually add lukewarm water and oil. Continue to beat on high speed until smooth dough.

Transfer to a lightly floured surface and knead until completely smooth. Form into a tight ball and wrap tightly in plastic foil. Set aside for one hour.

Line a baking dish with some parchment paper and set aside.

Roll out the dough with a rolling pin and transfer to the baking dish. Brush with tomato paste, and sprinkle with oregano, gouda, and button mushrooms.

Add a trivet inside your Instant Pot and Pour in 1 cup of water. Seal the lid, and cook for 15 minutes on High Pressure. Do a quick release. Remove the pizza from the pot using a parchment paper. Cut and serve.

# Mediterranean Meatballs with Mint Sauce

Serving Size: 4 | Total Time: 35 minutes

## Ingredients

1 lb lean ground beef
2 garlic cloves, crushed
¼ cup flour
1 tbsp fresh rosemary, crushed

1 large egg, beaten
½ tsp salt
3 tbsp olive oil
1 cup of water

*For sauce:*
1 cup Greek yogurt
2 tbsp fresh mint

1 garlic clove, crushed

## Directions

In a bowl, mix with hands ground beef, garlic, rosemary, 1 egg, ¼ cup flour, and salt. Lightly dampen hands and shape 1 ½-inch balls. Grease the instant pot with oil.

Transfer the balls to the pot. Add 1 cup of water. Seal the lid and cook on High Pressure for 13 minutes. Do a quick release. For the sauce, mix Greek yogurt, mint, and garlic. Stir well and drizzle over meatballs.

# Dill Marinated Gherkins

Serving Size: 6 | Total Time: 5 minutes

## Ingredients

1 pound cucumbers, sliced
2 cups white vinegar
1 cup water
1 cup sugar

¼ cup green garlic, minced
2 tbsp dill pickle seasoning
2 tsp salt
1 tsp cumin

**Directions**

Into the pot, add cucumbers, vinegar, water, sugar, green garlic, cumin, dill pickle seasoning, and salt. Stir well to dissolve the sugar. Seal the lid and cook for 4 minutes on High Pressure. Release the pressure quickly.

Ladle cucumbers into a large storage container and pour cooking liquid over. Chill for one hour.

# French Cheese & Spinach Quiche

Serving Size: 5 | Total Time: 30 minutes

**Ingredients**

1 lb spinach, chopped
½ cup mascarpone cheese
½ cup feta cheese, shredded
3 eggs, beaten
½ cup goat cheese

3 tbsp butter
½ cup milk
1 pack (6 sheets) pie dough
1 ½ cups water

**Directions**

In a bowl, mix spinach, eggs, mascarpone, feta and goat cheeses. Dust a clean surface with flour and unfold the pie sheets onto it. Using a rolling pin, roll the dough to fit your instant pot. Repeat with the other sheets.

Combine milk and butter in a skillet. Bring to a boil and melt the butter completely. Remove from the heat.

Grease a baking pan with oil. Place in 2 pie sheets and brush with milk mixture. Make the first layer of spinach mixture and cover with another two pie sheets.

Again, brush with butter and milk mixture, and repeat until you have used all ingredients. Pour 1 ½ cups water in your instant pot and insert the trivet. Lower the pan on the trivet and seal the lid.

Cook on High pressure for 6 minutes. Do a quick release. Place parchment paper under the pie to use it as a lifting method, to remove the pie. Serve cold.

# Creamy Turnips Stuffed with Cheese

Serving Size: 4 | Total Time: 20 minutes

**Ingredients**

4 small turnips, scrubbed clean
¼ cup whipping cream
¼ cup sour cream
½ cup chopped roasted red bell pepper

1 tsp Italian seasoning mix
1 ½ cups shredded mozzarella cheese
4 green onions, chopped
1/3 cup grated Parmesan cheese

**Directions**

Pour 1 cup of water into the pot and insert a trivet. Place the turnips on top. Seal the lid and cook on High for 10 minutes. Do a quick pressure release. Remove the turnips to a cutting board and allow cooling.

Cut the turnips in half. Scoop out the pulp into a bowl, mix in the whipping and sour cream using a potato mash until smooth. Stir in the roasted bell pepper, Italian seasoning, and mozzarella cheese.

Fetch out 2 tbsp of green onions and put into the turnips. Fill the turnip skins with the mashed mixture and sprinkle with Parmesan cheese. Arrange on a greased baking dish and place on the trivet.

Seal the lid and cook on High pressure for 3 minutes. Do a quick pressure release. Let cool for 5 minutes and garnish with the remaining onions.

# Spicy Turkey Meatballs in Red Sauce

Serving Size: 6 | Total Time: 30 minutes

## Ingredients

1 pound ground turkey
1 carrot, shredded
2 celery stalks, minced
¼ cup cotija cheese, crumbled
¼ cup hot sauce
¼ cup bread crumbs

1 egg, beaten
2 tbsp olive oil
½ cup water
4 tomatoes, chopped
Salt and black pepper to taste
2 tsp fresh basil, chopped

## Directions

In a bowl, combine turkey, carrot, celery, cotija cheese, hot sauce, bread crumbs, and egg. Season with salt and pepper. Shape the mixture into 12 meatballs. Heat oil on Sauté and fry the meatballs in batches until lightly golden. Pour in water, tomatoes, and salt. Seal the lid and cook on High Pressure for 5 minutes. Do a quick release. Sprinkle with basil and serve.

# Easy Camembert Cakes

Serving Size: 4 | Total Time: 45 minutes

## Ingredients

2 tbsp butter
1 small white onion, sliced
2 cups spinach, chopped
Salt and black pepper to taste
¼ cup dry white wine

1 pie pastry, thawed
1 cup Camembert cheese, cubed
1 tbsp thinly sliced fresh green onions
1 cup of water

## Directions

Melt 1 tbsp of butter on Sauté and cook onion and spinach for 5 minutes, or until tender. Season with salt and black pepper, then pour in white wine and cook until evaporated, about 2 minutes. Set aside.

Unwrap the pie pastry and cut into 4 squares. Prink the dough with a fork and brush both sides with the remaining butter. Share half of the cheese over the pie pastry squares.

Cover with the spinach and top with the remaining cheese. Arrange the tarts in a buttered baking dish, Pour 1 cup of water in the pot. Insert a trivet and lower the baking dish on top. Seal the lid and cook on High Pressure for 30 minutes. Do a quick release. Serve with green onions.

# Weekend Beef Balls

Serving Size: 4 | Total Time: 20 minutes

## Ingredients

1 lb ground beef
2 tbsp milk
3 tbsp oil
1 tbsp Italian seasoning mix

1 onion, chopped
2 eggs
2 slices wheat bread
Salt and black pepper to taste

## Directions

Place two slices of bread in a bowl. Add ¼ cup water and let soak for 5 minutes.

Mix beef, milk, oil, Italian seasoning mix, onion, eggs, salt, and pepper. Add soaked bread and shape balls with an approximately ¼ cup of the mixture. Flatten each ball with hand and place on a lightly floured surface.

Heat the oil on Sauté. Add the meatballs and fry for 3 minutes per side. Serve immediately with garlic sauce.

# Herby Shrimp with Garlic & Lemon

Serving Size: 4 | Total Time: 15 minutes

## Ingredients

1 pound shrimp, peeled and deveined
1 lemon, juiced
½ cup olive oil
1 tsp garlic powder
1 tsp fresh rosemary, chopped

1 tsp fresh thyme, chopped
½ tsp fresh basil, chopped
½ tsp fresh sage, chopped
½ tsp salt
1 tsp chili pepper

## Directions

Pour 1 ½ cups of water in the inner pot. In a bowl, mix oil, garlic, rosemary, thyme, basil, sage, salt, and chili. Brush the marinade over shrimp.

Insert the steamer rack, and arrange the shrimp on top. Seal the lid and cook on Steam for 3 minutes on High. Release the steam naturally, for 10 minutes. Press Sauté and stir-fry for 2 more minutes, or until golden brown. Stir in the lemon juice to serve.

# Paprika Chicken Wings

Serving Size: 4 | Total Time: 15 minutes

## Ingredients

2 lb chicken wings
¼ cup olive oil
4 garlic cloves, crushed
1 tbsp rosemary leaves
Salt and white pepper to taste

1 tsp paprika
1 tbsp fresh thyme, chopped
1 tbsp freshly grated ginger
¼ cup lime juice
½ cup apple cider vinegar

## Directions

In a bowl, mix oil, garlic, rosemary, white pepper, paprika, thyme, ginger, lime juice, and apple cider vinegar. Submerge wings into the mixture and cover.

Refrigerate for one hour. Remove the wings from the marinade and pat dry. Insert the steaming rack, 1 cup of water, and place the chicken on the rack. Seal the lid and cook on High Pressure for 8 minutes. Release the steam naturally, for about 10 minutes. Serve with fresh vegetable salad.

# Beef Layer Tart with Yogurt

Serving Size: 6 | Total Time: 35 minutes

## Ingredients

2 lb lean ground beef
4 garlic cloves, crushed
Salt and black pepper to taste
1 (16 oz) pack pie dough

½ tbsp butter, melted
1 tbsp sour cream
3 cups liquid yogurt

## Directions

In a bowl, mix beef, garlic, salt, and pepper, until fully incorporated. Lay a sheet of dough on a flat surface and brush with melted butter.

Line with the meat mixture and roll up. Repeat the process until you have used all the ingredients. Grease a baking dish and carefully place the rolls inside. In your instant pot, Pour in 1 ½ cups of water and place the trivet. Lay the baking dish on the trivet. Seal the lid and cook on High Pressure for 15 minutes.

Do a quick Pressure release, and transfer the pie to a serving plate. Mix sour cream and yogurt. Spread the mixture over pie and serve cold.

# Poached Eggs with Watercress

Serving Size: 1 | Total Time: 10 minutes

## Ingredients

2 eggs
1 cup watercress, chopped
½ cup water

¼ tsp garlic powder
Salt and black pepper to taste

## Directions

In a bowl, whisk eggs and water. Add the remaining ingredients and stir well. Transfer the mixture to a heat-proof bowl, that fits in your instant pot.

Add 1 cup of water in the pot. Set the steamer tray and place the bowl on top. Seal the lid and cook on High Pressure for 5 minutes. Do a quick release.

# Chicken Drumsticks with Hot Tomato Sauce

Serving Size: 6 | Total Time: 30 minutes

## Ingredients

2 lb chicken drumsticks, boneless skinless
1 ½ cups hot tomato salsa
Salt to taste

1 onion, chopped
1 cup feta cheese, crumbled

## Directions

Sprinkle salt over the chicken; and set in the instant pot. Stir in salsa to coat, add onion. Seal the lid and cook for 15 minutes on High. Do a quick Pressure release. Press Sauté and cook for 8 minutes as you stir until excess liquid has evaporated. Top with feta cheese to serve.

# Steamed Leek with Parmesan Topping

Serving Size: 2 | Total Time: 5 minutes

## Ingredients

3 leeks, cut into 2-inches long pieces
3 garlic cloves, crushed
1 tsp salt

¼ cup extra virgin olive oil
3 tbsp freshly squeezed lemon juice
½ cup Parmesan cheese, grated

## Directions

Pour 1 ½ cups of water in your instant pot and insert the trivet. In a baking pan combine leeks, oil, garlic, and salt. Lower the pan on the trivet.

Cook on High Pressure for 3 minutes. Do a quick pressure release. Transfer to a plate and sprinkle with freshly squeezed lemon juice and Parmesan cheese.

Tip: Add some dried herbs to the olive oil mixture for some extra taste.

# Tomato & Mozzarella Egg Scrumble

Serving Size: 2 | Total Time: 20 minutes

## Ingredients

4 eggs
½ cup fresh mozzarella cheese
1 cup button mushrooms, sliced
1 large tomato, chopped

2 spring onions, chopped
¼ cup milk
2 tbsp olive oil
½ tsp salt

**Directions**

Grease the pot with oil and set on Sauté. Stir-fry the spring onions for 3 minutes. Add tomato and mushrooms. Cook until liquid evaporates, for 5-6 minutes. Whisk eggs, cheese, milk, and salt. Pour into the pot and stir. Cook for 2 minutes, or until set.

# Sweet & Spicy Chili Dip

Serving Size: 6 | Total Time: 20 minutes

**Ingredients**

1 cup sour cream
2 cups tomato sauce
½ tsp dried oregano, ground
1 cup cream cheese

1 tsp cayenne pepper, ground
½ tsp chili pepper, ground
Salt and black pepper to taste

**Directions**

In a mixing bowl, add all ingredients and stir well to combine. Pour the mixture in the pot. Cook on High Pressure for 8 minutes.

When ready, do a natural Pressure release, for 10 minutes. Adjust the seasoning and transfer the dip into a serving dish. Serve with carrots, celery, or tortilla chips.

# Simple Cheese Spinach Dip

Serving Size: 6 | Total Time: 15 minutes

**Ingredients**

2 cups cream cheese
1 cup baby spinach, rinsed, torn into pieces
1 cup mozzarella cheese
1 tsp Italian seasoning mix

Salt and black pepper to taste
½ cup scallions
1 cup vegetable broth

**Directions**

Place all ingredients in a mixing bowl. Stir well and transfer to your instant pot. Seal the lid and cook on High Pressure for 5 minutes.

Release the steam naturally, for 10 minutes. Serve with celery sticks, or chips.

# Hard-Boiled Eggs with Paprika

Serving Size: 5 | Total Time: 20 minutes

**Ingredients**

1 cup water
5 large eggs

Salt and black pepper, to taste
A pinch of paprika

**Directions**

In the pot, add water and place a trivet. Lay your eggs on top. Seal the lid and cook for 5 minutes on High Pressure. Do a natural release for 10 minutes. Transfer the eggs to ice cold water to cool completely. Peel and season with paprika, salt and pepper before serving.

# Saucy Carrots with Crispy Bacon

Serving Size: 8 | Total Time: 30 minutes

## Ingredients

3 slices bacon, crumbled
4 pounds carrots, peeled and chopped
½ cup fresh orange juice
¼ cup olive oil

3 tbsp honey
1 tsp salt
2 tsp cornstarch
1 tbsp cold water

## Directions

Fry the bacon on Sauté mode until crispy, for about 5 minutes. Set aside. In a bowl, mix salt, olive oil, orange juice, and honey; add the mixture and carrots to the pot and mix well to coat.

Seal the lid, and cook for 6 minutes on High Pressure. Release the pressure quickly. Transfer carrots to a serving dish. Press Cancel, then press Sauté. In a bowl, mix cold water and cornstarch until dissolved.

Add to the liquid remaining in the cooker. Simmer sauce as you stir for 2 minutes to obtain a thick and smooth consistency. Ladle sauce over the carrots and scatter over the crumbled bacon.

# Picante Chicken Wings

Serving Size: 3 | Total Time: 25 minutes

## Ingredients

6 chicken wings
¼ cup cayenne hot pepper sauce
2 tbsp oil
4 tbsp butter

2 tbsp Worcestershire sauce
1 tsp tabasco
½ tsp salt
4 cups chicken broth

## Directions

Grease the pot with oil and place the chicken wings. Pour in broth and cayenne hot pepper sauce. Seal the lid and cook on Poultry for 15 minutes on High. Do a quick release and remove the wings from broth; set aside.

In the pot, melt the butter on Sauté on High. Brown the wings for 3 minutes, turning once. Add the Worcestershire sauce and tabasco. Stir and remove from heat. Serve hot.

# Four Cheeses Party Pizza

Serving Size: 4 | Total Time: 25 minutes

## Ingredients

1 pizza crust
½ cup tomato paste
¼ cup water
1 tsp dried oregano
1 oz cheddar cheese

5-6 slices mozzarella
¼ cup grated gouda cheese
¼ cup grated Parmesan cheese
2 tbsp extra virgin olive oil

## Directions

Grease the bottom of a baking dish with one tablespoon of olive oil. Line some parchment paper. Flour the working surface and roll out the pizza dough to the approximate size of your instant pot. Gently fit the dough in the previously prepared baking dish.

In a small bowl, combine tomato paste with water, and dried oregano. Spread the mixture over dough and finish with cheeses. Add a trivet inside your the pot and Pour in 1 cup of water. Seal the lid, and cook for 15 minutes on High Pressure. Do a quick release. Remove the pizza from the pot using a parchment paper. Cut and serve.

# Broths & Sauces

## Tasty Beef Neck Bone Stock

Serving Size: 8 | Total Time: 2 hours 10 minutes

### Ingredients

1 carrot, chopped
2 onions, chopped
2 cups celery, chopped
2 pounds beef neck bones
12 cups water, or more

1 tsp cider vinegar
2 bay leaves
10 peppercorns
Salt to taste

### Directions

Add carrot, peppercorns, salt, bay leaves, celery, vinegar, onions, and beef bones. Add enough water to cover ingredients. Seal the lid and cook on High Pressure for 120 minutes. Release pressure naturally for about 20 minutes.

Remove the bones and bay leaves, and discard. Use a fine-mesh strainer to strain the liquid. Allow the broth to cool. From the surface, skim fat and throw away. Refrigerate for a maximum of 7 days.

## Herby Chicken Stock

Serving Size: 8 | Total Time: 60 minutes

### Ingredients

2 pounds chicken wings
4 spring onions, diced
2 large carrots, diced
4 cloves garlic

1 small handful fresh parsley
1 small handful fresh thyme
1 bay leaf
6 cups water

### Directions

Add chicken, carrots, parsley, thyme, onions, garlic, and bay leaf. Pour in water. Seal the lid and cook on High Pressure for 45 minutes. Release Pressure naturally, for about 10 minutes. Use a fine-mesh strainer to strain the broth and allow to cool. Transfer the broth to containers and seal. Refrigerate for up to a week.

## Best Vegetable Broth Ever

Serving Size: 10 | Total Time: 55 minutes

### Ingredients

2 onions, chopped
2 cups celery, chopped
2 carrots, chopped
4 garlic cloves
1 cup kale
1 cup bell pepper, chopped

A handful of rosemary
A handful of parsley
10 peppercorns
2 bay leaves
Salt to taste
8 cups cold water, filtered

### Directions

Add onions, carrots, parsley, bay leaves, garlic, kale, celery, bell pepper, salt, rosemary, and peppercorns. Cover with cold water. Seal the lid and cook on High Pressure for 15 minutes. Do a natural release for 15 minutes. Use a wide and shallow bowl to hold the stock you strain through a fine-mesh strainer. Let cool to room temperature. Seal into jars and refrigerate for a up to 14 days.

# Ginger & Vegetable Beef Broth

Serving Size: 8 | Total Time: 1 hour

## Ingredients

2 pounds beef stew meat
2 leeks, chopped
1 onion, chopped
2 cups celery, chopped
2 red chilies, deseeded and chopped
2 carrots, chopped

1 tsp fresh ginger, grated
4 garlic cloves
8 cups water
1 tsp cider vinegar
Salt to taste

## Directions

In the pot, mix meat, celery, garlic, carrots, leeks, onion, red chilies, and ginger. Top with vinegar and water. Seal the lid and cook on High Pressure for 45 minutes. Release Pressure naturally for 10 minutes.

Use a fine-mesh strainer to strain the broth into a bowl; add season with salt. Store in sealable containers.

# Homemade Chicken Stock

Serving Size: 16 | Total Time: 40 minutes

## Ingredients

2 pounds chicken carcasses
4 carrots, cut into chunks
1 cup leeks, chopped
1 onion, quartered
1 cup celery, chopped
2 large garlic cloves

1 sprig fresh thyme
1 bunch fresh parsley
Salt to taste
10 peppercorns
2 bay leaves

## Directions

Add chicken, onion, peppercorns, thyme, celery, carrots, garlic, parsley, leeks, bay leaves, and salt. Cover with water. Seal the lid and cook for 30 minutes on High Pressure. Release the pressure quickly.

Use a colander to drain the broth and do away with solids. Allow cooling for about an hour before storing.

# Simple Beef Bolognese Sauce

Serving Size: 8 | Total Time: 45 minutes

## Ingredients

4 slices bacon, chopped
1 tbsp olive oil
1 onion, minced
2 celery stalks, minced
1 carrot, chopped
1 ½ pounds ground beef

3 tbsp red wine
28 ounces canned tomatoes, crushed
2 bay leaves
Salt and black pepper to taste
½ cup yogurt
¼ cup chopped fresh basil

## Directions

Set on Sauté, and cook bacon until crispy, for 4 to 5 minutes. Mix in oil, celery, carrot, and onion, continue cooking for about 5 minutes until vegetables are softened.

Mix in ¼ teaspoon pepper, ½ teaspoon salt, and beef, and cook for 4 minutes until golden brown. Stir in the wine and allow to soak, approximately 4 more minutes.

Add in bay leaves, tomatoes, and remaining pepper and salt. Seal the lid and cook for 15 minutes on High Pressure. Release Pressure naturally, for 10 minutes.

Add yogurt and stir. Serve alongside noodles and use basil to garnish.

# Cranberry Orange Sauce

Serving Size: 4 | Total Time: 15 minutes

## Ingredients

2 cups cranberries
1 tsp orange zest, freshly grated
½ cup orange juice, freshly juiced

¼ cup brown sugar
1 cup water
2 tbsp maple syrup

## Directions

Combine maple syrup, water, cranberries, and orange juice in the instant pot. Sprinkle with orange zest. Seal the lid, and cook on High Pressure for 5 minutes.

When done, release the Pressure naturally, for about 10 minutes.

Press Sauté, add brown sugar and stir until thick sauce mixture is formed. Turn off the heat and transfer the sauce to the serving dish. Serve cold.

# Herbed Squash Sauce

Serving Size: 3 | Total Time: 40 minutes

## Ingredients

3 beets, trimmed, peeled, cubed
3 carrots, peeled, cubed
2 cups butternut squash, peeled, cubed
1 cup red wine
1 tsp dried basil, ground

1 tbsp dried parsley, ground
1 tsp dried oregano, ground
½ tsp garlic powder
Salt and black pepper to taste

## Directions

Add all vegetables in the instant pot. Pour in 2 cups of water and seal the lid. Press Steam and set the timer to 10 minutes. Cook on High Pressure.

Do a quick Pressure release. Transfer to a food processor and pulse until smooth and creamy. Add the remaining ingredients and blend for a minute.

Return to the pot, Press Sauté and cook for 20 minutes, stirring occasionally.

# Authentic Neapolitan Sauce

Serving Size: 4 | Total Time: 50 minutes

## Ingredients

1 lb mushrooms
2 cups canned tomatoes, diced
1 carrot, chopped
1 onion, chopped
1 celery stick, chopped
1 tbsp olive oil

2 garlic cloves
1 tsp salt
½ tsp paprika
1 tsp fish sauce
1 cup water

## Directions

Heat olive oil on Sauté. Stir-fry carrot, onion, celery, and paprika, for 5 minutes. Add all remaining ingredients, except the tomatoes, and cook for 5-6 more minutes, until the meat is slightly browned. Seal the lid.

Cook on High Pressure for 20 minutes. When done, release the steam naturally, for about 10 minutes. Hit Sauté, and cook for 7-8 minutes, to thicken the sauce.

# Quick Zucchini Sauce with Greek Yogurt

Serving Size: 3 | Total Time: 10 minutes

## Ingredients

1 zucchini, chopped
1 cup Greek yogurt
1 cup sour cream
1 tsp garlic powder

¼ cup shallots, minced
1 tbsp ground dried parsley
Salt and black pepper to taste

## Directions

In a bowl, mix zucchini, sour cream, garlic, shallots, parsley, salt, and pepper. Stir until well combined. Transfer the mixture to the pot, and seal the lid.

Cook on High Pressure for 3 minutes. Do a quick release. Remove the sauce to a bowl and stir in the yogurt. Serve chilled.

# Garlic Red Bell Pepper Sauce

Serving Size: 3 | Total Time: 10 minutes

## Ingredients

3 red bell peppers, seeds removed, chopped
1 cup cherry tomatoes, diced
1 onion, chopped
1 tsp garlic powder
½ cup sour cream

2 cups vegetable broth
1 tbsp balsamic vinegar
1 tbsp cayenne pepper
1 tsp salt

## Directions

Combine all ingredients in a mixing bowl. Add the mixture to the instant pot, seal the lid and cook on High Pressure for 6 minutes. Do a quick release.

Transfer to your food processor and purée until the mixture is smooth.

# Caprese Sauce with Goat Cheese

Serving Size: 4 | Total Time: 15 minutes

## Ingredients

1 cup goat cheese, crumbled
1 cup tomatoes, diced
3 tbsp tomato paste
1 onion, finely chopped
3 tbsp apple cider vinegar

3 garlic cloves, chopped
¼ cup mozzarella cheese
2 cups vegetable broth
Salt and black pepper to taste

## Directions

Add all ingredients to your instant pot, seal the lid and cook on High Pressure for 6 minutes.

When done, Press Cancel and do a quick Pressure release.

# Homemade Honey Applesauce

Serving Size: 4 | Total Time: 45 minutes

## Ingredients

4 apples, cored, chopped
½ cup water

1 tsp ground cinnamon
1 tsp honey

## Directions

Add apples, cinnamon, water, and honey. Seal the lid and cook on High Pressure for 4 minutes. Release Pressure naturally, for 10 minutes.

If you desire a chunky blend, stir vigorously. For a smooth applesauce, puree the mixture in a blender.

Allow to cool before transferring in containers for storage.

# Basil Parmesan Sauce

Serving Size: 4 | Total Time: 10 minutes

## Ingredients

1 cup fresh basil, torn
1 cup cream cheese
2 tbsp Parmesan cheese, shredded

1 tbsp olive oil
Salt and black pepper to taste
2 cups vegetable broth

## Directions

In a bowl, stir in all ingredients. Transfer the mixture to the instant pot. Seal the lid and cook on High Pressure for 5 minutes. Do a quick Pressure release.

# Spicy Green Sauce

Serving Size: 4 | Total Time: 8 minutes

## Ingredients

4 oz green jalapeño peppers, chopped
1 green bell pepper, chopped
2 garlic cloves, crushed
½ cup white vinegar

1 tbsp apple cider vinegar
1 tsp salt
4 tbsp water

## Directions

Add all ingredients to the instant pot. Seal the lid and cook on High Pressure for 2 minutes. When done, release the steam naturally, for about 5 minutes. Transfer to a blender, pulse until combined and store in jars.

Tip: Strain the mixture if you prefer more liquid sauce.

# Mediterranean Tomato Sauce

Serving Size: 4 | Total Time: 15 minutes

## Ingredients

2 cups tomatoes, diced
½ cup tomato sauce
½ cup sun-dried tomatoes
1 medium onion, chopped
3 tbsp balsamic vinegar

3 garlic cloves, chopped
1 tsp dried oregano
½ tsp dried rosemary
1 tbsp olive oil
Salt and black pepper to taste

## Directions

Combine all ingredients in a mixing bowl and give it a good stir. Transfer to the instant pot and seal the lid. Cook on High Pressure for 6 minutes. When done, remove to serving bowls and serve with pasta or rice.

# Cheddar Cheese Sauce with Broccoli & Rosemary

Serving Size: 4 | Total Time: 15 minutes

## Ingredients

1 cup broccoli, chopped
1 cup cream cheese
1 cup cheddar cheese, shredded
3 cups chicken broth

Salt and black pepper to taste
1 tsp garlic powder
2 tsp dried rosemary

## Directions

Mix all ingredients in a large bowl. Pour the mixture in the instant pot, seal the lid and cook on High Pressure for 8 minutes. Do a quick release. Store for up to 5 days.

# Easy Onion Gravy

Serving Size: 4 | Total Time: 10 minutes

## Ingredients

1 onion, chopped
1 tsp onion powder
3 cups vegetable broth

2 cups cream cheese
2 tsp dried parsley, chopped
1 tbsp olive oil

## Directions

Heat oil on Sauté, and stir-fry the onion for 5 minutes, or until translucent.

Stir in the remaining ingredients. Seal the lid and cook on High Pressure for 5 minutes. Do a quick Pressure release and serve immediately.

# Two-Cheese Carrot Sauce

Serving Size: 4 | Total Time: 20 minutes

## Ingredients

1 carrot, shredded
1 cup cream cheese
½ cup Gorgonzola cheese
3 cups vegetable broth

1 cup Gruyere cheese, crumbled
Salt and black pepper to taste
1 tsp garlic powder
1 tbsp fresh parsley, finely chopped

## Directions

Combine all ingredients in a large bowl. Pour in the instant pot, seal the lid and cook on High Pressure for 8 minutes. Do a natural release, for 10 minutes. Store for up to 5 days.

# *Desserts*

## Vanilla Cheesecake with Cranberry Filling

Serving Size: 8 | Total Time: 1 hour

### Ingredients

1 cup coarsely crumbled cookies
2 tbsp butter, melted
1 cup mascarpone cheese, room temperature
½ cup sugar
2 tbsp sour cream

½ tsp vanilla extract
2 eggs, room temperature
1/3 cup dried cranberries
1 cup water

### Directions

Fold a 20-inch piece of aluminum foil in half lengthwise twice and set on the instant pot. In a bowl, combine melted butter and crumbled cookies. Press firmly to the bottom and about 1/3 of the way up the sides of a 7-inch springform pan. Freeze the crust while the filling is being prepared.

In a separate bowl, beat together mascarpone cheese and sugar to obtain a smooth consistency. Stir in vanilla extract and sour cream. Beat one egg and add into the cheese mixture to combine well.

Do the same with the second egg. Stir cranberries into the filling. Transfer the filling into the crust. Into the pot, add water and set the steam rack at the bottom. Center the springform pan onto the prepared foil sling. Use the sling to lower the pan onto the rack.

Fold foil strips out of the way of the lid. Seal the lid, press Cake and cook on High Pressure for 40 minutes. Release the pressure quickly. Transfer the cheesecake to a refrigerator for 3 hours. Use a paring knife to run along the edges between the pan and cheesecake to remove the cheesecake and set to the plate.

## Orange New York Cheesecake

Serving Size: 12 | Total Time: 1 hour

### Ingredients

*For the crust:*
1 cup graham crackers crumbs
2 tbsp butter, melted

1 tsp sugar
1/8 tsp salt

*For the filling:*
2 cups cream cheese, at room temperature
½ cup sugar
1 tsp vanilla extract

Zest from 1 orange
A pinch of salt
2 eggs

### Directions

Fold a 20-inch piece of aluminum foil in half lengthwise twice and set on the instant pot. Spray a parchment paper with cooking spray and line to the base of a 7-inch springform pan. In a bowl, combine melted butter, salt, sugar and graham crackers. Press into the bottom and about 1/3 up the sides of the pan.

Transfer the pan to the freezer as you prepare the filling. In a separate bowl, beat sugar, cream cheese, salt, orange zest, and vanilla until smooth. Beat eggs into the filling, one at a time. Stir until combined.

Add the filling over the chilled crust in the pan. To the pan, add 1 cup water and set steam rack into the pot. Carefully center the springform pan on the prepared foil sling. Lower pan into the inner pot using sling and place on steam rack. Seal the lid, press Cake and cook for 40 minutes on High Pressure.

Release the pressure quickly. Transfer the cheesecake to a refrigerator for 3 hours. Use a paring knife to run along the edges between the pan and cheesecake to remove the cheesecake and set to the plate.

# Walnut & Pumpkin Tart

Serving Size: 8 | Total Time: 1 hour 30 minutes

## Ingredients

3 eggs
½ cup sugar
1 cup flour
½ cup half-and-half
¼ cup olive oil
1 tsp baking powder

1 tsp vanilla extract
1 tsp ground cinnamon
½ tsp ground nutmeg
1 cup packed shredded pumpkin
½ cup chopped walnuts
2 cups water

*Frosting:*
4 ounces cream cheese, room temperature
8 tbsp butter
½ cup confectioners sugar

½ tsp vanilla extract
½ tsp salt

## Directions

In a bowl, beat eggs and sugar to get a smooth mixture; mix in oil, flour, vanilla extract, cinnamon, half-and-half, baking powder, and nutmeg. Stir well to obtain a fluffy batter; fold walnuts and pumpkin through the batter. Add batter into a 6-inch cake pan and cover with aluminum foil.

Into the pot, add water and set steamer rack over the water. Lay cake pan onto the trivet.

Seal the lid, select Cake and cook on High Pressure for 40 minutes. Release pressure naturally for 10 minutes, then release the remaining pressure quickly. As the cake cooks, beat cream cheese, confectioners' sugar, salt, vanilla extract, and butter in a mixing bowl until smooth; place in the refrigerator until needed.

Remove cake from the pan and transfer to a wire rack to cool. Over the cake, spread frosting and apply a topping of shredded carrots.

# Yogurt Cheesecake with Cranberry Topping

Serving Size: 8 | Total Time: 1 hour 10 minutes

## Ingredients

2 lb Greek yogurt
2 cups sugar
4 eggs
2 tsp lemon zest

1 tsp lemon extract
½ tsp salt
1 cheesecake crust

*For topping:*
7 oz dried cranberries
2 tbsp cranberry jam
2 tsp lemon zest

1 tsp vanilla sugar
1 tsp cranberry extract
¾ cup lukewarm water

## Directions

In a bowl, combine yogurt, sugar, eggs, lemon zest, lemon extract, and salt. With a mixer, beat well on low until well-combined.

Grease a springform pan with oil. Place in the crust and pour in the filling. Flatten the surface with a spatula. Leave in the fridge for 30 minutes.

Meanwhile, prepare the topping by combining cranberries, jam, zest, vanilla sugar, extract, and water in the inner pot. Simmer for 15 minutes on Sauté mode. Remove to a bowl and wipe the pot clean.

Fill in 1 cup of water in the pot, and insert a trivet. Set the pan on top and pour cranberry topping. Seal the lid, and cook for 20 minutes on High Pressure. Do a quick release. Run a sharp knife around the edge of the cheesecake. Refrigerate overnight.

# Homemade Lemon Cheesecake

Serving Size: 8 | Total Time: 3hr

## Ingredients

*Crust:*

4 ounces graham crackers

1 tsp ground cinnamon

3 tbsp butter, melted

*Filling:*

1 pound mascarpone cheese, at room temperature

¾ cup sugar

¼ cup sour cream, at room temperature

2 eggs

1 tsp vanilla extract

1 tsp lemon zest

1 tbsp lemon juice

A pinch of salt

2 cups water

1 cup strawberries, halved

## Directions

In a food processor, beat cinnamon and graham crackers to attain a texture almost same as sand; mix in melted butter. Press the crumbs into the bottom of a 7-inch springform pan in an even layer.

In a stand mixer, beat sugar, mascarpone cheese, and sour cream for 3 minutes to combine well and have a fluffy and smooth mixture. Scrape the bowl's sides and add eggs, lemon zest, salt, lemon juice, and vanilla extract. Carry on to beat the mixture until you obtain a consistent color and all ingredients are completely combined. Pour filling over crust.

Into the inner pot, add water and set in the trivet. Insert the springform pan on the trivet. Seal the lid, press Cake and cook for 40 minutes on High Pressure. Release the pressure quickly. Remove the cheesecake and let cool for 2 hours. Transfer to a serving plate and garnish with strawberry halves on top. Use a paring knife to run along the edges between the pan and cheesecake to remove the cheesecake and set to the plate.

# Pie Cups with Fruit Filling

Serving Size: 6 | Total Time: 35 minutes

## Ingredients

*For the crust:*

2 cups flour

¾ tsp salt

¾ cup butter, softened

1 tbsp sugar

½ cup ice water

*For the filling:*

1 apple

½ fresh peach

½ cup apples, chopped

¼ cup cranberries

2 tbsp flour

1 tbsp sugar

½ tsp cinnamon

1 egg yolk, for brushing

## Directions

Place all crust ingredients in a food processor and pulse until dough becomes crumbly. Remove to a lightly floured work surface. Divide among 4 equal pieces and wrap in plastic foil. Refrigerate for an hour.

Meanwhile, place all the filling ingredients in a bowl. Toss to combine and set aside.

Roll each piece into 6-inch round discs. Add 2 tablespoons of the apple mixture at the center of each disc and wrap to form small bowls. Brush each bowl with egg yolk and gently Transfer to an oiled baking dish.

Pour 1 cup of water in the pot and insert the trivet. Place the pan on top. Seal the lid, and cook for 25 minutes on High Pressure. Release the pressure naturally, for about 10 minutes.

# Walnut & Dark Chocolate Brownies

Serving Size: 6 | Total Time: 40 minutes

## Ingredients

1 ½ cups water
2 eggs
1/3 cup granulated sugar
¼ cup olive oil
1/3 cup flour
1/3 cup cocoa powder

1/3 cup dark chocolate chips
1/3 cup chopped walnuts
1 tbsp milk
½ tsp baking powder
1 tbsp vanilla extract
A pinch of salt

## Directions

Add water and set steamer rack into the cooker. Line a parchment paper on the steamer basket. In a bowl, beat eggs and sugar to mix until smooth. Stir in oil, cocoa, milk, salt baking powder, chocolate chips, flour, walnuts, vanilla, and sea salt. Transfer the batter to the prepared steamer basket.

Arrange into an even layer. Seal the lid, press Cake and cook for 20 minutes on High Pressure. Release the pressure quickly. Let cool before cutting into squares. Use powdered sugar to dust and serve.

# Cottage Cheesecake with Strawberries

Serving Size: 6 | Total Time: 8 hours 30 minutes

## Ingredients

10 oz cream cheese
¼ cup sugar
½ cup cottage cheese
1 lemon, zested and juiced
2 eggs, cracked into a bowl

1 tsp lemon extract
3 tbsp sour cream
1 ½ cups water
10 strawberries, halved to decorate

## Directions

Blend with an electric mixer, the cream cheese, quarter cup of sugar, cottage cheese, lemon zest, lemon juice, and lemon extract, until a smooth consistency is formed. Adjust the sweet taste to liking with more sugar.

Reduce the speed of the mixer and add the eggs. Fold in at low speed until fully incorporated. Make sure not to fold the eggs in high speed to prevent a cracker crust. Grease the springform pan with cooking spray.

Spoon the mixture into the pan. Level the top with spatula and cover with foil. Fit the trivet in the pot, and pour the water in. Place the cake pan on the trivet, seal the lid and select manual at High pressure for 15 minutes.

Mix the sour cream and one tablespoon of sugar. Set aside. Once the timer has gone off, do a natural pressure release for 10 minutes, then a quick pressure release to let out any extra steam, and open the lid.

Remove the trivet, place the pan on a flat surface, and open. Use a spatula to spread the sour cream mixture on the warm cake. Refrigerate for 8 hours. Top with strawberries; slice into 6 pieces and serve firm.

# Best Tiramisu Cheesecake

Serving Size: 12 | Total Time: 1 hour + chilling time

## Ingredients

1 tbsp Kahlua liquor
1 ½ cups ladyfingers, crushed
1 tbsp granulated espresso
1 tbsp butter, melted
16 ounces cream cheese, softened
8 ounces mascarpone cheese, softened

2 eggs
2 tbsp powdered sugar
½ cup white sugar
1 tbsp cocoa powder
1 tsp vanilla extract

### Directions

In a bowl beat the cream cheese, mascarpone, and white sugar. Gradually beat in the eggs, the powdered sugar, cocoa powder, and vanilla. Combine the first 4 ingredients, in another bowl.

Spray a springform pan with cooking spray. Press the ladyfinger crust at the bottom. Pour the filling over. Cover the pan with a paper towel and then close it with aluminum foil. Pour 1 cup of water in your pressure cooker and lower the trivet. Place the pan inside and seal the lid. Select Meat/Stew mode and set to 35 minutes at High pressure.

Wait for about 10 minutes before pressing Cancel and releasing the pressure quickly. Allow cooling completely before refrigerating the cheesecake for 4 hours.

# Walnut & Pumpkin Strudel

Serving Size: 8 | Total Time: 30 minutes

## Ingredients

2 cups pumpkin puree
1 tsp vanilla extract
2 cups Greek yogurt
2 eggs

2 tbsp brown sugar
2 tbsp unsalted butter, softened
2 puff pastry sheets
1 cup walnuts, chopped

## Directions

In a bowl, mix butter, yogurt with vanilla extract until completely smooth; set aside.

Unfold the pastry and cut each sheet into 4-inch x 7-inch pieces and brush with half of the beaten eggs. Place approximately 2 tbsp of pumpkin puree, sugar, and 2 tbsp of the yogurt mixture at the middle of each pastry, sprinkle with walnuts.

Fold the sheets and brush with the remaining eggs. Cut the surface with a sharp knife and gently place each strudel into an oiled baking dish.

Pour 1 cup of water in the pot and insert the trivet. Place the pan on top. Seal the lid and cook for 25 minutes on High Pressure. Release the pressure naturally, for about 10 minutes. Let it chill for 10 minutes. Carefully Transfer the strudels to a serving plate.

# Simple Apple Cinnamon Dessert

Serving Size: 5 | Total Time: 30 minutes

## Ingredients

*Topping:*
½ cup oat flour
½ cup old-fashioned rolled oats

½ cup granulated sugar
¼ cup olive oil

*Filling:*
5 apples, peeled, cored, and halved
2 tbsp arrowroot powder
½ cup water
1 tsp ground cinnamon

¼ tsp ground nutmeg
½ tsp vanilla paste
1 tsp salt

## Directions

In a bowl, combine sugar, oat flour, rolled oats, and olive oil to form coarse crumbs. Ladle the apples into the instant pot. Mix water with arrowroot powder in a bowl. Stir in salt, nutmeg, cinnamon, and vanilla.

Toss in the apples to coat. Apply oat topping to the apples. Seal the lid and cook on High Pressure for 10 minutes. Release the pressure naturally for 5 minutes, then release the remaining Pressure quickly.

# Easy Lemon Cookies

Serving Size: 10 | Total Time: 25 minutes

## Ingredients

2 eggs
2 cups sugar
2 cups vegetable oil

*Lemon topping:*
4 cups sugar
5 cups water
1 cup freshly squeezed lemon juice

½ cup all-purpose flour
1 tsp baking powder

1 tbsp lemon zest
1 whole lemon, sliced

## Directions

In a bowl, combine eggs, sugar, oil, and baking powder. Gradually add flour until the mixture is thick and slightly sticky. Shape balls with hands, and flatten them to half-inch thick.

Place in a baking pan that fits in the instant pot. Pour 2 cups of water, insert the trivet and lower the pan onto the trivet. Cover the pan with foil and seal the lid. Cook on High Pressure for 20 minutes.

Do a quick release and remove the pan and foil. Cool to a room temperature.

Add the remaining sugar, water, lemon juice, lemon zest, and lemon slices in the instant pot. Press Sauté and cook until the sugar dissolves. Pour the hot topping over the chilled dessert. Serve chilled.

# Grandma's Fruit Compote

Serving Size: 8 | Total Time: 35 minutes

## Ingredients

7 oz Turkish figs
7 oz fresh cherries
7 oz plums
3.5 oz raisins
3 large apples, chopped
3 tbsp cornstarch

1 tsp cinnamon, ground
1 tbsp cloves
1 cup sugar
1 lemon, juiced
3 cups water

## Directions

Combine all ingredients in the instant pot. Seal the lid and cook for 30 minutes on High pressure. Release the pressure naturally, for 10 minutes. Store in big jars.

# Catalan-Style Crème Brûlée

Serving Size: 4 | Total Time: 15 minutes

## Ingredients

5 cups heavy cream
8 egg yolks
1 cup honey

4 tbsp sugar
1 vanilla extract
1 cup water

## Directions

In a bowl, combine heavy cream, egg yolks, vanilla, and honey. Beat well with an electric mixer. Pour the mixture into 4 ramekins. Set aside.

Pour water in the pot and insert the trivet. Lower the ramekins on top. Seal the lid, and cook for 10 minutes on High Pressure. Do a quick pressure release. Remove the ramekins from the pot and add a tablespoon of sugar in each ramekin. Burn evenly with a culinary torch until brown. Chill well and serve.

# Classic French Squash Tart

Serving Size: 8 | Total Time: 30 minutes

## Ingredients

15 oz mashed squash
6 fl oz milk
½ tsp cinnamon, ground
½ tsp nutmeg

½ tsp salt
3 large eggs
½ cup granulated sugar
1 pack pate brisee

## Directions

Place squash puree in a large bowl. Add milk, cinnamon, eggs, nutmeg, salt, and sugar. Whisk together until well incorporated. Grease a baking dish with oil.

Gently place pate brisee creating the edges with hands. Pour the squash mixture over and flatten the surface with a spatula. Pour 1 cup of water in the pot and insert the trivet. Lay the baking dish on the trivet.

Seal the lid, and cook for 25 minutes on High Pressure. Do a quick release. Transfer the pie to a serving platter. Refrigerate overnight before serving.

# Old-Fashioned Apple Pie

Serving Size: 6 | Total Time: 30 minutes

## Ingredients

2 lb apples, cubed
¼ cup sugar
¼ cup bread crumbs
2 tsp cinnamon, ground
3 tbsp freshly squeezed lemon juice

1 tsp vanilla sugar
¼ tbsp oil
1 egg, beaten
¼ cup all-purpose flour
Pie dough

## Directions

Combine bread crumbs, vanilla sugar, granulated sugar, apples, and cinnamon, in a bowl. On a lightly floured surface, roll out the pie dough making 2 circle-shaped crusts.

Grease a baking sheet with cooking spray, and place one pie crust in it.

Spoon the apple mixture on top, and cover with the remaining crust. Seal by crimping edges and brush with beaten egg. Pour 1 cup of water in the instant pot and lay the trivet.

Lower the baking sheet on the trivet. Seal the lid, and cook on High Pressure for 20 minutes. Do a quick release and serve chilled.

# Banana & Vanilla Pancakes

Serving Size: 6 | Total Time: 20 minutes

## Ingredients

2 medium-sized bananas, mashed
1 ¼ cups milk
2 eggs
1 ½ cups rolled oats
1 ½ tsp baking powder

1 tsp vanilla extract
2 tsp coconut oil
1 tbsp honey
¼ tsp salt

## Directions

Combine the ingredients in a blender and pulse until completely smooth batter. Grease the inner pot with cooking spray. Spread 1 spoon batter at the bottom. Cook for 2 minutes, on Sauté mode, flip the crepe and cook for another minute. Repeat the process with the remaining batter. Serve immediately.

# Lemon-Apricot Compote

Serving Size: 8 | Total Time: 40 minutes

## Ingredients

2 lb fresh apricots, sliced
1 lb sugar
2 tbsp lemon zest

1 tsp ground nutmeg
10 cups water

## Directions

Add apricots, sugar, water, nutmeg, and lemon zest. Cook, stirring occasionally, until half of the water evaporates, on Sauté. Press Cancel, and transfer the apricots and the remaining liquid into glass jars. Let cool and close the lids. Refrigerate overnight before use.

# Chocolate Glazed Cake

Serving Size: 12 | Total Time: 45 minutes

## Ingredients

3 cups yogurt
3 cups flour
2 cups granulated sugar
1 cup oil

2 tsp baking soda
3 tbsp cocoa
1 cup water

*For the glaze:*
7 oz dark chocolate
10 tbsp sugar

10 tbsp milk
5 oz butter, unsalted

## Directions

In a bowl, combine yogurt, flour, sugar, oil, baking soda, and cocoa. Beat well with an electric mixer. Transfer a mixture to a large springform pan.

Wrap the pan in foil. Insert a trivet in the instant pot. Pour in water, and place the pan on top. Seal the lid and cook for 30 minutes on High Pressure. Do a quick release, remove the pan and unwrap. Chill well.

Meanwhile, melt the chocolate in a microwave. Transfer to a bowl, and whisk in butter, milk, and sugar. Beat well with a mixer and pour the mixture over the cake. Refrigerate for at least two hours before serving.

# Creme Caramel with Whipped Cream

Serving Size: 4 | Total Time: 30 minutes

## Ingredients

½ cup granulated sugar
4 tbsp caramel syrup
1 cup water
3 eggs

½ tsp vanilla extract
½ tbsp milk
5 oz whipping cream

## Directions

Combine milk, whipping cream and vanilla extract in your instant pot. Press Sauté, and cook for 5 minutes, or until small bubbles form. Set aside.

Using an electric mixer, whisk the eggs and sugar. Gradually add the cream mixture and whisk until well combined. Divide the caramel syrup between 4 ramekins. Fill with egg mixture and place them on top of the trivet. Pour in water.

Seal the lid, and cook for 15 minutes on High Pressure. Do a quick release. remove the ramekins from the pot and cool completely before serving.

# Cherry & Chocolate Marble Cake

Serving Size: 6 | Total Time: 30 minutes

## Ingredients

1 cup flour
1 ½ tsp baking powder
1 tbsp powdered stevia
½ tsp salt
1 tsp cherry extract

3 tbsp butter, softened
3 eggs
¼ cup cocoa powder
¼ cup heavy cream

## Directions

Combine all dry ingredients, except cocoa in a bowl. Mix well to combine and add eggs, one at the time. Beat well with a dough hook attachment for one minute. Add heavy cream, butter, and cherry extract.

Continue to beat for 3 more minutes. Divide the mixture in half and add cocoa powder in one-half of the mixture. Pour the light batter into a greased baking dish. Drizzle with cocoa dough to create a nice marble pattern. Pour in one cup of water and insert the trivet. Lower the baking dish on top. Seal the lid and cook for 20 minutes on High Pressure.

Release the pressure naturally, for about 10 minutes. Let it cool for a while and transfer to a serving plate.

# Pumpkin Pudding with Apple Juice

Serving Size: 4 | Total Time: 20 minutes

## Ingredients

1 lb pumpkin, chopped
1 cup granulated sugar
½ cup cornstarch

4 cups apple juice, unsweetened
1 tsp cinnamon, ground
3-4 cloves

## Directions

In a bowl, combine sugar and apple juice until sugar dissolves completely.

Pour the mixture into the pot and stir in cornstarch, cinnamon, cloves, and pumpkin. Seal the lid, and cook for 10 minutes on High Pressure. Do a quick release. Pour in the pudding into 4 serving bowls. Let cool to a room temperature and refrigerate overnight.

# Vanilla Buckwheat Pancake with Yogurt & Berries

Serving Size: 3 | Total Time: 15 minutes

## Ingredients

1 cup buckwheat flour
2 tsp baking powder
1 ¼ cups milk
1 egg
½ tsp salt

1 tsp vanilla sugar
1 tsp strawberry extract
1 cup Greek yogurt
1 cup fresh berries

## Directions

In a bowl, whisk milk and egg until foamy. Gradually add flour and continue to beat until combined. Add baking powder, salt, strawberry extract, and vanilla sugar.

Grease a baking pan with oil and spoon the batter in it. Pour 1 cup of water in the pot and place the trivet. Lay the pan on the trivet. Seal the lid and cook for 5 minutes on High Pressure. Do a quick release.

Top pancake with yogurt and berries.

# Sugarless Peach-Blueberry Clafoutis

Serving Size: 6 | Total Time: 50 minutes

## Ingredients

1 cup fresh blueberries
1 peach, chopped
1 cup flour
2 large eggs
1 tsp baking powder

½ tsp salt
¼ cup butter, softened
¼ cup powdered stevia
¼ tsp vanilla extract
2 tsp freshly squeezed lemon juice

## Directions

In a bowl, combine flour, baking powder, and salt. Mix well and set aside. In a separate bowl, combine eggs and powdered stevia. Using a hand mixer with a whisking attachment, beat well on high for 2 minutes until light and fluffy.

Place the flour mixture in a large mixing bowl. Add butter, vanilla extract, and lemon juice. Gradually add the egg mixture, beating constantly.

Transfer the mixture to an oiled baking dish. Spread the batter evenly with a kitchen spatula. Arrange the fruit on top. Pour 1 cup of water in the pot and insert the trivet. Place the pan on top. Seal the lid and cook for 30 minutes on High Pressure. Release the pressure quickly and let chill completely before serving.

# Homemade Walnut Layer Cake

Serving Size: 8 | Total Time: 20 minutes

## Ingredients

3 standard cake crusts
½ cup vanilla pudding powder
¼ cup granulated sugar

4 cups milk
1 (10.5 oz) box chocolate chips
¼ cup walnuts, minced

## Directions

Combine vanilla powder, sugar and milk in the inner pot. Cook until the pudding thickens, stirring constantly, on Sauté. Remove from the steel pot.

Place one crust into a springform pan. Pour half of the pudding and sprinkle with minced walnuts and chocolate chips. Cover with another crust and repeat the process. Finish with the final crust and wrap in foil.

Insert the trivet, pour in 1 cup of water, and place springform pan on top. Seal the lid and cook for 10 minutes on High Pressure. Do a quick release. Refrigerate overnight.

# Plum & Almond Dessert

Serving Size: 10 | Total Time: 1 hour 40 minutes

## Ingredients

6 lb sweet ripe plums, pits removed and halved
2 cups white sugar

1 cup almond, flakes

## Directions

Drizzle the plums with sugar. Toss to coat. Let it stand for about 1 hour to allow plums to soak up the sugar.

Transfer the plum mixture to the instant pot and pour 1 cup of water. Seal the lid and cook on High Pressure for 30 minutes. Allow the Pressure to release naturally, for 10 minutes. Serve topped with almond flakes.

# Molten Chocolate Cake

Serving Size: 8 | Total Time: 40 minutes

## Ingredients

1 cup butter
4 tbsp milk
2 tsp vanilla extract
1 ½ cups chocolate chips
1 ½ cups sugar

Powdered sugar to garnish
7 tbsp flour
5 eggs
1 cup water

## Directions

Grease the cake pan with cooking spray and set aside. Fit the trivet at the pot, and pour in water.

In a heatproof bowl, add the butter and chocolate and melt them in the microwave for about 2 minutes. Stir in sugar. Add eggs, milk, and vanilla extract and stir again. Finally, add the flour and stir it until smooth.

Pour the batter into the greased cake pan and use spatula to level it. Place the pan on the trivet, inside the pot, seal the lid, and select Manual at High for 15 minutes.

Do a natural pressure release for 12 minutes, then a quick pressure release. Remove the trivet with the pan on it and place the pan on a flat surface. Put a plate over the pan and flip the cake over onto the plate. Pour the powdered sugar in a fine sieve and sift over the cake. Cut the cake into 8 slices and serve immediately.

# Banana Chocolate Bars

Serving Size: 6 | Total Time: 25 minutes

## Ingredients

½ cup almond butter
3 bananas
2 tbsp cocoa powder

1 ½ cups water
Cooking spray

## Directions

Place the bananas and almond butter in a bowl and mash finely with a fork. Add the cocoa powder and stir until well combined. Grease a baking dish that fits into the pressure cooker.

Pour the banana and almond butter into the dish. Pour the water in the pressure cooker and lower the trivet. Place the baking dish on top of the trivet and seal the lid.

Select Pressure Cook mode, for 15 minutes at High pressure. When it goes off, do a quick release. Let cool for a few minutes before cutting into squares

# Quick Coconut Treat with Pears

Serving Size: 2 | Total Time: 15 minutes

## Ingredients

¼ cup flour
1 cup coconut milk

2 pears, peeled and diced
¼ cup shredded coconut, unsweetened

## Directions

Combine all ingredients in your Pressure cooker. Seal the lid, select Pressure Cook and set the timer to 5 minutes at High pressure. When ready, do a quick pressure release. Divide the mixture between two bowls.

# Amazing Fruity Cheesecake

Serving Size: 6 | Total Time: 30 minutes

## Ingredients

1 ½ cups graham cracker crust
1 cup raspberries
3 cups cream cheese
1 tbsp fresh orange juice
3 eggs

½ stick butter, melted
¾ cup sugar
1 tsp vanilla paste
1 tsp finely grated orange zest
1 ½ cups water

## Directions

Insert the tray into the pressure cooker, and add 1 ½ cups of water. Grease a springform. Mix in graham cracker crust with sugar and butter, in a bowl. Press the mixture to form a crust at the bottom.

Blend the raspberries and cream cheese with an electric mixer. Crack in the eggs and keep mixing until well combined. Mix in the remaining ingredients, and give it a good stir.

Pour this mixture into the pan, and cover the pan with aluminum foil. Lay the springform on the tray.

Select Pressure Cook mode and cook for 20 minutes at High pressure. Once the cooking is complete, do a quick pressure release. Refrigerate the cheesecake for at least 2 hours.